THE ART OF DYING

THE ART OF DYING

WRITINGS, 2019–2022

PETER SCHJELDAHL

FOREWORD BY STEVE MARTIN

INTRODUCTION BY JARRETT EARNEST

ABRAMS PRESS, NEW YORK

Originally published in hardcover by Abrams Press in 2024

ISBN: 978-1-4197-7325-9
eISBN: 979-8-88707-260-9

Printed and bound in the United States

10 9 8 7 6 5 4 3 2 1

ABRAMS The Art of Books
195 Broadway, New York, NY 10007
abramsbooks.com

CONTENTS

FOREWORD: PETER SCHJELDAHL

STEVE MARTIN

"Cézanne doesn't cut it."

When I heard Peter utter this sentence at a dinner party, I knew I was in over my head.

Peter, at these dinners, where no one was shy with opinions, would sit tolerantly, head tucked in, allowing us all to blather until our balloon heads had deflated. He would wait for the inevitable pause, raise his head, and speak so cogently that, if we had a stenographer present, he would have another readymade *New Yorker* essay.

In 2003, at one of those extravagant pier art fairs, I ran into Anne Stringfield, a *New Yorker* staffer who fact-checked my essays and contributed to the art listings. She was with Peter, the magazine's art critic. We were introduced, politely. Peter was as insightful with people as he was with art. He had picked up on something, and when I left, said to Anne, "Well, you run in some interesting circles." Five years later she and I were married.

Anne and I happily attended Peter's annual Fourth of July fireworks night in rural Bovina and played miniature golf at his wife Brooke's Rip Van Winkle–themed course (which is free for the whole community). In Manhattan, they hosted Anne and me at comfy home-cooked dinners with stellar company—artists (Vija Celmins, Martin Puryear, Thomas Nozkowski), writers and critics (Roberta Smith, Deborah Solomon, Jerry Saltz), notables (Ann Temkin, Kent Sepkowitz), and one comedian. Their apartment on St. Mark's Place was five flights up, accounting for Peter's trim figure and fleet walking pace.

Modest but potent art works that had gravitated to Peter and Brooke through the years hung cockeyed on the royal-blue walls: Bruce Nauman, Susan Rothenberg, Cindy Sherman. A de Kooning painting on newsprint—a gift from the artist—worth ten years' rent, stayed firmly in place, despite its potential on the auction block.

Peter's writing was exemplary. Finding a gem is almost too easy: simply open any of his books of collected essays to a random page and put your finger down. Which I have just done:

"Kippenberger's nihilism blew through the world like a yakking ill wind."

Peter's goal, per him, was to have one idea, at least, per sentence. His best mentoring, he said, came from journalists, which makes sense. His reviews have an urgent quality. Breaking news!

"There's a new old painter in town: Hans Holbein the Younger . . ."

Peter luxuriated in rare words. He liked dormant but appropriate vocabulary that otherwise might languish in the dictionary. Startling words occurred in sentences as if to say, "Perhaps you'd like to try *this* wine instead?" Always perfect, they could jar a sentence midway, unless you wanted to skip over them and miss out on the prize. I recently ran across the phrase "Kandinsky's epigones." *Epigone: A less distinguished follower or imitator of someone, especially an artist or philosopher*. He turned twelve words into one with a wave of his wand. "What a useful word," you think; an epigone is not just a follower, but a *less distinguished* follower, especially of an artist. And here I am using it.

It's easy to think you can write like Peter, intrepidly flinging words around, but it's dangerous. Even as I type his sentences it's like slipping on someone else's clothes: "Hey, this almost fits!" But an observer will tell you that you look odd. It's one thing to learn the word "epigone," but it's another to find out you are one.

One September day in 2010, Anne and I received an urgent communication from Peter. The Frick's Rembrandt self-portrait from 1658—"the best painting in the museum, if not the world," according to Peter—was in the process of being courtesy cleaned at the Met. Would we like to drop in on the conservation lab and see the work in progress? Oh yes. Peter had written nimbly about Rembrandt. On the intricacies of Rembrandt's drawing of Cain killing Abel:

"The drawing establishes that murder requires concentration, a sure method, and that it hurts."

We went through the bowels of the Met, past a scattershot assortment of paintings undergoing restoration—Rubens, Stanley Spencer, O'Keeffe—and finally up into the sunny atelier of the conservation room. And there it was.

Unadorned on an easel, the painting, out of its frame, loomed. There was a clear feeling that the artist was with us but invisible, that his brush had just lifted from the canvas. Peter approached the painting, absorbing it, looking up and down, and we waited for the perfect comment, epigrammatic and quotable. He turned, gleeful: "Where are his knees? He has no knees! His knees are somewhere out here in the room." Then he held his thumb up at arm's length, covering and uncovering Rembrandt's right eye. "See that white dot in his right eye? Cover that and the face loses its vitality."

In 2019, Peter was diagnosed with advanced lung cancer and began experimental treatment. He wrote his final salute-to-life essay, which was published in *The New Yorker*. It caused a stir in the art world, which marveled at its grace, candor, and delicate phrase-turning.

Anne suggested we form a group around Peter and Brooke and head off to Spain and the Prado for a farewell confrontation with his obsession, Velázquez's *Las Meninas*. Deborah Solomon and Kent Sepkowitz would join, and the six of us would dare to spend five days with one another, though we had never previously traveled together. We set a date five weeks ahead, not confident about what the future would bring.

Then we learned that the experimental cancer treatment was working. Peter, miraculously, sprang back to full energy.

We all saluted science, which saved our friend and the world's own essayist, and subsequently landed in Madrid. Peter, embracing jet lag, bounded off the plane and raced off to our first stop. Several hours later we were standing beneath Goya's early frescoes at the Real Ermita de San Antonio de la Florida, hushed within a holy—in my case, secular—silence.

In Spain dinners start late, but the time change worked for us perfectly. Anne and I went from low-key mom-and-pop dinners in New York at six, to glamorous and wide-eyed Madrid dinners at ten. Our group of six gelled, and soon we were a community of smart travelers, now plotting agendas, timetables, entrance times, and evaluating possibly lengthy queues.

We finally arrived at the hallowed Prado, where Peter got us an expedited entrance—a noted art critic's perk, not a comedy actor's—and we were off and literally running. At first the group clung together, then adventurously separated, relying on accidental meetups. Seeking out Goya's family portrait of Charles IV of Spain, I felt quietly pleased that Peter reconsidered the ostensibly conventional royal portrait after I extolled the jewels of light that subtly shimmer in the painting's middle.

The Prado cafeteria, airy and fun, with a Wayne Thiebaud-esque display of luscious cakes and tarts, was in the main lobby and became a hub from which we would fan out to see endless roomfuls of Goyas and the still lifes of Meléndez and Chardin, about whom Peter once said, "Were I a rival of Chardin, I would briefly consider hanging myself."

But Peter's home base was *Las Meninas*. He was magnetized to it. If he strayed, even in the maze of the Prado, he eventually found his way back like a mouse to cheese on a trap, moving closer, farther, his contemplation punctuated by indecipherable looks back to us. What we saw was no doubt different than what he saw, though he once wrote: "The only way to miss Velásquez is to be blind." Regarding his many encounters with the painting, he wrote: "Pity the fool I was when I last viewed his work. This time I get it!"

After the Prado and his Velásquez injection, Peter soared. All of us, his wife and his friends who accompanied him, felt the trip had cleansed his mind and body, but probably his second wind was provoked by spotting the finish line. He came back from the Prado energized, but two years later, according to Brooke, he returned from the Met's Cubism show mortally exhausted.

Peter used his health reprieve well, publishing forty-five more essays after he had published his own premature eulogy in *The New Yorker*. Yes, forty-five.

And that is this book.

INTRODUCTION: FOR A LIVING

JARRETT EARNEST

Peter had just received the diagnosis: six months to live. In early September 2019 we met in one of his favorite haunts in the East Village, a grubby Ukrainian restaurant where we'd eaten countless times over the last few years. I'd gotten into the habit of recording conversations while hanging out with my friends. Always haphazard, and without a goal beyond some open-ended Warholian reportage. "Peter, mind if I record?" "Sure." Switching on Voice Memos, laying the iPhone on the table, the process weirdly goes out of mind. Now, eight months after Peter's death, almost four years after the diagnosis, I can hear the sounds of that evening again for the first time: the clattering dishes and chattering patrons, the waiter setting down dinner. We ordered the same thing, blueberry blintzes—I wouldn't have remembered that. Here's a stretch from the beginning; we're discussing a few artworks in the Frick Collection:

PS: But it took me a long time to start looking at the Velázquez and the Rembrandt. I remember I fell in love with one painting they don't always have up by Théodore Rousseau, a little landscape.* It's a kind of village in the woods—I mean there are trees and there is a road coming forward and a horseman coming forward and it's raining, there's a little puddle in it—I love Rousseau, actually, I love Barbizon—and there is a kind of odd lumpiness. It all feels kind of, I don't know, organic, or like maybe there can be an earthquake or

* Théodore Rousseau, *The Village of Becquigny*, circa 1857.

something. It isn't *still*. And I thought: I'm sitting here looking at this and I bet nobody has looked at this in four months. They haven't spent any time with it. I'm spending half an hour with it.

JE: When you find something that isn't famous, you're free to develop your own relationship with it.

PS: Yeah!

JE: You've never heard anyone else talk about it, and then it almost seems like a whetstone for sharpening your own perceptions of art.

PS: That's what I was doing—not consciously, but that is exactly the spirit in which I discovered art and kept at it. Trying to see something new. Or seeing newly. Going back and back to the Frick over years, realizing that art doesn't change but we do. It's like a different painting at different times, but that was all about me. We've talked about narcissism as workshop equipment; you look at yourself and see how it affects you, monitoring your own feelings . . .

JE: How did that Rousseau landscape change for you over the years?

PS: I don't know now. I know it did. But that is part of the physiology of memory: I only remember the last time I saw it, with a sense of nostalgia for previous things I can't feel anymore. Memory overwrites.

JE: In terms of professional equipment, then, it might be useful to keep a little notebook when you see art, but neither of us keeps a journal that way.

PS: That would seem vain to me. That would be embarrassing. I'm a self-denigrating narcissist. You know, I've never written a page of a journal. I've tried at times, and I think, this isn't me—first of all I should put on a smoking jacket and have a dog sitting in front of a fire. You know, I'm just a kid from Minnesota . . .

Here's the voice readers of Peter's art criticism will recognize—he really talked like that—except in person it was funnier, and more freewheeling. After about an hour of this, and not wanting to avoid the matter at hand, I hear myself trying to shift the conversation.

JE: If you want to talk about ground zero of meaningfulness, you and I are sitting at a table in the East Village and talking about art. And that gesture has always been one that is inherently meaning-making for me: we've set time aside and this is what we're doing with it. In the context of you now having a much more urgent sense of mortality—

PS: You got that right!

JE: —that becomes clarifying.

PS: It's very clarifying.

JE: We haven't really spoken about that since you've gotten this medical information, so how are you processing it?

PS: Dr. Sam says, "The prospect of being hanged in the morning concentrates a man's mind wonderfully." You know that saying? So my mind is concentrated rather wonderfully. Which, with my mind, doesn't mean pursuing any kind of path to a particular question. But a very heightened noticing.

JE: I guess I'm asking what matters to you—what do you want to do in the next few months?

PS: I want to do everything I would do anyway, with more appreciation. I was thinking, *What do I want from the world now?* I can't think of a single thing. You know, it's pure gratitude—gratitude defined as wanting what you have. I see no gaps. It has nothing to do with ideals, but with real stuff.

After we left the restaurant Peter walked me to the train, past his apartment. Along the way we stopped to discuss the visual merit of a square of crumbling sidewalk, enacting his "heightened noticing," testing the theory that the validity of any kind of aesthetic experience lies in the quality of attention brought to bear upon it. In the days following, Peter was almost euphoric, reconciling complex relationships, tying up some loose ends and letting others remain undone with magnanimity and aplomb. He also started writing short personal vignettes in a kind of rapture.

Peter was peculiar about writing. A working critic, he proudly explained that he never wrote "for himself" but only and always on deadline for publication. Whatever these new fragments would add up to remained unclear, whether they'd "become something," paid for and published. At the time he said, "I could go on writing this forever." The magic window lasted a few weeks, slammed shut by an electrical fire in his building on St. Mark's Place that October. Beginning in the apartment below, it consumed the contents of Peter's crammed office, right next to the bedroom where he and his wife, Brooke, were sleeping. Luckily they woke up and got out, huddling on the street in their nightclothes while the firefighters rushed in.

With the records of his writing life gone, displaced from the comfortable and deeply ingrained routines of nearly fifty years, Peter couldn't continue writing those beautiful little aphorisms. Instead, in a sublet on Avenue C, he threw himself into shaping them into what became "77 Sunset Me," published in the print edition of *The New Yorker* just before Christmas 2019 and posted to the magazine's Web site as "The Art of Dying." A multifaceted memoir about a life in art, it was instantly hailed a classic—the reigning critical voice of his generation bidding the world adieu, with a few jokes and a lot of style.

Neither the diagnosis nor the fire interrupted Peter's commitment to writing. He had a job to do. A month and a half after "The Art of Dying" appeared, he resumed his column with a review of painter Peter Saul's retrospective at the New Museum. He dove headlong into Saul's Day-Glo grotesquerie, even laughing about a painting that depicts Peter blowing his brains out beside another art critic (it wasn't in the show; he asked for it to be reproduced in the magazine). Peter had known Saul's work for years but never engaged. The piece heralded an expansive generosity—borne no doubt by the sense of gratitude he'd described—returning to art and artists he'd thought little of, seeking capacities for renewed thinking and feeling. This setup for his epic essay on Jasper Johns's retrospective is characteristic of the tone: "In past writing, I've complained about those frailties in the face of pious praise of everything from his hand. I guess I wanted him, great as he is, to be greater still. Now, amid his art's abounding glories, I declare unconditional surrender."

In conversations he often referenced the fourteenth-century mystical tract *The Cloud of Unknowing*, which teaches a method of contemplation where one willfully releases all prior conceptions of life, pushing into a great "unknowing" wherein God becomes manifest. It gave theological word to the techniques he'd developed for encountering art. This long-standing habit of mind, which enabled him to grapple with new art, as well as reconsider canonized masters, was reinforced by Peter's diagnosis. Here, in column after column, was an opportunity to think it all anew.

As he neared the six-month mark, Peter discovered that his body was responding to an experimental immunotherapy. This good news was greeted by the onset of the COVID-19 pandemic, with New York City entering lockdown in mid-March, an apocalyptic setting for Peter's personal saga. He and Brooke decamped to their house in upstate New York. The timetable he'd reconciled himself to was replaced with a receding horizon, in a world suddenly altered beyond recognition. Museums and galleries desperately tried to adapt their programs online, to mostly weak effect. In response he wrote "Mortality and the Old Masters," a companion to "The Art of Dying" and a meditation on painting and history. The essay ends by imagining the reencounter with art in the aftermath of calamity: "Here's a prediction of our experience when we are again free to wander museums: Everything in them will be other than what we remember. The objects won't have altered, but we will have, in some ratio of good and ill. The casualties of the coronavirus will accompany us spectrally. Until, inevitably, we begin to forget, for a while we will have been reminded of our oneness throughout the world and across time with all the living and the dead."

It wasn't until late summer 2020 that Peter was experiencing art again directly, beginning with a tour of the comparatively COVID-safe sculpture park Storm King Art Center in New York's Hudson Valley. This inaugurated a sequence of essays about the experience of being with art in person, reveling in a joyful sensitivity. Take the incandescent review of an exhibition with the unlikely pairing of the still lifes of Giorgio Morandi—a longstanding passion—with the hard-edged abstractions of Josef Albers, whom he had largely written off. It proved a revelation: "To my amazement, viewing them together electrifies, as their works' extremes play off each other. Think of it as a pas de deux of a drill sergeant (Albers) and an enchanter (Morandi). There's a crackle in perception when you turn from works by one artist to those of the other." The narrative ends with a deeply felt credo in the midst of the pandemic: "Nearly a year of being disheartened by the online garishness and promotional smarm of digitized images has set me up to rediscover the pungency of direct aesthetic experience. There can be no meaningful discourse about art divorced from that. Intellectual appreciation starves for want of it. The less you see, the dumber you get."

Peter's writing always foregrounds his experience of the work at hand, attending to his immediate perceptions and associations as a firsthand account of art's effects—what he'd meant by calling narcissism a professional tool. These responses provide a framework for retelling events from an artist's life, adding context for choices made. The result is criticism that models both *how* and *why* art matters. Three eventful years passed, encompassing not only the COVID-19 pandemic, but also the intensification of the ongoing Black Lives Matter protests and growing movements for social justice, the election of Joe Biden over Donald Trump amid political polarization, and the war in Ukraine: these upheavals, along with the tremors they sent through the art world, also registered in Peter's writing. He carried on doing what "I would do anyway, with more appreciation."

In October 2022 Peter drove the three hours to the Museum of Modern Art from his place upstate with a young neighbor, Kaz. We met at the retrospective of German photographer Wolfgang Tillmans. Peter had always been thin, and now as he was nearing the end, he was starting to resemble one of his favorite Munch paintings, a comically intense skeletal Norwegian. He walked in coughing, assuring, "It's not COVID!" Later he found out it was pneumonia, which had also plagued him through writing his penultimate piece, a terrific review of a biography of Mondrian, an artist he loved.

Peter seemed poised to deflate what appeared to him to be a lot of commercial and critical hype: big pictures, pretty people, money all around. It was a normal day, and the gallery was mobbed, especially with young people, hyper-styled, enthralled, which for Peter was a key sign that the artist was connecting with an important new impulse in the culture. As we moved around the first gallery containing the earliest works, he was enraptured. They were so fresh, without simple explanation. Peter reflected on some of his favorite photographers, about whom he'd written so thoughtfully over the years—Diane Arbus, Stephen Shore, Nan Goldin—measuring the distance between their work and what we were seeing, attempting to register the nature of Tillmans's achievement. We stopped at works that were by turns breathtaking and consternating. Peter was busy scribbling words in a little notebook like a reporter in a noir movie, bits of description, disconnected phrases that seemed apt.

He spent a long time with pictures that he thought were flawed, attending to his dislikes as actively as his loves, knowing those were more indicative of what was new. And he wrote through these ambivalences and contradictions in what turned out to be his final column—he died on October 21, eleven days after it was published in the magazine. It opens: "'To Look Without Fear,' the immense, flabbergastingly installed retrospective of the German photographer Wolfgang Tillmans, at the Museum of Modern Art, persuades me that the man is a genius. There's a downside to the concession—it dampens my quarrels of taste with certain items, among the show's predominantly brilliant several hundred, that I do not like." For a proclamation of genius there is a lot of critique. It is bracing to watch a mind grapple with serious art, conceding greatness yet able to leave questions on the table.

It's often remarked that Peter had an almost freakish gift for the English language—critic as artist, poet-journalist. As he thought of it, he just had this facility, discovered as a small child in rural Minnesota, for doing things with words. Where it came from mystified him, contributing to his conviction that talent is fundamentally impersonal. Even with this marvelous ability, he worked very hard to make it matter: alone in a room, just him and the words, coaxing order out of the pigsty of ordinary sensation. "Taking a sick sentence and making it better," as he once put it. Technical acuity irradiated, more and more over time, by love.

The Tillmans review concludes with a passage that captures the critic's specific gift. Peter is discussing pictures of random detritus scattered on windowsills and studio floors after parties. "These photographs shouldn't amount to much, but to me they are stunningly lovely and, with only trace elements of melancholy, poetically more telling of communal ecstasy than any shots of the originating events could be. Think about mornings. They're when the purest sense of what we are doing, or not doing, with our temporary habitation of the Earth sinks in." Now think about how Peter spent his own mornings: chain-smoking in his office, writing about art.

THE ART OF DYING

Lung cancer, rampant. No surprise. I've smoked since I was sixteen, behind the high-school football bleachers in Northfield, Minnesota. I used to fear the embarrassment of dying youngish, letting people natter sagely, "He smoked, you know." But at seventy-seven I'm into the actuarial zone.

I know about ending a dependency. I'm an alcoholic twenty-seven years sober. Drink was destroying my life. Tobacco only shortens it, with the best parts over anyway.

I got the preliminary word from my doctor by phone while driving alone upstate from the city to join my wife, Brooke, at our country place. After the call, I found myself overwhelmed by the beauty of the passing late-August land. At mile eighty-one of the New York State Thruway, the gray silhouettes of the Catskills come into view, perfectly framed and proportioned. How many times had I seen and loved the sight? How many more times would I? I thought of Thomas Cole's paintings, from another angle, of those very old, worn mountains, brooding on something until the extinction of matter.

Patsy Cline was playing on the car radio: "Walkin' After Midnight." Not a great song, but performed in Cline's way of attending selflessly to the sounds and the senses of the words. Showing how art should be done. She was thirty when she died in a plane crash, consummate.

I was at the wheel of my first brand-new car since 1962, a blue Subaru Forester that I dote on. I wanted for nothing. I want for nothing. The other night, I dreamed that I fetched the car from a parking lot only to find that it was another Subaru Forester, with two hundred thousand miles on it, dirty and falling apart. (That's diseased me now, I suppose.) But the real one sits gleaming on East Seventh Street today.

Twenty-some years ago, I got a Guggenheim grant to write a memoir. I ended up using most of the money to buy a garden tractor. I failed for a number of reasons.

I don't feel interesting.

I don't trust my memories (or anyone's memories) as reliable records of anything—and I have a fear of lying. Nor do I have much documentary material. I've never kept a diary or a journal, because I get spooked by addressing no one. When I write, it's to connect.

I am beset, too, by obsessively remembered thudding guilts and scalding shames. Small potatoes, as traumas go, but intensified by my aversion to facing them.

Susan Sontag observed that when you have a disease people identify you with it. Fine by me! I could never sustain an expedient "I" for more than a paragraph. (Do you imagine that writers speak "as themselves"? No such selves exist.) Playing the Dying Man (*Enter left. Exit trapdoor*) gives me a persona. It's a handy mask.

I've lost the scraps of my aborted Guggenheim memoir, but I remember that it started something like this:

> On September 9, 1956, in the very small Minnesota town of Farmington, my family of seven settled in, as we did every week, to watch "The Ed Sullivan Show." We had the living-room lights off because we were still confusing TV with film. Elvis Presley came on. My grandmother said, "Disgusting!" My parents made discontented sounds. When Presley finished, I left the house and started walking over to my friend Richie Sievers's

house. Autumn leaves covered the sidewalks and ground. I met Richie coming the other way. One of us said, “Did you see that?” “Yeah, what do you think?” “I don’t know. What do you think?” “I don’t know.” We stood silent, kicking at leaves. Something had happened.

I thought I’d braid my life into cultural history. That went nowhere.

Death is like painting rather than like sculpture, because it’s seen from only one side. Monochrome—like the mausoleum-gray former Berlin Wall, which kids in West Berlin glamorized with graffiti. What I’m trying to do here.

Swatted a fly the other day and thought, Outlived *you*.

I grew up in small-town Minnesota being regarded as the rich kid, because my father’s firms (first manufacturing plastic bags, then engineering inventions including the NASA Echo 1 and Echo 2 Mylar-balloon satellites) were the biggest businesses around. I had no sense of this, thinking that the kids who sucked up to me and the others who bullied me were reacting to my true self. This left me deeply confused. Years later, I asked my mother if she had been aware of the pattern. She said yes. I asked why she hadn’t said anything to me about it. She said, “Because people shouldn’t be like that.”

The Midwest!

My mother was a prairie princess, the only child of a school superintendent who doubled as a postmaster, from a tiny town in North Dakota. My father was a railroad worker’s son from another. I was born in Fargo. In the summer of 1945, when I was three and a half, alone in the kitchen of my great-uncle Martin's farmhouse—water by hand pump; chamber pots and an outhouse—a grizzled man came in and tried to grab me. I ran screaming. It was Dad, home from the war.

My mother maintained a peaceful home, and neither she nor my father was ever physically abusive. But they were wrapped up in themselves and each other to the extreme of being jealous of their five kids, of whom I'm the oldest. From my father's point of view, God forbid my mother should waste affection on me that could go to him. Zero sum. Everything that he had went into his work, and everything that she had went into him. The one and only way I could attain his attention was to be insolent, to make my mother cry. Then he'd rage but at least make eye contact.

I grew up with a craving for and a resentment of authority. This bedevils me still.

In love letters, my mother addressed him as the President, and he called her the Student Body.

What my parents were doing having children mystifies, beyond the given, during the Depression and the war eras, that marriage required it. My father was a self-made extraordinary inventor and engineer and a successful but credulous—i.e., exploitable—entrepreneur. He may have suffered lifelong post-traumatic stress from his ordeals as a grunt in the Battle of the Bulge. He wouldn't talk about it except in bursts now and then. But he had nightmares.

My father's fragmentary stories from the war left big gaps in time. Here's what I can piece together. He was a private in a division, the 84th, that helped to roll back the German advance. He was hunkered down in snow on the day that my sister Ann was born, two days before Christmas, 1944. His infantry units would creep to the edge of villages to suppress any anti-tank fire ahead of armored advances. Once, one of our own tanks churned across a foxhole he was in, burying him and killing the man, a close friend, next to him. My father was a radio operator until, ordered to take a radio to a cutoff platoon, he and another soldier came under mortar fire. They dived into a shell hole. The mortars zeroed in, "like someone bouncing a basketball around the hole," he said. A near-hit wounded his partner. Making a break for it, my father helped the man and lugged the radio, which, when they reached the platoon, was found to be wrecked by shrapnel. He was awarded a Bronze Star and spent the rest of the war as a rifleman.

I have a photograph of him with some of his comrades outside a battered church. He grins rather maniacally and holds a lectern—inexplicable loot from the church. He brought home a German helmet and uniform, a German rifle-cleaning kit, a piece of transparent plastic from the cockpit canopy of a downed Messerschmitt, an artillery-shell casing, a large fragment of an exploded grenade, and a steel ammunition box on which he had painted, in his elegant engineer's hand, his division logo and the names of the places where he had fought. I played continually with those objects as a boy, fantasizing about military glory.

Once, he spoke of being under artillery bombardment in a forest. It frightened me. His tone hinted at still-unrelieved, helpless terror.

Late in life, going dotty (or dottier than usual), my father contemplated returning to the battle zone of the Ardennes and seeking out German privates who had fought on the other side. He wanted to test his theory that they had hated their officers as much as he had hated his—whose sole aim, from his perspective, was to squander the lives of their men.

I recounted this plan to the German painter Anselm Kiefer, who was born in 1945. As I recall, though he doesn't, he said, "Don't tell your father. Our men loved their officers."

I was friends with Kiefer for a while, as I was with many artists over the years, until about twenty years ago. The friendships fell apart. Closeness is impossible between an artist and a critic. Each wants from the other something—the artist's mojo, the critic's sagacity—that belongs strictly to the audiences for their respective work. It's like two vacuum cleaners sucking at each other.

My father was on a cutting edge—quite literally, as one of the first to discover how to simultaneously cut and seal polyethylene with a hot knife, experimenting in the basement of our modest house. He invented the plastic-lined paper sickness bag for airplanes, for which he received a dollar. (The patent belonged to the company he was working for.) What remained of the family fortune when he died has all but gone to the care of my mother, who is chipper at the age of a hundred and two.

Too much about my dad? Exactly! His charisma bleached the identities of his five children. I spent years of my childhood trying to win his approval and years of my adolescence trying to provoke his disapproval, until I had to accept that he didn't care either way. When I told him on the phone, in 1998, that I'd been hired by *The New Yorker*, there was a long silence. Then he said, "Oh, you kids!"

Too little about my mother? Exactly again. My memories of her from my childhood amount to a uniform haze of bland niceness punctuated with flares of incomprehensible anger or tears and almost no sense of emotional connection. She was, and remains, a constant reader without a trace of intellectual curiosity. She tells everybody that she's proud of me. I'm a credit to her.

I was set up to be the tower-of-strength big brother, a surrogate parent, and my three younger sisters and my younger brother bought into it. But my heart was a loveless void. I broke free at the cost of hating myself for letting my siblings down. Estrangements ensued that now, one by one, are healing. Ann, Don, Peggy, Mary, and me: an accountant, a geographer, a massage therapist, a chef, and an art critic. We've done all right.

Still, people I know will roll their eyes—same old Peter!—at how little of their deserved shrift they're receiving from me here as, alone, I linger again with my lifelong lover: you, reader.

I was a kid crazy about language and an omnivorous reader. At breakfast, I'd pore over every word on a cereal box as if it were holy writ. The first poem I remember writing was at a class picnic on the last day of sixth grade. I lay back on the grass, looking up. A hawk soared overhead. This wasn't unusual, but it gave me an odd feeling. I rolled over and wrote what I knew was a poem because it looked like one. All I recall of it is a chorus: "Winged avenger from the skies!" I'm not sure that I even knew what an avenger was. I took the poem to my teacher, who said, "Peter, this is very unpleasant." That smothered my literary drive for some years.

In a car with high-school classmates after a picnic party somewhere in rural Minnesota—a bottle had been passed, and I would have proof that Cheetos were on the bill of fare—I said to stop. I tumbled out and barfed beside the road. The vomit was bright orange. It puddled on bright-green grass. The summer sky was bright blue. I thought I had never seen anything so beautiful.

My rags-to-riches-to-fewer-riches father decided that his children should make their own way in the world, as he had. So no financial support beyond college and such emergency aid as was required to pay a fine, say, rather than have me spend a year in jail (pot bust in Maine) and, oh, yes, the funds for the little yellow Austin-Healey Sprite in which, dropping out of college in Minnesota, I drove east on a slim chance. That was in 1962. I was twenty.

I had wanted out of school and, after a landlocked upbringing, yearned to see an ocean. In those days, cities of any size had dailies. I sent letters to papers in small cities near big ones, three on the East Coast and three on the West. Only the Jersey *Journal*, in Jersey City, replied, offering an interview. I drove through a day and a night, my tiny car drafting behind barrelling trucks, to Journal Square, which glistened in the sun after a night rain. An editor asked where I was staying. I think I mumbled something. He said, "You don't have a place to stay, do you?" Then he said, "Oh, hell, take a desk."

Hudson County, New Jersey, was epically corrupt. Several Jersey City mayors have gone to jail. One day, in 1963, a reporter hung up the phone and announced, "Tony Pro is having another press conference." Mysteriously, everybody laughed. "Let's send the kid," someone said.

At the Teamsters headquarters in Union City, Tony (Pro) Provenzano sat behind an immense desk, flanked by central-casting bodyguards. Other reporters lounged and smoked. Only I had a notebook ready. Tony Pro told a series of obscene jokes about Attorney General Robert Kennedy, who was crusading against the Mob. And that was that. Tony Pro stood at the door shaking hands with us. *Crinkle*. In my palm was the first fifty-dollar bill I had ever seen. I said thanks, but I really couldn't. I set the bill down when he wouldn't take it back.

Staring eyes greeted my return to the paper, and the editor-in-chief called me into his office and shut the door. He said, "I don't know what you did or what you said, and I don't want to know. Never do it or say it again."

Later that year, when Provenzano was on trial in Newark for extortion, he sat down beside me during a break and chatted amiably about something, maybe baseball.

I acquired the most useful writing discipline of my life from fat, cigar-chewing Jersey *Journal* copy editors—burned-out reporters—at desks in a half circle facing the city editor. With No. 1 pencils, like black crayons, they'd eviscerate my copy. I'd rewrite, and they'd do it again. Finally, they sent it down to the Linotype—the old racketing, reeking contraption for setting type from molten lead. Those men still sit by as I write, pencils in their itching paws.

"Sleeping the big sleep." Raymond Chandler proved that the American form of Montaigne-grade aphorism is the wisecrack.

Wisecracks in Chandler are existential rescues of imperilled self-possession. Worth the risk to the detective of a punch in the gut. And conserving calm for noticing the world.

"A slanting gray rain like a swung curtain of crystal beads."

"A few windows were lit and radios were bleating at the dusk."

I lost my interminably heavy-petting virginity with the recently graduated fiancée of a college friend who was still at school, a senior. I had been invited to my friend's parents' penthouse on Sutton Place South, an apartment that was deluxe beyond my dreaming. A spotlighted Willem de Kooning painting stunned me: wild but somehow purposeful, clinching an unstated argument. The woman and I left together and fell to making out in the elevator, then proceeded to a cheap hotel on Lexington Avenue. We had a frenzied affair, only about sex. It was what's now termed empowering.

I went back to college in Minnesota for a year, dropped out for good, returned to the Jersey City job for three months, unwisely married, spent an impoverished and largely useless year in Paris, had a life-changing encounter with a painting by Piero della Francesca in Italy, another with works by Andy Warhol in Paris, returned to New York, freelanced, stumbled into the art world, got a divorce, which, while uncontested, entailed a solo trip to a dusty courthouse in Juárez, Mexico, past a kid saying, "Hey, hippie, wanna screw my sister?," to receive a spectacular document with a gold seal and a red ribbon from a judge as rotund and taciturn as an Olmec idol.

When I started writing criticism, in 1965, in almost pristine ignorance, I discovered that I was the world's leading expert in one thing: my experience. Most of what I know in a scholarly way about art I learned on deadlines, to sound as if I knew what I was talking about—as, little by little, I did. Educating yourself in public is painful, but the lessons stick.

In 1966, after a few months of writing mostly one-sentence reviews for *The Art News*, I was hired as the art critic of the *Village Voice*, for the first of three stints with the often marvellous weekly. (The others spanned 1980–81 and 1991–98.) I had a problem besides inexperience: a question of priorities, between meeting deadlines and doing lots of drugs—a no-brainer in more than one way. I lasted in that job for only a few weeks. Meanwhile, the poetry scene, centered on St. Mark's Church, was both expanding and unravelling, as rock songs displaced poems as soul food for young hearts and minds. But the art scene boomed. Art parties were immeasurably more fun than poetry parties.

Starting in 1967, I began writing regularly for the *Times*' Sunday Arts & Leisure section. The section's editor, Seymour Peck, a flinty New Yorker, had me write columns on movies, theatre, rock music, and television as well as on art, extending my capacities, while cracking down on my flakiness. He practically invented me as a functioning professional.

My uptown feats didn't impress people whom I looked up to in the downtown art scene, where anti-bourgeois hardheadedness and minimalist disdain for the "literary" reigned. They were contemptuous of the *Times*. I was Peter the poet, a relative nobody. Advice to aspiring youth: in New York, the years that you spend as a nobody are painful but golden, because no one bothers to lie to you. The moment you're a somebody, you have heard your last truth. Everyone will try to spin you—as they should, with careers to think of. For about a dozen years, I hung out, drank, and slept with artists who didn't take me seriously. I observed, heard, overheard, and absorbed a great deal.

One drunken night, a superb painter let me take a brush to a canvas that she said she was abandoning. I tried to continue a simple black stroke that she had started. The contrast between the controlled pressure of her touch and my flaccid smear shocked me, physically. It was like shaking hands with a small person who flips you across a room.

At a time, in the early seventies, when I slept a lot, I kept track of my dreams, writing a book distilling some of them. For example, "Conceptual Art":

> I am in Cleveland on a sort of official art junket. With the head of the local museum—a handsome, dapper black man—I visit a young artist in his new loft. The loft is large and sunny; facing its dozens of windows are dozens of old, uncomfortable-looking armchairs.
>
> Jokingly, I suggest that the artist could create "a terrific Conceptual art-work entitled 'Golf'" by placing a golfball on each of the chairs, then, with a golf club, hitting it through a closed window.
>
> To my surprise, I am taken seriously. The artist agrees to perform the work the very next day.
>
> As for the police, who will obviously be called when the street below is showered with golfballs and broken glass, the museum director has a plan. There is a secret passage from the loft to a building next door, he says, and in that building a large sum of money is hidden that we can use to finance our escape from Cleveland.
>
> We all agree that "Golf" will be an event of tremendous artistic importance.

That prose-poetic experiment ended when I entered Jungian therapy and presented my dreams for interpretation. They all made abundant sense, which was entertaining but not terribly helpful. My problem was not a lack of connection with the collective unconscious. I was a fucking poet. My problem was getting out of bed in the morning.

The birth of Brooke's and my daughter, Ada, on St. Patrick's Day, 1976, saw to that. When your baby cries, you're out of bed before being fully awake.

Ada was present when my oncologist, at Memorial Sloan Kettering, gave me six months or so to live. Ada asked me what I wanted to do. Revisit Rome? Paris? I would forget that I said, "Nah. Maybe a ballgame." She arranged it, with family and friends: Mets versus Braves, at Citi Field. Glorious. Grandson Oliver caught a T-shirt from the mid-game T-shirt cannon. Odds of that: several thousand to one.

Writing consumes writers. No end of ones better than I am have said as much. The passion hurts relationships. I think off and on about people I love, but I think about writing all the time.

Writing is hard, or everyone would do it.

You're reading an exception, which is pouring out of me. It's the first writing "for myself" that I've done in about thirty years, since I gave up on poetry (or poetry gave up on me) because I didn't know what a poem was any longer and had severed or sabotaged all my connections to the poetry world. An impermeable block has crumbled, my muse being, I guess, the grim reaper.

I'm given pause here by my unreconstructed reverence for extreme states of mind and feeling. Think William Blake and Edgar Allan Poe. Huysmans. I've often quoted Baudelaire: "I cultivated my hysteria with terror and delight." But I also thrilled to the august sanities of Paul Valéry ("Stupidity is not my strong suit") and Auden ("Poetry makes nothing happen"). Another extreme.

Extremity was the spirit of my drug-using, which I never really enjoyed: pot, acid, DMT, and downers taken pragmatically, in service to "systematic derangement of the senses" (Rimbaud). Did the drugs help? I don't know. The acid taught me things about the mind by making all of its workings simultaneously perceptible, though to no one—ego dissolving like Alka-Seltzer in warm water.

I dodged the Vietnam draft by staying awake for three days and nights on speed, taking any other drugs that came to hand, rolling in dirt, presenting myself at the induction center on Whitehall Street, and trying to coöperate. The draft officials discarded me like a used condom. I felt guilty. I brooded that some guy would have to go in my place. I had faked psychosis so well that my sanity teetered for months afterward.

Baudelaire wrote of having been "brushed by the wind of the wing of madness." I have felt that breeze at times, though not in a great many years now. I still have the occasional thought that what is commonly deemed sanity is absurd; but I let that slide.

I met Susan Sontag once, at a party. She came up and praised something that I had written. Thrilled, I began chattering about I don't remember what. Sontag froze. She retreated, taking backward steps before turning away. It dawned on me that receiving her blessing was supposed to have been enough: a solemn initiation. I had presumed on it.

At the end of my multi-drug sixties, I figuratively put all the chemicals in a funnel, and they came out bourbon. Jack Daniel's-on-the-rocks, with a splash, except when scarce funds reduced me to Heaven Hill. Alcohol was liberating for me at first. A standard progression: great, good, fair, poor, bad, very bad, and then a phase for which any word but "hell" fails. Halfway through the second drink, there may be a flicker of the old euphoria, quickly snuffed. You chase it in vain for the rest of a wretched night. It's over for you. A line has been crossed. Yet you cannot imagine yourself not drinking. The obsession is at one with your core sense of self.

Brooke drinks. We keep a full liquor cabinet. I mix drinks for guests without a qualm. The booze is a different chemical in their bodies from what it would be in mine. Pleasant for them, poison for me.

Free. Sort of free. Who's free? I can see the paragraphs I'm writing as little jail cells, penning me into perspectives, conceits, ideas, jokes, and memories—stories! Not an original type of anxiety, for a writer.

Writers can be only so conscientious about truth before becoming paralyzed.

I remember thinking in the sixties that becoming emotionally paralyzed could be cool if one were in an interesting enough position. Coolness was the holy grail then. I was hopeless at it. Sincerity is my accursed default.

I had a rage of ambition and an acrid dissatisfaction that, along with a love of the world, were bound to come out somehow. The self-centered motives have waned. It's harder to pitch into writing with less to prove or avenge. To start a critical essay, I must prod myself until the old mesmerized flow resumes.

When I finish something and it seems good, I'm dazed. It must have been fun to write. I wish I'd been there.

In my drinking years, I took to saying, for a laugh, "The only thing I want in life is a written apology from everyone I've ever met." Arrogant! But, truth to tell, arrogance—as a placeholder for confidence, of which I had none—enabled me to brave the world when I was young.

The same goes for snobbery, a necessary stage for the insecure until we acquire taste that admits and reflects the variety of experience.

To limber your sensibility, stalk the aesthetic everywhere: cracks in a sidewalk, people's ways of walking. The aesthetic isn't bounded by art, which merely concentrates it for efficient consumption. If you can't put a mental frame around, and relish, the accidental aspect of a street or a person, or really of anything, you will respond to art only sluggishly.

I like to say that contemporary art consists of all art works, five thousand years or five minutes old, that physically exist in the present. We look at them with contemporary eyes, the only kinds of eyes that there ever are.

I retain, but suspend, my personal taste to deal with the panoply of the art I see. I have a trick for doing justice to an uncongenial work: "What would I like about this if I liked it?" I may come around; I may not. Failing that, I wonder, What must the people who like this be like? Anthropology.

I assess art by quality and significance. The latter is most decisive for my choice of subjects, because I'm a journalist. There's art I adore that I won't write about, because I can't imagine it mattering enough to general readers. It pertains to my private experience as a person, without which my activity as a critic would wither but which falls outside my critical mandate.

I write for readers and not for artists, who can buy the magazine and read me like anyone else if they're interested. I didn't always. When I was young, I had personal and coterie loyalties. Then I decided to see how responsible a critic I could be, open to ideas but never prescriptive or proscriptive. By academic measure, this makes me not a true critic at all. I can live with that.

Family and friends are being wonderful to me in my sickness. I've toiled all my life, in vain, to like myself. Now the task has been outsourced. I can't go around telling everybody they're idiots.

I always said that when my time came I'd want to go fast. But where's the fun in that?

True story: a friend received a preliminary diagnosis suggesting advanced breast cancer. Normally shy, she took this as license to tell or show everyone in her circle how little she liked or respected them. False alarm. It was cat-scratch fever. She moved overseas.

"When a man knows he is to be hanged in a fortnight, it concentrates his mind wonderfully," per Samuel Johnson.

"Why isn't Schjeldahl's copy in?" "He's dead." "Uh, O.K., then."

The best excuse.

The most delicious poem about someone dying is Auden's "In Memory of W. B. Yeats" (1939), with these lines:

> But for him it was his last afternoon as himself,
> An afternoon of nurses and rumours;
> The provinces of his body revolted,
> The squares of his mind were empty,
> Silence invaded the suburbs,
> The current of his feeling failed; he became his admirers.

The poet Ron Padgett pointed out to me the technical shrewdness of the compound last line: the all-time best use of a semicolon in place of a line break. Then there's the sterling "became": nothing is left of Yeats but others' thoughts of him, and the thoughts of him enhance the others, like badges.

We wear as many such badges as there are dead people we admire. The Shakespeare badge. The Jesus one, though he cheated on Easter morning. At what hour did the Saviour reopen his eyes? At dawn? Before it, with time to kill?

Seeing Hans Holbein's *Dead Christ* (1520–22) shook Dostoyevsky's Christian belief: a two-days-gone corpse in a warm climate, a *thing*.

Simone Weil said that the transcendent meaning of Christianity is complete with Jesus' death, sans the cherry on top that is the Resurrection. I think so.

"I believe in God" is a false statement for me because it is voiced by my ego, which is compulsively skeptical. But the rest of me tends otherwise. Staying on an "as if" basis with "God," for short, hugely improves my life. I regret my lack of the church and its gift of community. My ego is too fat to squeeze through the door.

Disbelieving is toilsome. It can be a pleasure for adolescent brains with energy to spare, but hanging on to it later saps and rigidifies. After a Lutheran upbringing, I became an atheist at the onset of puberty. That wore off gradually and then, with sobriety, speedily.

I had a moment, while anticipating my diagnosis, of feeling special. But what's as commonplace as dying? Everybody does it. I also had an instant of fancying that I could drink again. That evanesced in a flash. Fellow-alcoholics know that the beast, though out of mind, survives. My thought was a foul little burp from a cave.

Life doesn't go on. It goes nowhere except away. Death goes on. Going on is what death does for a living. The secret to surviving in the universe is to be dead.

Self-knowledge! Almost better never than this late. (I don't mean that at all. But I enjoy the sound of it.) I am endeavoring to practice self-forgiveness. I believe it's recommended.

As for folks out there in resentful and envious circles who will be glad to have me out of the way, they, by their pleasure, afford me a bonus credit for increasing human happiness.

"Everyone, it seems, loves Peter Schjeldahl," an art Web site opined recently. I know for dead sure that's not so. To the extent that it's plausible hyperbole and because I believe in a balanced universe, the people who hate me do so with enough intensity to square up the sums.

I think of righteous nonsmokers "in the hospital dying of nothing." That's a line for a role that Brooke played, as a chain-smoking coroner, in a not-great movie, *Just Cause* (1995), with the great Sean Connery, who may or may not have had a say in cutting the line from the released film because it stole the scene. Soon after that, she proved her ability, which I've lacked, to break habits by quitting both smoking and acting. Her subsequent enterprises have ranged from an antiques-and-whatnot store, Brooke's Variety, to a spectacularly unusual mini-golf course on land that we own in the Catskills.

Nicotine stimulates *and* relaxes. Beat that. I understand that it teaches the brain to prefer it to a natural neurotransmitter, acetylcholine, which, among other boons, promotes mental agility. Nicotine does the same, better. How many quitters never miss smoking? (Liars line up on the left.) The times I tried to stop, I wondered what writers do.

L., who is no longer alive, became pregnant on our second date, in 1963. A backstreet abortion in Chicago left her sterile. I married her out of guilt mixed with infatuation. (She was wild and adored me while sleeping around, as I did, too, but I couldn't keep up.) We lasted for most of five years, possibly because a man I disliked had said that he gave us three months.

Lee Crabtree. Jairus Lincoln. Jeff Giles. You don't know about them. They were friends of mine who died young. I'll get over Lee's suicide, in 1973, only when I've joined him. I was harsh the last time I saw him, hiding my love.

Lee was the pianist and musical arranger for the Fugs. One night after an awful fight with L., in which for emphasis I punched out a window, I showed up at Lee's, bleeding. He bandaged and calmed me. He had a big plastic toy horn that I started to toot on. Lee sat at his electric keyboard, and we jammed. Later, he showed me sheet music that he had printed of our improvised creation: "The Red Horn Polka." We collaborated on a song, "Police State," that became the Fugs' first-act closer but isn't on any album, perhaps because it was too dirty, even for them.

Lee was the gentlest, most generous person amid a prevalence of shitheads, who, at the worst possible moment, included me. I knew that he was struggling with his repressed homosexuality. Having been so good a friend, he sorely needed friendship.

At a temporary job on the twelfth floor of a building in midtown, he was seen, at a window, to wave affably to a random person in another building. Then he climbed out the window and stepped into space.

Bury me. Nix to cremation. I want an address that people know they can visit even if they never do. Phooey to dust on a random sea breeze or strewn on a field of unoffending vegetation. Or in a jar? Think about it.

Though cemeteries waste real estate. Better a Walmart parking lot?

Really, do as you please with the corpse—not me, not mine. I believe in earnestly agreeing to deathbed wishes and then forgetting about them, unless it's to satisfy those among the living.

Between bulletins from my body that say this isn't so, I still feel like a kid inside. Four and a half years ago, while rushing to catch a bus ("Don't run for a bus" was a rule for longevity in Mel Brooks's "2000 Year Old Man"), I tripped trying to leap, gazelle-like, over a chunk of broken asphalt and must have caught a toe. When I came to on the street, surrounded by strangers, I had no memory of falling or of much else (who I was, where I was). There was blood. My glasses were smashed. I said, "I'm O.K." The strangers strenuously disagreed. An ambulance had arrived.

I was mostly conscious when wheeled on a gurney into an emergency room in Greenwich Village. A scrawny old-time Village-hipster type was driving the nurses crazy about something, likely trying to wheedle drugs. Strolling past and glancing down at me, he said tenderly, "Die, baby." That didn't seem like a terrible idea, right then, and it struck me in a remote sort of way as the funniest thing I'd ever heard.

A CAT scan to check out a suspicion that my neck was broken (weird story short: my neck was found to have broken and healed sometime in the past, unbeknownst to me) incidentally discovered a spot in my left lung. This later led to hospital visits for scans and tests, including a needle biopsy (ouch), all of them inconclusive. Fed up with the rigmarole, I refused further investigation. Shouldn't have? Live and learn.

Shakespeare wrote of "desiring this man's art and that man's scope." I find this comforting. But who was he thinking of? Marlowe? Someone forgotten although evidently fucking incredible?

Originality is overrated, except by people who have it. It's like an untamed, ungrateful beast you're trapped with. If people praising you knew the half of it, they'd think twice.

I think of Lee Crabtree and of all suicides. What happens? One night in the early seventies, I perched on a tenement-roof edge despite my fear of heights, legs dangling, and ordered myself to let go. It was amid a love disaster. I truly thought I'd jump. But something inside me laughed derisively. Who was I kidding? Humiliated, I went downstairs. Some, in a crisis, must lack the laugh or muffle it for long enough.

Twice I've been to Oaxaca during the Day of the Dead, when the departed members of families have their favorite food, drinks, and perhaps cigarettes set out for them at meals. It's understood that, at the table, the dead consume the immaterial goodness of these things. The families visit them overnight in graveyards. I was deeply moved by the implication that death may be a major life event, such as birth, confirmation, and marriage, but that it doesn't mean you're *gone*. We spare the dead a bit of the life in us. I shuddered suddenly during my second walk among placid, candlelit groups. It hit me that the dead were reciprocating: a bit of the death in them for us. Never fully dead, never fully alive.

I may have this wrong, but I'm savoring the idea. Today, the little bit of death in me has sat up in bed and is pulling on its socks.

I remember arriving in an Italian village by train after midnight and walking past a cemetery where candles burned at every grave, with no one around. Or I think I remember it.

We have lousy memories. Proust had a lousy memory. (There is no "little patch of yellow wall" in Vermeer's *View of Delft*.) Memory is a liar. It's a heap of dog-eared, smudged, incessantly revised fictions. The stories make cumulative lies—or, give us a break, conjectures—of our lives. This is O.K. because it had darn well better be.

Who's "we"? You know.

Meaning is a scrap among other scraps, though stickier. Meaning is so much better than nothing, in that it defines "nothing" as everything that meaning is not. Meaning prevents nothing from being only nothing. The "nothing that is not there and the nothing that is," Wallace Stevens noticed. The same nothing, but a difference of attitude.

A random shame: I was visited in New York by P., a soft-souled, brilliant friend from high school and college, a concert pianist. High on speed, I was arrogant and callous, watching the effects on P. with cold-blooded detachment. Finally, he said in a hurt tone, "I always thought you had a modesty about you. But not so." I could have said something, admitted my drugged state, made amends the next day. But a devil in me exulted.

Years later, a scene occurred that might work well in a novel set in the early seventies, in case you're writing one. I was seeing a terrific artist, H., at least as prone to defiance as I was. I saw that P. was giving a concert. I asked H., my not-really, because she was so independent, girlfriend to attend with me. She got the message, which was not fully conscious but true: besides wanting to make up with P., I relished the prospect of showing her off. Usually downtown casual, she showed up in heels, a stunning dress, diamonds or what looked like them, and a mink coat.

After the terrific music, especially Liszt, we joined P. and some other people in champagne toasts. P. facilitated introductions by asking the men—only the men—to say what they did. H. let that develop for about half a minute and detonated, "Let's start this over! Let's play *What do the women do?*" The company gawked. She was magnificent! With a flourish, she left the theatre. I tagged along moments later, stricken. Out on the street, she was gone. I limped home. I saw her only in passing after that. I didn't try again to reconcile with P.

The shock of feminism came none too soon for guys, including me, who had lorded in a sixties bohemia that mandated women be doting helpmeets to their entitled—because genius—men. Those domesticities went down like a row of dominoes at the first breath of female revolt. With no new model for relationships, libertinage reigned. I guess it was fun for some people, but it piled up emotional wreckage left and right.

The art scene was always a third or more gay—often the best third. My chief poet heroes were Frank O'Hara and John Ashbery. John complained to me that he had thought that with success he'd have his pick from a meat rack of young poets. "How come you're all *straight*?"—stretching out the last word to sound like something nasty going through a mangle.

How straight was I? I'd always been nervous about homosexuality. Didn't that mean I was repressing it? Given that everybody seemed to be having sex with everybody, not to mention being soused or stoned nightly, I decided to face the facts. A gay friend I approached would have nothing to do with me in that way. Well! I hooked up with a bisexual friend, but too much to drink made whatever happened a blur. So I seduced a straight friend. It was interesting. Nice, but obvious. I didn't rule out doing it again, but I never have.

There were brief affairs that I think neither the woman nor I really wanted; but this wasn't an adequate excuse then. An entropy of the heart grew in me, as did, which I didn't suspect, a yen for monogamy.

My last bachelor fling was semi-scandalous, in the art world, and volcanically erotic. I like to say that it burned the carbon out of my cylinders. She broke up with me on a street corner, denouncing me and storming off. I stood there for a spell grinning from ear to ear. I figured that I had mastered swinging singledom. Then I met Brooke.

I remember, in rehab, on the Upper East Side in 1992, an alum of the place, a tough guy from Queens, addressing the nightly A.A. meeting. He told us of once showing up at some clinic, drunk and filthy and soiled with his own diarrhea, and throwing a fit because the doctor was ten minutes late. "If you're a real alcoholic," the guy said to us, "no matter how low you go, you *will* have an attitude." He added, "If you're a real alcoholic, you will never feel quite right. Whatever you want will be a little bit out of reach. Can't handle that? Get the fuck out of here and get drunk." I went up to him afterward, in tears, to thank him. He said, "You heard me?" I said yes. "Good," he said, turning and walking away as if from some crap on a sidewalk. Saved my life.

The rehab was crowded with crack addicts, some of them felons. I was the rare middle-aged, middle-class white man in the joint. It was loud at all hours. Scared, I couldn't sleep. I told Brooke, on the building's pay phone, that I had to get out. She said, "Cope," and hung up. Saved my life.

See, Brooke is a child of alcoholics, as I'm not. I grew up and became one. She grew up and married one. She knew I was a mess but thought the drinking part was normal, until she got wise and kicked me out of the house. (Note to anyone who knows an active alcoholic: never, ever sympathize. If you suspect you're going to, shut your eyes, plug your ears, and hum.)

I bottomed out in the rehab, where I had gone as a condition for being allowed back home. I thought I was serious. I always had been when, previously, I was dry for periods of up to thirteen months: going to meetings at first, dewy with pity for people who plainly had been far worse off than I was. I wouldn't admit that we shared the identical fate, wherever we ranked along its descending scale.

On the third or fourth of my twenty-eight days there, I was climbing stairs and paused, too exhausted for another step. I harbored a nebulous conviction that I could tolerate only so much pain, short of a red zone in which I would go mad or die or something terrible would happen. And that anyone should see as much and want me to do anything—have a drink or a drug, for starters—to make it stop.

I thought, They say one day at a time. How about one second? I stared at my ticking watch. A black abyss opened. I was numbly aware that I wasn't insane. I wasn't dying. Reality was droning on as usual, with impartial sunlight streaming through a nearby window and picking out swirls of dust motes.

A perfectly demented thought blazed up. Roughly: What if they find out I'm not really an alcoholic and throw me out of here? I need this place! I believe it was the last, deepest rootlet of my denial, expelled. Not an alcoholic?

My daughter, Ada, has told me that in her childhood she spent years trying to interest me. I hadn't noticed. She was sixteen when I got sober. She said, "Let's see if I get this straight. *Now* you want to be my dad?" It took a lot of time and change and is still under way. I don't know if it's a consolation prize for Ada, or what it is, that she turned out to be fantastically interesting.

Meeting Brooke, having Ada, and getting sober are my life's top three red-letter days.

Cigarette brands I remember smoking for at least a few months running: Alpine, Salem, Newport, Camel, Lucky Strike, Parliament, Kent, Gauloises, Benson & Hedges, Nat Sherman. Finally (and I do mean finally), Marlboro Gold (formerly Lights), the crack cocaine of tobacco products, containing all sorts of cunning chemicals and a somewhat insulting whisper of sugar.

Doing the math, I reckon that I have smoked about a million cigarettes—and enjoyed every one of them, not that you care.

Tried gum, patches, and e-cigarettes. Not the same. I use nicotine lozenges to not be twitchy on airplanes, while driving with family, and indoors anywhere except in my offices in our city apartment and country house, with exhaust fans in opened windows—challenging during summer heat and winter cold. Smoking today requires grit.

Quit now? Sure, and have the rest of my life be a tragicomedy of nicotine withdrawal.

Mishaps. I had polio when I was eleven, in one of the last big epidemics before the Salk vaccine. I remember riding my bike home from school, every bump like a knife through my brain. Rushed to the local hospital for a spinal tap—every bit as horrible as you may imagine, but the one sure means of diagnosis then—and throwing up in the back of the family station wagon on the way to the polio-specializing Sister Kenny Institute, in Minneapolis.

I had a bed, but there were too many kids, so some were laid out in halls. Screaming all night. Dying. And always the mechanical sucking noise of iron lungs. I had no paralysis, but I was much weakened, spending seven weeks in the hospital and subject to physical therapy for months. Meanwhile, my family was quarantined at home. Food was left at the doorstep.

For a summer just out of high school, I worked at a resort in Glacier National Park, in the Montana Rockies. I hitchhiked on days off with a copy of *On the Road* in my back pocket and a big jackknife that I practiced opening in a flash in preparation for the lethal fights that I fantasized about. I told one truck driver, in what I imagined to be the right accent, that I was from Lexington, Kentucky. He said, "Lexington, Kentucky, boy, my home town!" I feigned sleep.

Another time, I climbed a manageable-looking mountain, setting out at dawn with pockets full of candy bars. It became steep, then close to vertical. As I clung to a rockface, an eagle launched, shrieking, from a ledge just above me and sailed into the blue distance. Higher up, there was snow, and there were bear tracks in the snow. I thought the mountaintop was a sloping ridge. I crawled up it and found a sheer drop facing the inaccessible summit. Had I had acrophobia before, or did my subsequently lifelong case of it begin then and there? I hugged rock and sobbed. The next thing I remember is striding and tumbling down a side of the mountain covered in deep gravel, grabbing bushes to slow myself. I alighted in brambled woods, disoriented. I had the sense to follow a trickling stream, and I was kept on course by the feel of the water as night fell. I emerged, a tattered scarecrow, on the park's one highway. Cars sped up at the sight of me in their headlights until one stopped.

I'm not in physical pain as I write, though I tire quickly and nap often. I have been receiving, every three weeks, an immunotherapy infusion—not chemo, and not a cure—which, at the outset, the doctor said had a thirty-five-per-cent chance of slowing the disease. (At those odds in Vegas, you're broke within an hour, but in baseball you're a cinch for the Hall of Fame.) A recent scan shows marked improvement, likely extending my prospect of survival. But I have to wonder if, whatever betides, I can stay upbeat in spirit. A thing about dying is that you can't consult anyone who has done it. No rehearsals. No mulligans.

At a bar when I was first in New York, I smirked dandyishly at my reflection in the mirror behind the bottles. I looked handsome! I was stirring my drink, Scotch-on-the-rocks, with my right index finger, which in the mirror became my left one. The moment seemed ineffably cool. Clown!

I ordered coffee at a diner. The guy said, "Regular?" I said, "Well, sure." Surprise: milk and sugar. In the Midwest, coffee was black, no sugar. Brooke remembers being a Texan newbie in New York and seeing a store sign that read "COFFEE RICE & BEANS." Fascinated, she asked for a pound of coffee rice. You get to be clueless in a new place only briefly. Don't waste the chance to have truths, great and small, burst upon you.

Brooke was an actress and standup comic from Dallas. Introduced at a Whitney Museum opening by A., a woman connected to both the art and the entertainment worlds, we despised each other immediately. I deemed Brooke a bubblehead, and she noticed that I was a jerk. Then she attended a poetry reading I gave, which, whatever its quality, turned out to be the best of my life, because she liked it. Next, A. invited me out to dinner and then, perhaps getting cold feet at what it implied, asked if she could bring Brooke. I said something like "Sure, why not?"

It's forty-six years later. Brooke is in bed rereading *Pride and Prejudice*, as she does two or three times a year, with a Mets game muttering on the radio. I have no doubt that our two cats cuddle beside her. It's night at our place in the Catskills, moonless and clear. I could turn off my office light and look out a window at the sky choked with stars.

Brooke has Texas grit: respecting everyone and taking no shit from anybody, least of all her spouse. When she's mad, it's scary, tapping a rage that once fuelled her escape from an awful family. There's no recourse but to duck and wait for it to pass, which it does. The sun began to shine on my life when I gave up arguing with Brooke. She is also very funny and brings out the fun in others, her spouse not excluded.

Ada asked her mother how to stay married. Brooke said, "Don't get divorced." If you don't divorce, you are a hundred per cent married no matter what's going on. I am so glad we stayed together that, for once in my verbose life, words to express it fail me.

Oddly, or not, I find myself thinking about death less than I used to. I thought that I might be kidding myself in my explorations of the subject while my life stretched ahead of me to an invisible horizon. But no. The thinking cut channels in which I now slip along. They involve acceptance. Why me? Why not me? In point of fact, me. Dying is my turn to survey life from its far—now near—shore. These extra months are a luxury that I hope to have put to good use. "To have put." See? While here, not here. Like a camera situated nowhere and taking in every last detail of the pulsating world.

God creeps in. Human minds are the universe's only instruments for reflecting on itself. The fact of our existence suggests a cosmic approval of it. (Do we behave badly? We are gifted with the capacity to think so.) We may be accidents of matter and energy, but we can't help circling back to the sense of a meaning that is unaccountable by the application of what we know. If God is a human invention, good for us! We had to come up with something.

Take death for a walk in your minds, folks. Either you'll be glad you did or, keeling over suddenly, you won't be out anything.

Published in the December 23, 2019, issue of *The New Yorker*, with the headline "77 Sunset Me."

THE IN-YOUR-FACE PAINTINGS OF PETER SAUL

Surprisingly, the timeliest as well as the rudest painting show of this winter, opening at the New Museum, happens to be the first New York museum survey ever of the American aesthetic rapscallion Peter Saul. The earliest of the works date from the early sixties, when Saul, who's from San Francisco, was a bohemian-dreaming expatriate in Paris: blowsy pastiches of Abstract Expressionist brushwork and proto-Pop imagery. Recognition so delayed bemuses almost as much as a reminder of the artist's current age: eighty-five, which seems impossible. Saul's cartoony style—raucously grotesque, often with contorted figures engaged in (and quite enjoying) intricate violence; caricatures of politicians from Nixon to Trump that come off as much fond as fierce; and cheeky travesties of classic paintings by Rembrandt, Picasso, and de Kooning—suggest the gall of an adolescent allowed to run amok. It takes time to become aware of how well Saul paints, with lyrically kinetic, intertwined forms and an improbable approximation of chiaroscuro, managed with neon-toned Day-Glo acrylics. He sneaks whispery formal nuances into works whose predominant effect may be as subtle as that of a steel garbage can being kicked downstairs. Not everyone takes the time. Saul's effrontery has long driven fastidious souls from galleries, including me years ago. Now I see him as part of a story of art and culture that has been unspooling since the nineteen-fifties; one in which, formerly a pariah, he seems ever more a paladin.

Saul, who now lives in upstate New York, was the only child of an oil executive and a federal-government secretary who appeared to take little interest in him. A nursemaid saw to much of his upbringing. He was packed off at ten to a rigid boarding school in Canada, where beatings were frequent and he was assumed, based on his last name, to be Jewish. Only after six years of enduring abuse as the school's rare "kike" did he learn that he wasn't. (Saul says that his name may be derived from his father's ancestral home, in England: the village of Saul, in Gloucestershire.) That strange tale feels both inconceivable and revelatory, considering the mixture of aggressive absurdity and armor-plated defiance with which Saul, after studying at the California School of Fine Arts and at Washington University School of Fine Arts, in St. Louis, entered into a tough-love romance with modern painting. He was already primed for affront by a love of hellacious comic books, such as the standout series, from the forties and early fifties, "Crime Does Not Pay." Those books were so gruesome that threats from Congress forced self-censorship on the industry, which in 1954 instituted the Comics Code Authority. Saul thrilled, too, to figurative painters who had fallen from fashion in New York as abstraction became well-nigh obligatory: Salvador Dalí, Thomas Hart Benton, Paul Cadmus, George Tooker. Saul says that when he was five years old he was deeply affected by a reproduction of Cadmus's rhapsody of human ugliness, *Coney Island* (1934). In it, a wobbling pyramid of gross bathers pose for a snapshot. Others writhe or sprawl, contributing to a sort of carnal junk yard, though with the homoerotic garnish of one good-looking young man in the background.

Tyro ambition pointed Saul toward Europe, where he spent eight years in England, the Netherlands, Paris, and Rome. He took to painting jam-packed brushy images of consumer goods, body parts, and (inspired by his discovery of *Mad*, in 1957 or so) lampooned comic characters, including Superman and Donald Duck, who tend to meet awful fates on his canvases. (Only oldsters like me will remember the revolutionary effect, on young minds, of the early *Mad*'s scorched-earth hilarity.) Art historians have striven to categorize those works by their affinity to Expressionism, Surrealism, and English Pop art, but, as with everything Saul, including his drive-by relation to funk and psychedelia in San Francisco, in the hippie sixties, the links don't hold. (He turned down overtures from R. Crumb and other cartoonists to collaborate in the underground-comics movement of the time.) His adamant individualism is keyed precisely to his rejection of similitude to the manners of anyone else.

Especially futile are comparisons to the New York Pop of Warhol and Lichtenstein, who tempered the shock of vernacular images with modernist formal cool—far more in tune with the sang-froid of Minimalism than was initially noticed. Saul brought heat, with goofball and/or monstrous, teeming imagery that makes sensation a means and an end in itself. His pictures mount furious assaults on the eye, leaving you with indescribable (art critics aren't supposed to say that, but I give up) choreographies of one damned thing after another. Where Emanuel Leutze carefully arrayed the constituent parts of *Washington Crossing the Delaware*, his 1851 commemoration of American valor, Saul's 1995 parody keeps the elements more or less in place—but mostly, vertiginously, less. That boat is doomed. Compared with him, Lichtenstein is Ingres. Saul came to function as an exterminator of the kind of refined sensibility that separated the sophisticates from the yahoos in haut-bourgeois twentieth-century America. Maybe think of him as a yahoo's yahoo, by design.

As a malcontent, Saul tends toward a policy of not so much getting mad about anything in particular as of getting even across the board. In 1996, he made a topical exception with *Art Critic Suicide*, which is not in the show. It features me and the conservative critic Hilton Kramer (1928–2012) as Siamese twins gravely blowing our brains out with bullets whose wandering malice isn't sated by plugging us only once. Saul tells me that he forgets the proximate motive, but it may have had to do with how paintings of his in the 1995 Whitney Biennial were received. I was amused at being paired with a writer who was so much an intellectual antagonist of mine that you'd have been unlikely to encounter us sharing the same city street, let alone what amounts to a history painting. At any rate, I was taking hot lead for belonging to a New York critical establishment that had condescended to the wrong guy.

The timeliness of the New Museum's show strikes me as threefold. First, there's an air of canonical dignity that hasn't exactly been earned but has irresistibly descended. Decades of aesthetic, social, and political democratizing have collapsed the redoubts of consensus good taste. (If you think Rembrandt is a better painter than, say, Richard Prince, as I certainly do, be ready to make the case.) Second, young painters are on board. The various returns to (or re-volcanic-eruptions of) figurative image-making in current art make Saul's multifarious tropes a handy visual thesaurus for engaging the mind through corporeal mimesis. (Never mind the heart, though. Saul's emotional tone, with no exception that occurs to me, is a polar vortex.)

Finally, we may have here a test of political correctness. Although the show's selection of works is ecumenically misanthropic, it admits wildly stereotypical renderings of African-Americans, Asians, and women—defensible, if they are, by being so far over the top of any detectable attitude as to self-destruct. Where apparent, Saul's satirical spleen is default leftist—he was America's most graphically anti-Vietnam War painter, as witness the storming pageant of American-soldier depravity that is *Saigon* (1967)—but with an antic panache that gainsays righteousness. *Crucifixion of Angela Davis* (1973), in which the activist is stuck with knives and sports a halo, might equally be seen as tweaking the left's deification of Davis as protesting her persecution. Either way, or neither, sheer visual impact seems to be Saul's aim, in service to an ever-seething personal rage that finds release and takes refuge in double-down buffoonery. He is like one of Dostoyevsky's irrepressible fomenters of chaos. Is moral equivocation for art's sake O.K.? The temerity is echt Saul, who, whatever you choose to think of him, definitely disagrees with you. Is raw intensity a malady or a purgative? Does it kill or cure?

Published in the February 17 & 24, 2020, issue of *The New Yorker*, with the headline "Target Practice."

THE LASTING INFLUENCE OF MEXICO'S GREAT MURALISTS

The title of a thumpingly great show at the Whitney, "Vida Americana: Mexican Muralists Remake American Art, 1925–1945," picks an overdue art-historical fight. The usual story of American art in those two decades revolves around young, often immigrant American aesthetes striving to absorb European modernism. A triumphalist tale composed backward from its climax—the postwar success of Abstract Expressionism—it brushes aside the prevalence, in the Depression thirties, of politically themed figurative art: social realism, more or less, which became ideologically toxic with the onset of the Cold War. What to do with the mighty legacy of the time's big three Mexican painters, Diego Rivera, José Clemente Orozco, and David Alfaro Siqueiros? As little as possible has seemed the rule, despite the seminal influence of Orozco and Siqueiros on the young Jackson Pollock. Granted, there's the problem of appreciating muralists in the absence of their murals. (A mural is a picture that is identical with a wall, and a wall belongs to a building that, besides not being portable, has meanings of its own.) But, with some two hundred works by sixty artists and abundant documentary material, the Whitney curator Barbara Haskell reweaves the sense and the sensations of an era to bring it alive.

Start the story with Emiliano Zapata, the peasant leader from a village in the central state of Morelos, who was tricked into a military ambush and martyred in 1919. This was a year before the decade-long, staggeringly bloody Mexican Revolution, which had begun with an attempt to overthrow the dictatorial and oligarchic President Porfirio Díaz, finally culminated in the election of Álvaro Obregón. (At least a million of the country's fifteen million citizens lost their lives.) The agrarian rebel

Zapata became an iconic figure for a new order that was merging social reform with a celebration of folkways and traditions—in striking contrast to the urban-industrial character of the Russian Revolution. (Shifting views of the Soviet Union regularly roiled the Mexican intelligentsia, many of whom welcomed the exiled Leon Trotsky to the capital, in 1937, before some effectively condoned his murder by a Stalinist agent, in 1940.) Nearly every artist had a go at exalting Zapata for his deep rootedness in native soil as well as for his dashing militance. Orozco's *Zapatistas* (1931) lyricizes the rural force. A *Zapatistas* made the following year, by Alfredo Ramos Martínez, conveys a lot with witty economy: a packed composition of overlapping sombreros affording incomplete glimpses of peasant faces and rifle barrels. It radiates a sort of ecstatic menace.

Ramos Martínez, who immigrated to Los Angeles in 1930, is one of a number of lesser-known artists who impress in the show's opening sections. The Italian-born photographer Tina Modotti, who journeyed the opposite way, from Los Angeles to Mexico, in 1923, is represented with crisp images, including a still-life of a sickle, a loaded bandolier, and an ear of corn. But the exhibition centers on the three leaders of the mural movement and their galvanizing effects north of the border. The star, of course, is Rivera, whose panache in an epic style of sophisticated populism won him world fame. In 1931, he was given the newly founded Museum of Modern Art's second monographic show (the first was devoted to Matisse) and created a remarkable suite of portable frescoes. Among them were a magnificent portrayal of Zapata appropriating the white horse of a slain foe and *The Uprising*, in which a woman with a baby defends a worker from a sword-wielding soldier. I once underrated that work, but this time it affected me with its cinematic immediacy. Rivera keeps looking better in retrospect, after a long period in which his standing declined while that of his wife, Frida Kahlo, soared. I prefer Kahlo myself, though by a narrower margin now. The show includes only two works by her. One jolts. The self-portrait *Me and My Parrots* (1941) communicates a force of personhood beyond that of any of the hundreds of other faces on view here.

Rivera notoriously enchanted American financiers and industrialists, engaging in a dizzying dance of co-optation that extended to adulatory coverage in *Forbes* and peaked with his masterpiece murals, completed in 1933, in the Detroit Institute of Arts, of a Ford plant in full-tilt operation. This celebrity proved tricky for him at home, where Siqueiros, among others, denounced him as a sellout to class enemies. Rivera countered by painting a head of Lenin into his grand mural suite for Rockefeller Center, in 1933. Ordered by Nelson Rockefeller to remove the Bolshevik, Rivera refused. (Light verse by E. B. White in this magazine had the mogul objecting, "After all / It's my wall," before it concluded, "'We'll see if it is,' said Rivera.") The work was destroyed in 1934. The same year, Rivera painted a new version, *Man, Controller of the Universe*, in Mexico City. The Whitney show features a full-size (nearly sixteen feet high by thirty-seven and a half feet wide) digital reproduction of the surviving mural, printed on a single sheet of vinyl glued to a wall. I don't know what to make of that except as an instance of technical whoop-de-do. Much as I empathize with Haskell's yen for a pièce de résistance, I swear by the physical integrity of painting, here betrayed by a smooth-as-silk illusion.

Rivera inspired American painters to create tableaux of laboring or protesting workers (police brutality figures often) and of historical events and themes. The work of the African-American artist Charles White is notable; give an eye to his *Progress of the American Negro: Five Great American Negroes* (1939–40), which works such heroes as Booker T. Washington and Marian Anderson into a baroque panorama. The show also includes ten temperas from Jacob Lawrence's *Migration Series*, of 1940–41: little pictures, narrating the northward exodus of Southern Blacks, that reverberate with intense color, clenched design, and a quiet power of conviction that makes much other work here seem forced and fustian.

But America already had a prominent public artist: the ebullient neo-Mannerist Thomas Hart Benton, who hailed Rivera until he was alienated by his Marxism. Benton's output might be termed liberal-nationalist with a heaping side order of Hollywood. His bravura series *American Historical Epic* (1924–27) has the virtue of featuring noble Indians along with the vice of casting them as perennial losers. He could be callous. But he was right on time for certain popular moods of the thirties—so much so that his reputation crashed soon thereafter. He has come to be mentioned most often as a teacher of Jackson Pollock—a status that happens to be at the beating heart of the Whitney show.

The young Pollock was a student, too, of Siqueiros, who was at once the mural movement's most adamant Stalinist (in 1940, he led a failed attempt, with machine guns, to assassinate Trotsky) and its most experimental, indeed avant-garde, painter. Pollock attended a workshop that Siqueiros conducted in New York, in 1936, teaching innovative techniques: using non-paint materials, airbrushing, and, among other heterodox procedures, dripping and pouring. Meanwhile, Pollock emulated Orozco's dark, fierce, rhythmic Expressionism to the point of making works that are almost—but not quite—hard to distinguish from it. Relatively neutral politically, Orozco favored mythological subjects in such explosively composed works as *Prometheus*, a mural at Pomona College, in California, which the Whitney represents, at about half scale, in another digital reproduction. Juxtapositions of paintings by Orozco and Siqueiros with contemporaneous ones by Pollock amount to a riveting show within the show: a crucible in which the apolitical American found ways around the crushing authority of Picasso, Matisse, Miró, Mondrian, and other European paragons. The vehemence of the Mexicans matched his volcanic temperament; and the heft of their gestural forms showed him how to rival, while evading, the tinkered unities of Cubism. I recommend comparing and contrasting the seething intensity of Pollock's *Composition with Flames* (1936) with that of *The Fire* (1938), by Orozco, and Siqueiros's *The Electric Forest* (1939).

"Vida Americana" valuably augments standard histories of modern art. Without the Mexican precedents of amplified scale and passionate vigor, the development of Abstract Expressionism in general, and that of Pollock in particular, lacks crucial sense. As for the politics, consider the persistently leftward tilt of American art culture ever since—a residual hankering, however sotto voce, to change the world.

Published in the March 2, 2020, issue of *The New Yorker*, with the headline "Wall Power."

THE COLD, IMPERIOUS BEAUTY OF DONALD JUDD

I would tell you my emotional responses to the gorgeous works in the Donald Judd retrospective that has opened at the Museum of Modern Art if I had any. I was benumbed, as usual, by this last great revolutionary of modern art. The boxy objects (he refused to call them sculptures) that Judd constructed between the early nineteen-sixties and his death, from cancer, in 1994, irreversibly altered the character of Western aesthetic experience. They displaced traditional contemplation with newfangled confrontation. That's the key trope of Minimalism, a term that Judd despised but one that will tag him until the end of time. In truth, allowing himself certain complexities of structure and color, he was never as radically minimalist as his younger peers Dan Flavin (fluorescent tubes) and Carl Andre (units of raw materials). But Judd, a tremendous art critic and theorist, had foreseen the change (imagine, in theatre, breaking the fourth wall permanently) well before his first show of mature work, in 1963, when he was thirty-five. Slowly, by erosive drip through the nineteen-sixties and seventies, the idea that an exhibition space is integral to the art works that it contains took hold. It is second nature for us now—so familiar that encountering Judd's works at MOMA may induce déjà vu.

We are talking about, for example, an untitled piece from 1964: a wall-mounted, square-sectioned, polished brass tube, seven feet long, from which descend five vertical tubes in iron, lacquered blue. Of the same vintage, there's a rectangular box, almost four feet long, with a top and sides of translucent orange Plexiglas and ends of hot-rolled steel. The works register as material propositions of certain principles—chiefly, openness and clarity. They aren't about anything. They afford no traction for analysis while making you more or less conscious of your physical relation to them, and to the space that you and they share. As installed by the curator Ann Temkin, with perfectly paced samples of Judd's major motifs—among them, floor-to-ceiling "stacks" of shelflike units, mostly of metal-framed, tinted Plexiglas, which expose and flavor the space they occupy—the second of the show's four big rooms amounts to a Monument Valley of the minimalist sublime. Don't miss it. Less enchanting, though expertly appointed, are a room of tentative early work and two that feature such later developments as boothlike, angled constructions, at joins of wall and floor, in raw plywood; large aluminum boxes containing differently oriented, lushly colored sheets of Plexiglas; and a huge congeries, nearly six feet high by more than twenty-four feet long, of stacked, bolted, and multicolored horizontal aluminum open boxes.

Not represented are Judd's curatorial adventures, which included an exquisitely revamped building at 101 Spring Street, where he lived for a time and experimented with ways of installing art. It has been preserved as a museum. Then came the artist's Bayreuth, his Mecca, in the remote (from anywhere!) desert town of Marfa, West Texas. There, starting in 1971, he converted old military, civic, commercial, and domestic buildings to house permanent and temporary installations of his work, that of artists he favored, and his collections of Navajo blankets and other choice craft objects. He also created studios, guest quarters, and his own living space, tucked into one end of a former gymnasium.

Works by Judd are almost routinely beautiful, but coldly and even imperiously so, as if their quality were none of your business. If you have any feeling, it might be chagrin at being underqualified to cope with so rigorous a visual intelligence. He's Donald Judd; you're not. He came on as a Savonarola of art in early writings and interviews, preaching a chastened aesthetic that should be "non-naturalistic, non-imagistic, non-expressionist," in addition to "unrelational," "nonillusionistic," and "neither painting nor sculpture." That dispenses with an awful lot of what normally appeals to people about art, leaving, in my case, a state of chilled awe. The one solid pleasure still provided is that of decoration: art that is meant not to be looked at but to be seen in relation to the environments that it enhances—keeping in mind that Judd's ideal environments are voids. (Come to that, we owe to Minimalism the stubborn fashion in architecture and design of hygienically spare, white-walled interiors and sleekly simplified commodities.) Success did not mellow him. Nor was he much given to humor. His statement of purpose, in 1986, for the Chinati Foundation, which he instituted for Marfa, admits no doubt about the grandeur, and the grandiosity, of his enterprise: "Somewhere, just as the platinum-iridium meter guarantees the tape measure, a strict measure must exist for the art of this time and place." Visiting those places, you're not an art lover. You're a pilgrim.

Judd was born in 1928 in Excelsior Springs, Missouri, the son of a Western Union executive. In 1948, after Army service, he began studies that led to a degree in philosophy and—but for a thesis—one in art history, from Columbia University. His early work evolved from so-so abstract painting to such tentative three-dimensional experiments as the relief of a yellow, concave, plastic letter from a sign embedded in a Masonite panel painted Cadmium Red Light (a favorite Judd hue). Manually, he was a klutz. Nothing quite fits in his initial constructions, and his drawing style is rudimentary. His first really strong works—woodblocks, from 1961, of tine-like vertical stripes contained by a diagonal shape—were executed by his father, Roy (who co-signed the backs). Starting in 1964, almost everything Judd made was commercially fabricated. He was a thinker and a designer of far-seeing intellect and, if you will, profound taste. Indeed, his main holdover from modernism was a high seriousness in matters of discrimination, asserting preferences as gauges of integrity that expand beyond the aesthetic to the moral. You can't know now from looking only at his work that his politics were left-libertarian, but he seemed sure that sophisticated viewers would implicitly understand his stance. The populism of Andy Warhol repelled him, but he found Roy Lichtenstein's formal prowess "hugely satisfying."

Judd's extraordinary connoisseurship shines in the reviews he wrote—some six hundred of them—between 1959 and 1965, most for *Arts Magazine*. Gathered in a cherishable book, *Donald Judd: Complete Writings 1959–1975*, they combine lucid description and fearless judgment in a bracingly forthright, no-nonsense style that makes other critics of the time, and most of us since then, seem flabby by comparison. Almost always, when an artist is familiar to me Judd's assessment is penetrating and dead-on correct, while never gentle. (Imagine being Charles Cajori, a fair-to-middling second-generation Abstract Expressionist, and reading a review of your work that begins "The color is gray, varied some, and a little grayed blue and orange. It could not be less considered.") Judd's later writing, from the seventies to the nineties, runs to jeremiads against the thick-headedness and what he deemed the incompetence of art-world institutions. He regularly had good reason to complain of damage to his works returned from museum shows. Minimalist art was long vulnerable to art handlers and viewers who barely saw it as art, and to children who mistook it for playground equipment. Absolute physical perfection, destructible by a nick or a fingerprint, is as essential to Judd's aesthetic as it was, before him, to Brancusi's, and, more recently, to that of Jeff Koons.

A wonderment of the MOMA show is that it is installed with no physical, or even indicated, barriers. Temkin, fingers crossed, acknowledged to me that the presence of the works would be compromised otherwise. It's worth pausing to note that probably only MOMA commands the clout, the cash, and the expertise to gather, from many collections, the number and quality of so many fragile treasures. The chance surely won't recur to take the measure—platinum-iridium grade or not—of an artist whose influence on our art and, sub rosa, our lives in common, remains beyond large, engulfing.

Published in the March 9, 2020, issue of *The New Yorker*, with the headline "The Shape of Things."

THE DARK REVELATIONS OF GERHARD RICHTER

Birkenau. The dread name —of the main death facilities at Auschwitz—entitles four large abstract paintings and four full-size digital reproductions of them in the last gallery of "Painting After All," a peculiarly solemn Gerhard Richter retrospective at the Met Breuer. The works are based on four clandestine photographs that were smuggled out of the concentration camp in 1944. Two, taken from the shadowed exit of a gas chamber, show naked corpses strewn on the ground and smoke rising from bodies afire in a trench beyond them. Men in uniform stand at ease—two appear to chat—amid the shambles. Richter first saw the images in the fifties. He encountered them again in 2008 and kept the worst of them hanging in his studio in Cologne. In 2014, he projected them onto canvas and traced them. As he worked, they became illegible. The finished paintings exemplify Richter's frequent style of densely layered, dragged pigments. They are unusually harsh in aspect, with clashing red and green, sickly whites, and grim blacks. But you'd hardly guess, by looking, their awful inspiration.

Richter's *Birkenau* is a provocation—who dares take history's ultimate obscenity as a theme, or even an allusion, for art?—but one that makes biographical sense. Born in Dresden in 1932, Richter is haunted, like many of his German contemporaries, by memories and associations from the Third Reich and the Second World War. Previously indirect in his references to the horror, he has reason to focus on it now, for a show that comes late in his life, and which he says might be the last one of his six-decade career as a chameleon stylist and visual philosopher of painting. (He's eighty-eight and, not well enough to travel, did not attend the opening.) The shock of *Birkenau* retroactively exposes a thread of sorrow and guilt through an art of invariably subtle, at times teasing, ambiguities. His photographic images transposed to canvas and painterly techniques that exploit chance have often seemed deliberately arbitrary, as if to forswear feeling. He brings to everything an attitude of radical skepticism. But it has dawned on many of us, over the years, that plenty of emotion, like banked fire, underlies his restless ways.

Heretofore, Richter's only overt reference to the Holocaust was a suite of touching illustrations for an edition of *The Diary of Anne Frank*, picturing Frank's face in a range of styles, which he made in 1957, while he was unhappily apprenticed as a Socialist Realist painter in East Germany. (The illustrations are not in the show.) Having glimpsed free-world art when he was permitted visits to exhibitions in the West, he fled via East Berlin in 1961, shortly before the Wall went up. He was soon in Düsseldorf, in the thick of an avant-garde that was both piqued and excited by Pop art and the traditions of Dada. "Capitalist Realism," he and some new friends, including the brilliant Sigmar Polke, termed their response, which, among other things, degraded the glossiness of advertising material to matte grunge. Richter took to painting copies of banal black-and-white photographs, smearing the paint to emphasize the change of medium. Among a number of these in the show are paintings from family snapshots that touch on Richter's and Germany's dire past.

One, *Uncle Rudi* (1965), is of a relative—in uniform and smiling goofily—who died fighting in the war. Another, *Aunt Marianne* (painted in 1965 and rendered as a luminous digital print in 2018), shows a woman cradling baby Gerhard in her arms; she was adjudged schizophrenic, imprisoned, and then killed in a Nazi eugenics program. Keeping company with those poignancies is *Mr. Heyde* (1965), taken from a news photograph of the concentration-camp psychiatrist Werner Heyde being arrested, in 1959, after fourteen years of maintaining a false identity. (He hanged himself in prison in 1964.) Richter wouldn't have expected viewers to recognize those subjects readily, and he was at no pains to explain them. Their meaning stayed personal, with roots in his boyhood, when he was enlisted in the junior auxiliary of the Hitler Youth and his father served in the Wehrmacht. Not until *Birkenau* would he palpate the wound again.

It feels heavy-handed of me (though on this occasion Richter quite asks for it) to be zeroing in on some specific content of his art, which always shades subjects with undecidable intention. That goes for early images of tabloid sensations, such as yearbook-style portraits of eight nurses who were murdered on a single night in Chicago, in 1966, and forty-eight deadpan copies of photographs of famous artists and intellectuals. The latter served, perhaps, as marmoreal father figures for a largely fatherless generation. (It's estimated that more than four million German men died in the war.) Uncertainty clings, as well, to later works, including jittery cityscapes that may be bombed ruins or simply indistinct views of an intact metropolis; landscapes that could be either sarcastic or sincere revisitations to German Romanticism (I vote for wistful); funereal paintings of candles and skulls; and ravishing photo-realist pictures, true to the hues of color film, of subjects including members of his family. One of these last, from 1988, portraying his daughter Betty from behind, seems to me the single most beautiful painting made by anyone in the last half century. It is not in the present show. Nor is *October 18, 1977*, Richter's famous series drawn from photographs of the Baader-Meinhof terrorist gang, in life and, as suicides in prison, death. Those darkling images will always tug at our general assessments of Richter. Whatever his reason for taking on a subject that was charged, at the time, with conflicting political passions, I believe that the work asserts an artist's license to transcend partisan judgment, independent of opinions that may even include his own.

Irony blankets Richter's career. He is a darling of the contemporary art market, with his works selling at auction for tens of millions of dollars. But his longtime best friend, and a co-curator of this show, is the critic Benjamin H. D. Buchloh, a hard-bitten apostle of Frankfurt School anti-capitalist, all but anti-aesthetic, political theory. In a notorious interview, in 1986, Buchloh insisted on interpreting Richter's art as historical critique skewering the bourgeois decadence of painting, and Richter placidly declared his wholehearted allegiance to Western painting's grand tradition. Richter said, "The reason I don't argue in 'socio-political terms' is that I want to produce a picture and not an ideology." He declines to claim any subversive intent, even for his occasional work in odd formats, such as stark charts of random colors and the use of transparent glass in place of canvas—two predilections that came together in his successful commission, in 2007, of an immense stained-glass window for Cologne Cathedral, proving that the experiments had been exploratory rather than tendentious. I like to imagine Buchloh as a negative conscience perched on Richter's shoulder, amusingly scandalized as the artist hews again and yet again to ancient values of meaningfulness and pleasure.

While never forsaking representation—as seen at the Met Breuer in portraits of his third wife, Sabine Moritz, and their three children, which radiate Titianesque color—Richter took up chromatic abstraction in the seventies, overlaying brushed, slathered, and scraped swaths of paint. I remember hating those on my first sight of them, circa 1980. They seemed to me sloppy travesties of Abstract Expressionism, and pointless: inferior coals to the Newcastle of Willem de Kooning. Gradually, I caught their drift as pragmatic explorations of painterly phenomena: ur-paintings. Not only condoning but soliciting accident, Richter attends to the multifarious effects of layered paint that has been repeatedly smashed and dragged, wet-in-wet. He appraises the results with an exercise of taste, deciding what to keep and what to efface. In this, his true predecessor is Jackson Pollock, who, dripping paint, collaborated with chance and monitored the results.

At last I saw, as I still see, Richter's abstractions as miraculously, often staggeringly, beautiful, with an air of having come into being through a will of their own, happening to—rather than issuing from—their creator. They provide the chief pleasures of the show, which excludes the more brazen of his subjects—there are none of his early borrowings from pornography, for example—and the most seductive of his color-photograph transformations, including floral still-lifes. The selection favors eerie minor keys, as seems appropriate for being a retrospective bathed in the terrible resonance of *Birkenau*.

Published in the March 16, 2020, issue of *The New Yorker*, with the headline "Painting History."

MORTALITY AND THE OLD MASTERS

We will have so much to say to one another when the coronavirus crisis is over: distillations from solitude, in cases like mine. At seventy-eight, with bad lungs, I'm holed up with my wife at our country place until a vaccine is developed and becomes available. It's boring. (Remember when we lamented the distracting speed of contemporary life?) On the scale of current human ordeals, as the pandemic destroys lives and livelihoods, mere isolation hardly ranks as a woe. It's an ambivalent condition that, among other things, affords time to think long thoughts. One of mine turns to the art in the world's now shuttered museums: inoperative without the physical presence of attentive viewers. Online "virtual tours" add insult to injury, in my view, as strictly spectacular, amorphous disembodiments of aesthetic experience. Inaccessible, the works conjure in the imagination a significance that we have taken for granted. Purely by existing, they stir associations and precipitate meanings that may resonate in this plague time.

Why does the art of what we term the Old Masters have so much more soulful heft than that of most moderns and nearly all of our contemporaries? (I place the cutoff between the murderous scourges of war that were witnessed by Francisco Goya and those that Édouard Manet, say, read about in newspapers.) I think the reason is a routine consciousness of mortality. Pandemic diseases and innumerable other causes of early death haunted day-to-day life, even for those creators who were committed to entertainment. Consider the heaps of bodies that accumulate in Shakespeare's tragedies: catharses of universal fear. The persistence of religion in art that was increasingly given to secular motives—Bible stories alternate with spiritually charged themes of Greek and Roman mythology—bespeaks this preoccupation. Deaths of children were a perpetual bane. Paintings of the Madonna and Child, most grippingly those by Giovanni Bellini, secrete Mary's foreknowledge of her son's terrible fate. The idea that God assumed flesh, suffered, and died was a stubborn consolation—Mary's to know and ours to take on faith or, if we're atheists, at least to marvel at as mythic poetry.

An ineffably sacramental nuance in paintings from the Dutch seventeenth century, which luxuriate in the ordinary existence of ordinary people, evokes the impermanence of human contentment. Never mind the explicitness of that time's memento mori, all the skulls and guttering candles. I am talking about an awareness that's invisible, but palpable, in Rembrandt's nights—his fatalistic self-portrait in the Frick Collection comes to mind—and in Vermeer's mornings, when a young wife might open a window and be immersed in delicate, practically animate sunlight. The peculiarly intense insouciance of a Boucher or a Fragonard—the sensuous frolics of France's ancien régime, immune to concern about absolutely anything disagreeable, including, God forbid, social unrest—protests, in favor of life, rather too much. (Young folk dallying at court provide the sole but turbulent drama in Fragonard's *The Progress of Love*, a marvellous suite of paintings that is also at the Frick.) Only as the nineteenth century unfolds, with improvements in sanitation and other living conditions (for the rising middle classes, at least), does mortal insecurity wane—barring such episodic ravages as tuberculosis and syphilis, which, like AIDS a century later, could seem to the unaffected to be selective of their victims—and death start to become an inconvenience in the lives of other people.

Now, in our world of effective treatments for almost anything, death obtains at the extremes of the statistical and the anecdotal, apart from those we love, of course. People slip away, perhaps with the ripple of an obituary: celebrity news items. What with the dementias attendant on our remorselessly lengthened lives, many slip away before the fact. Cancer is an archipelago of hospital medicine, normalized across the land. (I have cancer, but with fading awareness of it as immunotherapy gives me an unexpected lease on continued life.) The twentieth century shifted our sense of mass death to the political: war, genocide, and other numerical measures of evil, lately focussed on terrorism, opiates, and guns. Our mourners are respected—and lavished with optimistic therapy, as an aspect of a zeal for mental hygiene that clears away each night's corpses before every workaday morning. We may well return to shallow complacency when the present emergency passes. (There's the baffling precedent of the 1918–19 influenza pandemic, which killed as many as fifty million people, largely young, and left so little cultural trace.) But right now we have all convened under a viral thundercloud, and everything seems different. There's a change, for example, in my memory of Diego Velázquez's *Las Meninas* (1656), which is the best painting by the best of all painters.

In December, I spent most of two days studying *Las Meninas* during a visit to Madrid, when I believed that my end was near. I had set myself the task of ignoring all received theories about this voluminously analyzed masterpiece and, on the spot, figuring out its maddening ambiguities. It's big: more than ten feet high by about nine feet wide. Its hanging in the Prado allows for close inspection. (The picture's illusion of a space that is continuous with the one that you occupy can make you feel invited to walk into it.) The work's conundrums orbit the question of who—situated where in space and when in time—is beholding this placid scene in a large room at the court of the Hapsburg king (and Velázquez's employer) Philip IV which captures life-size presences with the instantaneity of a snapshot. The painter? But he's in the picture, at work on a canvas, with its back to us, that can only be *Las Meninas*. Some characters, mildly startled, lock eyes with ours; others remain oblivious of us. (But who are we?) There's the riddle of a distant mirror that doesn't show what you would assume it shows.

Presuming to grasp the whole is like hazarding a unified theory of relativity and quantum physics. Despite ending as I had started—mystified—I congratulated myself on parsing evidence of the artist's chief ingenuity: a perspectival scheme that resolves at a viewing point not centered but offset to the right, face to face with a jowly dwarf and opposite Velázquez's rendered position to the left. (Speculations that he must have painted the scene with the aid of a large mirror requires one to believe, implausibly, that he and a number of other visibly right-handed characters were southpaws.) I was in aesthete heaven. But, three months on, marooned by fear of the virus, I'm interested by an abrupt shift in my attitude toward the painting: from lingering exhilaration to vertiginous melancholy. *Las Meninas* is tragic, as an apotheosis of confidence and happy expectation that teeters precariously—a situation that Velázquez couldn't have known at the time but which somehow, subliminally, he wove into his vision.

At the lower middle of the painting stands the stunningly pretty five-year-old Infanta Margarita Teresa, coolly self-possessed and attended by two maids. She is a vessel of dynastic hope, which proved not to be entirely misplaced. Unlike three other children of Philip IV and his queen (and niece), Maria Anna, she survived childhood, and, unlike her remaining sibling, a younger brother, she seems to have escaped the genetic toll of Hapsburg inbreeding. (When her brother ascended the throne, as Charles II, his ruinous disabilities, impotence among them, ended the dynasty in Spain, amid the country's steep decline as a European power.) Margarita Teresa lived to the ripe age of twenty-one, married off for diplomatic reasons, at the age of fifteen, to become the Empress of the Holy Roman Empire and to bear four children, only one of whom outlasted infancy. Her reputed charms did not include her vicious anti-Semitism. (She encouraged her husband, Leopold I, to expel Jews from Vienna and to convert the city's main synagogue into a church.) But the glory of her promise in *Las Meninas* suddenly casts, for me, a shadow of ambient and forthcoming death and disaster. There would never be another moment in the Spanish court so radiant—or a painting, anywhere, so good. It's the second to last of Velázquez's greatest works. He all but discontinued painting, in favor of taking on more prestigious court duties, and died in 1660, at sixty-one. Philip IV survived him by five years.

This sort of reëvaluation can happen when events disrupt your life's habitual ways and means. You may be taken not only out of yourself—the boon of successful work in every art form, when you're in the mood for it—but out of your time, relocated to a particular past that seems to dispel, in a flash of undeniable reality, everything that you thought you knew. It's not like going back to anything. It's like finding yourself anticipated as an incidental upshot of fully realized, unchanging truths. The impression passes quickly, but it leaves a mark that's indistinguishable from a wound. Here's a prediction of our experience when we are again free to wander museums: Everything in them will be other than what we remember. The objects won't have altered, but we will have, in some ratio of good and ill. The casualties of the coronavirus will accompany us spectrally. Until, inevitably, we begin to forget, for a while we will have been reminded of our oneness throughout the world and across time with all the living and the dead. The works await us as expressions of individuals and of entire cultures that have been—and vividly remain—light-years ahead of what passes for our understanding. Things that are better than other things, they may even induce us to consider, however briefly, becoming a bit better, too.

Published in the April 13, 2020, issue of *The New Yorker*, with the headline "Out of Time."

DOROTHEA LANGE AND FÉLIX FÉNÉON AT MOMA, AND ONLINE

Two terrific shows that languish in darkened galleries at the Museum of Modern Art should not pass uncelebrated—or unvisited, to the extent that MOMA's Web site ameliorates the lockdown. It helps that both shows feature a good deal of verbal content and may well incite Googling of their brilliant subjects: Dorothea Lange, the premier photographer of the human drama of the Great Depression, and Félix Fénéon, a shadowy French aesthete and political anarchist. Fénéon was also a sometime art critic, dealer, collector, and journal editor, and a legendarily sardonic wit—not an artist but an art-world sparkplug. Best known for having coined, in 1886, the term "neo-Impressionism," and for his championing of Georges Seurat, he is characterized in the show's catalogue as "implacable, inscrutable, meticulous, and mysterious." Lanky and sporting an Uncle Sam-like goatee (Henri de Toulouse-Lautrec portrayed him in profile at the Moulin Rouge, accompanied by a rotund Oscar Wilde), Fénéon merits nothing so much as the latter-day American honorific "cool." There's a mystery about Lange, too, which owes to her evasiveness about being called an artist, rather than a documentary photographer. In fact, she was a supreme artist, whose pictures lodged the Depression in the world's imagination and memory at least as much as John Steinbeck's writing did: with truths to life on a scale of everlasting myth.

Lange was born in Hoboken, New Jersey, in 1895, and went to school on New York's Lower East Side, a rare Gentile among thousands of Jewish schoolmates at P.S. 62, on Hester Street. Her father abandoned the family when she was twelve. A childhood bout of polio left her with a lifelong limp, which, she said, "formed me, guided me, instructed me, helped me, and humiliated me." Determined to become a photographer even before she first used a camera, she assisted at studios throughout the city and studied the medium at Columbia University. In 1918, would-be world travels with a friend stalled in San Francisco, after the two women were robbed. There Lange found patrons for a studio of her own and became a successful portraitist of the city's élite. (She also married a painter, Maynard Dixon, and had two children.) Her grounding in portraiture seems key to her subsequent singularity. With the onset of the Depression, she took to the streets. Her photograph *White Angel Bread Line, San Francisco* (1933), of a dejected man turned aside from a mass of others, became a public sensation. Between 1935 and 1939, she drove the back roads of the West and the South as part of a program that promoted the New Deal by distributing the resulting material to newspapers and magazines.

Lange stood out from the start. Her sensitivity to faces individualizes each of her subjects. The encounter is an event in that subject's life—and in Lange's own. Her images defy generalization. Facts of poverty and exhaustion speak for themselves. Lange cuts through them to specific presences, whose thoughts we seem to know, and which she enhanced with vernacular quotations that she compiled, with her second husband, the economist Paul Taylor, in the book *An American Exodus: A Record of Human Erosion*, in 1939. The MOMA show has a subtitle, "Words and Pictures"—Lange insisted that photographs complete their meaning in tandem with verbal information. That amounts to heresy for a modernist, which Lange intuitively was in formal discipline, with her masterly compositions and eloquent gradations of light. Yet she shrugged off the aesthetic appeal of her work, determined not to stand between her subjects and their effects on the broadest possible public.

One day in 1936, at a blighted pea field in Nipomo, California, she came upon the subject of what is perhaps history's most famous photograph, *Migrant Mother*—a thirty-two-year-old Cherokee woman, Florence Owens (later Thompson). With three children huddled against her in an open tent, the woman's mingled anxiety and resilience transfix a viewer's mind and heart. No sentimental response is possible in the evocation of vast, rock-hard realities that have come down, for an instant, to one synoptic point. Publication of the picture in the San Francisco *News* spurred a rush of food aid to Nipomo, where today a public school is named for Lange. It emerged later that Lange had got details about her subject wrong. Not a pea picker, Owens had stopped at the field briefly, awaiting a car repair. She was not identified as the image's subject until forty-two years later, when she had risen to tolerably comfortable circumstances. This instance of Lange's faulty reporting suggests to me that her declared deference to verbal supplementation was a feint, hiding the transcendent artistry of her eye in plain sight.

On a side note, I felt a twinge as I was looking on my laptop at pictures by Lange, which include a series taken of Japanese-Americans about to be sent to internment camps during the Second World War—work that was commissioned and then suppressed by the federal government. One of the best known is a shot of children, Japanese-Americans and others, with hands on hearts, apparently reciting the Pledge of Allegiance. Lange's images show the detained as regular people who had to cope with an outrageously unjust confinement—and who, in doing so, were buoyed by being together, at least. Among other strengths, Lange was a poet of the ordinary but imperious human need, under any conditions, for mutual contact.

The first intriguing fact that's new to me about the unpredictable Félix Fénéon is that he never liked the carnivalesque Pointillist portrait, painted by Paul Signac, in 1890, that makes him look like a dandyish magician pulling a lily from a hat against a blazing vortex of abstract patterns. Given the picture by Signac, Fénéon kept it hanging in his home until his death, fifty-four years later, but airily pronounced it one of Signac's weaker pieces. The MOMA show displays it with works by other of Fénéon's favorite artists—twenty-one by Seurat, several each by Matisse and Bonnard—as well as objects that reflect his pioneering interest in African, Native American, and Oceanic tribal art. Less than enthusiastic about Picasso, he greeted *Les Demoiselles d'Avignon*, in 1907, by advising the artist to stick to caricature. But he hailed Cubism for its extreme radicalism.

Any dramatic change in art might foreshadow a social revolution, by Fénéon's anarchist lights—never mind if the art was arcane and destined for museums. Fénéon generally despised museums. His life abounded in apparent contradictions. He was the chief clerk of France's Ministry of War when, in 1894, he was arrested on suspicion of conspiring with a cohort of terrorists and stood trial with twenty-nine others. Bomb-making materials had been discovered at his office. His defense turned less on evidence than on a stream of witticisms that enchanted the Parisian public. Accused of having "surrounded" himself with two notorious characters, he objected mildly that it takes at least three people to surround anyone. In effect, he won an acquittal on grounds of being exasperating. For a time, he edited the avant-garde journal *La Revue Blanche*. Though not rich, he shrewdly bought and sold art, impervious to imputations of commercialism even as he joined the Communist Party. Little that might pose a problem to others troubled Fénéon. He died in 1944, possessed of an immense collection, much of which was sold off three years later, after the death of his widow.

Fénéon's most startling departure was to write, as a daily feature in a Parisian newspaper, in 1906, more than a thousand unsigned, usually salacious items. Titled "Nouvelles en Trois Lignes," these were diamond-cut in style, featherweight in tone, and exquisitely cruel. In one, he wrote, "Scheid, of Dunkirk, fired three times at his wife. Since he missed every shot, he decided to aim at his mother-in-law and connected." In another: "Pauline Rivera, 20, repeatedly stabbed, with a hatpin, the face of the inconstant Luthier, a dishwasher of Chatou, who had underestimated her." I've found the online Fénéon show a waterslide into the lore of a staggeringly clever man who epitomizes a heyday of audacities in pell-mell, modernizing Paris. He never wrote a book. He cut a practically invisible figure in public. But, once you've made his acquaintance, he may pester any thoughts you have of the era, like something that is glimpsed and then, when you look, isn't there.

Published in the May 18, 2020, issue of *The New Yorker*, with the headline "Out of the Dark."

SUSAN ROTHENBERG'S ASTEROIDAL IMPACT ON THE NEW YORK ART WORLD

Susan Rothenberg, who died this week, at the age of seventy-five, in Galisteo, New Mexico, her home for thirty years, was the best thing that happened to the art of painting in New York in the nineteen-seventies. I say "thing" because the effect of the horse paintings that Rothenberg sprang on the world in 1975, at the scruffy loft gallery 112 Greene Street, in a nascent SoHo, in a city wracked by poverty and chaos, was like an asteroid impact. It triggered mass extinctions among the time's dinosaur species of mannerly formalist abstraction. There were rebellious realist styles at the time, and infusions of conceptualist ideas. But nothing prepared us for the powers of a young woman from Buffalo—trained as a sculptor and, small and lithe, sometimes a dancer—who had been painting for barely two years.

Married to the sculptor George Trakas at the time, Rothenberg started with small works in water-soluble mediums—fields of broken brushwork with lines down the middle, stabilizing silhouette images of horses—so that she could wash her hands quickly when their baby daughter, Maggie, cried. She and Trakas later divorced. (It would be good to have a month-by-month chronology—what ensued in her life from then until the Greene Street show—to enhance the major museum retrospective that, shockingly, Rothenberg has yet to be given, despite her secure fame.) At 112 Greene, her huge paintings in acrylics made some of us laugh with sheer wonderment. In stentorian blacks and orangeish browns, they had formal rigor aplenty, as flat and integral as any current abstraction. But that was perfunctory, a nod to the tradition that Rothenberg commenced to blow sky high. The great horses loomed, ranging in form from crude cartoonishness to hints of plausible equine anatomy. All seethed with emotion—the isotope that had gone missing from the mandarin styles of the day, in which carefulness had displaced suggestions of anything worth caring about. The works conveyed anger, exaltation, and self-abandoning intrepidity. They felt personal, albeit on a grand scale. In an era preoccupied with what to do in art and how to do it, Rothenberg addressed and answered a rarer question: Why? She palpably made the pictures not only because she could but because she had to. The historic upshot was a rebirth of Expressionism, with kinetic force and unmistakable authenticity. So it seemed to me then and seems to me now.

The rest is a long story replete with changing imagery—heads and human figures, usually fragmentary, as well as animals—and ever more eloquent touch. (One of her masterpieces is a vision of Piet Mondrian dancing the foxtrot, as was his wont, in a blizzard of feathery strokes.) Tiring of acrylics, Rothenberg mastered oil paints, which brought fugitive beauty and aching tenderness to her furiously worked surfaces. I take pride in having introduced Bruce Nauman to her work in a show at the superb, now bygone Willard Gallery, in 1981. (It was fun to watch his stony skepticism of painting crack a little.) They met subsequently, married in 1989, and moved to Nauman's ranch outside Santa Fe, living on familial terms with horses, chickens, dogs, cats, and ambient treasures of ancient Indian petroglyphs and pottery shards. Rothenberg seldom revisited New York except for periodic shows of her work at the Sperone Westwater gallery, rendering her rather ghostly, while legendary, as a presence on the contemporary scene. But stand in front of one of her paintings. She's fully there, with a jolt of what permanently rearranged my sensibility, and the art world's, in 1975.

Published on *The New Yorker* Web site May 20, 2020.

EDWARD HOPPER AND AMERICAN SOLITUDE

I've been thinking a lot about Edward Hopper. So have other stay-at-homes, I notice online. The visual bard of American solitude—not loneliness, a maudlin projection—speaks to our isolated states these days with fortuitous poignance. But he is always doing that, pandemic or no pandemic. Aloneness is his great theme, symbolizing America: insecure selfhoods in a country that is only abstractly a nation. "E pluribus unum," a magnificent ideal, thuds on "unum" every day throughout the land. Only law—we're a polity of lawyers—confers unity on the United States, which might sensibly be a Balkans of regional sovereignties had the Civil War not been so awful as to remove that option, come what may. Hopper's region is the Northeast, from New York to parts of New England, but his perceptions apply from coast to coast. Born in Nyack in 1882, and dying in 1967 after living for half a century in an apartment on Washington Square, he couldn't conceivably have developed as he did in any other culture. His subjects—atomized persons, inauspicious places—are specific to his time. But his mature art, which took two decades to gestate before consolidating in the nineteen-twenties, is timeless, or perhaps time-free: a series of freeze-dried, uncannily telling moments.

Though termed a realist, Hopper is more properly a Symbolist, investing objective appearance with clenched, melancholy subjectivity. He was an able draftsman and masterly as a painter of light and shadow, but he ruthlessly subordinated aesthetic pleasure to the compacted description—as dense as uranium—of things that answered to his feelings without exposing them. Nearly every house that he painted strikes me as a self-portrait, with brooding windows and almost never a visible or, should one be indicated, inviting door. If his pictures sometimes seem awkwardly forced, that's not a flaw; it's a guarantee that he has pushed the communicative capacities of painting to their limits, then a little bit beyond. He leaves us alone with our own solitude, taking our breath away and not giving it back. Regarding his human subjects as "lonely" evades their truth. We might freak out if we had to be those people, but—look!—they're doing O.K., however grim their lot. Think of Samuel Beckett's famous tag "I can't go on. I'll go on." Now delete the first sentence. With Hopper, the going-on is not a choice.

I haven't seen "Edward Hopper: A Fresh Look at Landscape," a large show at the lately reopened Beyeler Foundation, Switzerland's premier museum of modern art, outside Basel. I take its fine catalogue, edited by the exhibition's curator, Ulf Küster, as occasion enough for reflecting anew on the artist's stubborn force. I rely as well on memories that we likely share of encountering *Nighthawks* (1942) and *Early Sunday Morning* (1930), but also, really, anything from his hand. Once you've seen a Hopper, it stays seen, lodged in your mind's eye. The reason, beyond exacting observation and authentic feeling, is an exceptional stylistic cleverness. Hopper was explicit on this score, saying, in 1933, "I have tried to present my sensations in what is the most congenial and impressive form possible to me." Exasperated by questions of what his works meant, he squelched one interviewer by exclaiming, "I'm after ME." The remark reflects his debts to European Romanticism and Symbolism, which he absorbed in depth while stripping away any stylistic resemblances. Highly literate, he read and reread nineteenth-century German and French poetry all his life. His poetic liberties in a realist mode point back to one of his favorite predecessors, Gustave Courbet. And a certain smoldering vehemence in Hopper puts me in mind of Théodore Géricault, except tamped down to static views of drab actualities. Hopper imported, or smuggled, some emotive powers of European traditions to unforgiving American soil.

Having studied in New York with Robert Henri and other preceptors of the Ashcan School, who addressed modernity with vernacular realism, he had three sojourns in Paris. There he emulated minor post-Impressionists with restless variations of tonal contrasts and off-kilter compositions. Back home, while supporting himself as a commercial illustrator, he found a way forward by way of etching. Heavily inked cows, railroad tracks, and a banal house in *American Landscape* (1920) presaged a direction unlike that of any of his contemporaries. The closest was his mystically inclined acquaintance Charles Burchfield, whose rapturous treatments of unprepossessing sites in western New York State have aged very well, informing a trend today among young painters toward potent representation. Less imitable, Hopper has never ceased to influence the thinking, at the very least, of subsequent artists. Willem de Kooning, as Küster recounts in the catalogue, praised him to an interviewer in 1959. De Kooning noted a startling effect of the summarily brushed woods in the background of *Cape Cod Morning* (1950), in which a woman is seen from the side leaning forward at a bay window and staring at something beyond the picture's right edge: "The forest looks real, like a forest, like you turn on it and there it is, like you turn and actually see it." That's on the mark with Hopper: thereness that becomes hereness, in a viewer's eye and mind.

A catalogue essay by David M. Lubin, the esteemed scholar of art history in relation to popular culture, makes a connection that I've often thought about myself: Hopper and Alfred Hitchcock. The Yank painter and the Brit cinéaste display remarkable parallels as visual storytellers. Hitchcock, learning American experience from scratch after immigrating to Hollywood in 1939, at the age of thirty-nine, acknowledged the influence. The Bates house in *Psycho* reproduces, with simplifications, the already suitably ominous Victorian in Hopper's *House by the Railroad* (1925). Lubin concentrates on suspenseful narrative tactics, which I would enlarge to cover methods of composition and aspects of temperament. Hitchcock storyboarded scenes and shots for his films. Hopper (incidentally, an addicted moviegoer) as much as did the same for his paintings. I once got to inspect a stack of studies that he'd made on paper. Some sheets bore only drawn rectangles: seeking the right proportions for what he had in mind. Then there were congeries of details with which he auditioned, in effect, particular body parts, architectural features, or other elements that would be knitted into dramatic wholes. Both he and Hitchcock aimed for the soundness and the suddenness of sights that compress time in service to a pre-imagined vision. Each knew the feeling—because he felt it—that the effort would trigger in viewers.

Hitchcock shares with Hopper a predilection for jarring relations of backgrounds to foregrounds in pictorial space: perhaps someone or something relatively innocuous is nearby and something less calming is yonder. Lubin offers the example, from *North by Northwest*, of the distant crop-dusting plane at work "where there ain't no crops." In certain pictures of rural dwellings by Hopper, woods (like those in *Cape Cod Morning*) or topographical formations subtly menace a human intrusion. But in Hitchcock's work, and in Hopper's, especially, the unnerving relation of the far to the near is often reversed, and what's mysterious, if not sinister, becomes identical with our point of view. What are we doing here, seeing that? Voyeurism—the saddest excitement—may be suggested. The emotional tug of many of Hitchcock's characters and all of Hopper's requires their unawareness of being looked at. To see them is to take on a peculiar responsibility. Hopper often produces the unease even in unpeopled landscapes and views of buildings, as if catching nature and habitation defenselessly exposed in disarray, mundanity, or squalor. The New England coastlines, lighthouses, and sailboats that he painted on summer excursions get off relatively easy. He liked them. But they, too, feel taken by surprise, depicted from odd angles of vision. No judgment is passed on anyone or anything, one way or another. The naked fact of their existence is provocative enough. "Why is there something rather than nothing?" cosmologists wonder. Hopper is all ears for the answer.

Politically, Hopper was "a sort of McKinley conservative," his friend the novelist John Dos Passos remarked. The artist scorned the New Deal art programs of the thirties as sops to mediocrity. Interrupting a vacation on Cape Cod in 1940, he returned to New York to register to vote in order to cast his ballot against Franklin Roosevelt. The orientation leaves no mark in his work that I can detect—Hopper's artistic passion disallowed the trivia of opinionating—but it chimes with a wary individualism that could seem to refuse agreement about practically everything with almost everybody except his painter wife, Josephine Nivison. Having first met as art students around 1905, they married in 1924 and were symbiotically a unit. (Their closeness strikingly recalls that of Hitchcock's taut, creatively collaborative marriage with the screenwriter Alma Reville.) Nivison supervised a detailed ledger of all Hopper's works and served, at her insistence and with his consent, as his only model when he painted nudes. She was as vivacious as he was taciturn. (She once joked that talking with him was like dropping a rock down a well and waiting to hear it hit, in vain.) Hopper's last painting, *Two Comedians* (1965), pictures the pair of them in commedia-dell'arte costume as Pierrot and Pierrette on a stage, taking a bow.

Nivison aside, or standing guard, Hopper's independence feels absolute, repelling attempts to associate him with any other artist or social group. In this, he updates and passes along to the future the spirit of a paradigmatically American text, "Self-Reliance," minus Ralph Waldo Emerson's optimism. The free, questing citizen has devolved into one or another of millions rattling around on a comfortless continent. Can you pledge patriotic allegiance to a void? Hopper shows how, exploring a condition in which, by being separate, we belong together. You don't have to like the idea, but, once you've truly experienced this painter's art, it is as impossible to ignore as a stone in your shoe.

Published in the June 8 & 15, 2020, issue of *The New Yorker*, with the headline "Apart."

RETURNING TO STORM KING

What's with the metal-band-worthy name of Storm King, the marvellous sculpture park—or, better, landscape with sculptures in it—about fifty miles north of Manhattan, in Cornwall, New York? I've just spent some happy hours there, sprung from months of art deprivation, on the occasion of the Storm King Art Center's reopening to visitors with timed tickets. The setting is thundery enough, under the mighty brow of one of the highest mountains of the Hudson Highlands, in a valley of variegated hills, lawns, meadows, forest, and waters, along with elegant alterations that include arboreal allées and plantings with deference to native flora—some five hundred acres hosting roughly a hundred art works. I hadn't known, until I was told during my visit, that the park's name owes its provenance to the Romantic exasperation of a writer who, in 1853, pressed locals to rebrand their principal mountain Storm King from—get ready—Butter Hill. That nineteenth-century embrace of the hyperbolic anticipated the moxie, in 1960, of two art-loving businessmen, Ralph E. Ogden and his son-in-law H. Peter Stern, who gradually acquired much of the valley. They founded the park as a nonprofit entity, made a museum of an existing château on a hilltop, and pondered the ambient possibilities of the terrain.

In 1967, Ogden bought thirteen works from the estate of America's greatest sculptor, David Smith. Mostly made of welded steel, they deploy a repertoire of shapes, from the surreally animate to the nobly abstract, gracing dancerly postures with lyrical drawings in space. A suite of eight of them, currently installed under cathedralesque oak and black-walnut trees, is modestly scaled. Not so the vista-dominating, gestural arrays of mostly steel elements by a favorite of the collectors since 1968, Mark di

Suvero, which at times suggest playground facilities for giants. Nine of those were supplemented last year by a three-year loan of *E=mc²* (1996–97)—a tower, more than ninety-two feet high, whose converging I-beam legs are topped by flaring forms in stainless steel that grab at the sky. Also monumental are two maximum-size stabiles by art's foremost bejeweller of air, indoors or out, Alexander Calder. There are major works, as well, by Richard Serra, Andy Goldsworthy, and, most recently, Maya Lin, whose earthwork *Storm King Wavefield* (2007–08) represents a vast expanse of mid-ocean waves, up to fifteen feet high, with grassy undulations.

Sculpture parks proliferated, worldwide, in the second half of the twentieth century, in the wake of an identity crisis for large three-dimensional art. Modernist austerity had stripped sculpture of its traditional architectural and civic functions: there were no more integrated niches and pedestals, few new formal gardens, and an epochal apathy regarding statues—until lately! (We are now practically neo-Victorian in our awakenings—rude, for the most part—to symbolism in statuary.) Never mind the odd plaza-plunked, vaguely humanist Henry Moore. Where could one put outsize works that were almost invariably abstract—modernism's universalist ideals persisting—to give them a chance of seeming to mean something? In nature! Conjoining the made with the unmade, gratifying both. Sculpture parks emerged as game preserves and laboratories for big art. Storm King's early concentration of works by relevant artists of the late nineteen-sixties and seventies includes some formulaic banalities, tending to presume a surefire magic in embowered angular geometry, but even there you may savor the zest of a moment when sculpture jumped into nature's lap. The history is complicated and obscured, in the art world, by the contemporaneous development, in the sixties, of Minimalism, which, by engaging the physical presence of viewers, shrugs off its surroundings. (The park's chastely white modular piece by Sol LeWitt doesn't mind a bucolic site one way or another.) As a consequence, Minimalism sidelined poetic potencies that prove their lasting worth at Storm King.

Prior visitors won't be kept away by learning that few installations in this pandemic summer are new. The park's changing light, breezes, and theatre of clouds will do for novelty. The best recent addition, on view until November 9th, is *River Light* (2019), a ring of nine high-flying cyan-blue silk flags that Kiki Smith derived from a sun-sparkled film she made on a walk along the East River. Wind stirs the fabric to rippling, soft applause. The ensemble suggests a rallying point for angels. Also new is *A stone that thinks of Enceladus* (2020), a piece by a young New York-based artist, Martha Tuttle, which consists of a mowed field studded with boulders and cairns and rather hectically festooned with carved rocks and molded glass stones. Close by, propped on an island in a pond, is a startling curio, the hull of an America's Cup-grade racing boat that, in 1994, was prettily decorated with a mermaid motif by Roy Lichtenstein. Its abrupt presence, which you may less look at than gawk at, invokes the metaphysical truth that everything has to be somewhere. Storm King's prevalent rectitude might serve as a foil for other sorts of interesting shocks, within appropriate limits.

I can't remember why, on a visit many years ago, I was unimpressed by *Storm King Wall* (1997–98), by Andy Goldsworthy—perhaps residual fatigue with a fashion, in the seventies and eighties, for back-to-the-land schmaltz. The work strikes me now as rigorously intelligent as well as ecstatic. Made of rocks that were gathered from the surrounding region, impeccably hand-laid, the wall snakes nearly half a mile through the park's roughest terrain—clinging to slopes, plunging into ravines, ostensibly even passing underwater. The gratuitous labor-intensiveness generates a paean to the first human being who placed one stone atop another, and to every other since then and in time to come. Hiking the erratic land, you chance upon discontinuous views of the wall, proceeding at the pace of a waking dream. Similarly inexhaustible is the authority of Serra's *Schunnemunk Fork* (1990–91), four rectangular steel plates protruding from the sides of a gentle rise. The work looks smaller than I remember, from a time when I wrote that it induced "consciousness of the earth's sullen, immemorially surging mass." It turns out that a few years ago Serra decided to forgo any mowing around the plates, which now peek out almost shyly from rustling grasses: less imposing, their aggressiveness a kept secret, and very beautiful.

The Maya Lin *Storm King Wavefield*, just beyond sight of the Serra, is a tour de force by the designer of, to my mind, the single most successful work of American public art in contemporary memory, the Vietnam Veterans Memorial—a cenotaph for shared mourning—in Washington, D.C. (Still, it proved divisive enough—we are talking about America—to acquire the neighboring complement of a statuary group of three heroic G.I.s.) At Storm King, Lin extends the idea of form that exists simultaneously upon and within—and, in this case, as—the ground it occupies. The effect that she achieves, in common with Serra's *Fork*, is a placeness that centers the world while you are in its vicinity. Neither work could have a home more hospitable than Storm King.

Repeatedly, there are medium-size objects that, spotted from a distance and drawing you to them, precipitate new relations of yourself to the landscape at large. It's like a recurrent bonus for tiny pilgrimages. Louise Bourgeois's writhing cluster of silvered-bronze eyeball shapes that electrically light up from within now and then—*Eyes* (2001)—requires a bit of a climb to be viewed properly. You may then be reluctant to move along, so engrossing is the work's rambunctious grotesquerie and smack-on-the-ground adamancy at the edge of a lovely wood. That's a happenstantial quality of the finest things at Storm King: art that, beyond looking good, feels keenly aware of where it is and what it's doing there. It's a forgiving standard for lesser art, which gets by on seeming eager to please if ever you find yourself in a mood for it. Every piece hints at a story of its curatorial nomination and election, inviting judgment on the judgments that were made—a perambulatory discourse, if you're so inclined.

In lockdown times, there's euphoria in going much of anywhere, not to speak of a journey to a tract of paradise. You could say that I was primed for giddiness on this occasion. I noticed unaccustomed intensity in my responses to the art works that I encountered, taking them in like gulps of air after escaping a miasma. It was a gift of refreshed aesthetic innocence, which I think awaits us all when we are set free in even non-curated environs—I've been feeling apologetic to certain trees, near my home, for my past indifference to their beauty—and a lesson in joys that we used to take for granted. We will have peeled eyes. I should warn that attendance at Storm King is limited right now: visitor tickets are capped at three hundred per day, from Wednesday to Monday. But the place, which will stay open into December this year, is very apt to exist for at least as long as you do. And just to know and to think about it brightens a world, our present one, that is crisscrossed with shadows.

Published in the August 31, 2020, issue of *The New Yorker*, with the headline "The Great Outdoors."

THE JOYS OF NINETEENTH-CENTURY FRENCH DRAWINGS

"Lines from Life: French Drawings from the Diamond Collection," at the Clark Art Institute, in Williamstown, Massachusetts, is a pleasant show of forty-three drawings and a lithograph, largely middling studies for figure paintings, by thirty-three nineteenth-century French artists, some of whom were unfamiliar to me. I loved it! It proved to be just my speed as I return to savoring art in person after half a year's diet of digital gruel. (The pandemic has schooled us, by deprivation, in the indispensable materiality of art works as made things.) Thirty-two of the drawings, many of them gifts to the Clark, were collected by Herbert and Carol Diamond, who have a house near Williamstown and exercise generally conservative taste with catchy zeal. Styles in the show range from orthodox figure studies, favored by the École des Beaux-Arts, in Paris, and the Académie de France, in Rome, to examples of Realism and early onsets of Symbolism. There aren't many surprises in the works by the show's big names—Ingres, Géricault, Delacroix, Degas, Morisot, Millet, Redon, Toulouse-Lautrec, Cézanne—but one, by an artist who is little regarded now, Jean-François Raffaëlli, *Man in the City's Outskirts* (circa 1885), stands out. The energetic limning, in black chalk and pastels, of a rough workman feels poised at an eclectic intersection of Realism, Impressionism, and Symbolism, and hints at the raw expressiveness that Edvard Munch would unclench a few years later. In 1880 and 1881, Edgar Degas tried to induct Raffaëlli into the inner circle of the Impressionists, over grumbling from the group. An artist whom Claude Monet disdained as a "dauber" here merits a consolatory star turn.

The show's charm, over all, resides in the purity of its preoccupations. The Diamonds aren't trophy hunters. They respond to personalities, cherishing the signature qualities, rather than the crowning feats, of artists who made nineteenth-century Paris the global epicenter of contemporary art, powered by one competitive, temporarily commanding manner after another. (All but one of the artists are men. Think of the selections as notes in bottles washed up from a land bygone, such as Atlantis.) I felt admitted to backstage company with both marquee thespians and creditable troupers. During my visit, I spent only a little time with the Clark's terrific permanent collections—notably, in Impressionism and nineteenth-century American art—because I was in a mood less for Sunday punches than for the gentle touches of a show that suited a tranquil weekday afternoon. But I paid renewed reverence to the jewel in the Clark's crown, Piero della Francesca's *Virgin and Child Enthroned with Four Angels* (circa 1460–70), the most consummate of Madonnas. Under Mary's gaze, the naked baby Jesus reaches toward a symbol of the Crucifixion, attended by hauntingly cognizant angels. By contrast, the drawings, as drawings will, let me pursue thoughts about how art comes to be before it turns ceremonious.

To put it clumsily, I did connoisseurship—anyone can; it's calisthenics for sensitivity—which is always more fun with minor than with major art. (Masterpieces traffic in the inexplicable.) It avails best with drawings, which speak directly from the artist in pre- and mid-creation, hatching little big bangs of ideas that any finished work tends to diffuse. We can register the makers' period sensibilities, with resemblances to other art, and winkle out differences, the subtler the better. The Clark's show reinvigorates the old story of a sea change in French cultural fashion from Beaux Arts artifice to modes of engagement with lived reality. Senses of space evinced this. I may never have got more of a kick from less to look at than I did with a sheet of undated, faint pencil sketches, *Women in the Garden*, crudely outlined figures with fugitive indications of a background, that probably took Camille Pissarro about twenty seconds to dash off. I relished a break from the blank ground—the idealist non-atmosphere—of images like the one by Alexandre Cabanel, *Study for Florentine Poet* (circa 1853), of a carefully posed prone figure. Pissarro immediately activates an entire surface, from edge to edge: the modern picture. The trifle is like a little pill that, dropped in the proper liquid, could exfoliate a world. I imagined glimpsing it among other scraps on a studio visit to Pissarro—a fantasy spurred by the Diamonds' spirit of infectious fandom.

Two minuscule mythological drawings, on a single sheet, by Théodore Géricault, of the rape of Antiope by Jupiter, riveted me. They date from roughly 1815–16, shortly before this supreme artist began work on *The Raft of the Medusa* (1819), his colossal canvas, a touchstone of the Louvre, that dramatizes desperation, death, and cannibalism among survivors of an 1816 shipwreck off the northwest coast of Africa. In the drawings, a god grapples with a lividly naked nymph. The clarities of mass in pictorial depth, achieved with sharply contrasting dark and light, that sculpturally define the convulsive action and turn its scale from tiny in the eye to monumental in the mind astonish. (Is the subject upsetting? Upset was Géricault's flywheel.) I found myself aching anew at his death, in 1824, from a slew of maladies, at the age of thirty-two. With psychological acuity to match his vehemence, and ambition pitched to the skies, he seemed destined to reach the unexplored far shores of Romanticism—imagination flooded with subjectivity while addressing subjects of real-world importance (he had plans for an epic composition on the African slave trade)—and perhaps beyond, to something we will never know. Absent him, leadership in the movement fell to Eugène Delacroix, a virtuoso with paint who, except on inspired occasion, tended toward formulaic theatrics that needed critical boosterism from Charles Baudelaire to ennoble them. The show includes two Delacroix drawings, one of which is an entertaining melee, like a mud wrestle, with motifs from Rubens.

There are lovely things, such as the portrait drawing (circa 1867) of a young woman by Degas, striking for the Ingres-esque, crisp contour of the softly appealing face. That kind of decisive line had intoxicated artists of Ingres's time, for good and for strange. Ingres famously said, "Drawing is the probity of art." Bushwa. No one ever drew better, but to a befuddling effect that allowed him to get away with high-handed distortions of the human anatomy. (You must look long and skeptically at Ingres's paintings to detect the weirdnesses.) But I understand the yen, reported to me by a friend who has seen the show, to steal and take home the artist's *A Couple Embracing* (circa 1813–14), a tender subject seized upon with chilly efficiency. Ingres's linear sorcery is addictive. Degas would integrate it into more spontaneous forms—again, modern pictures—with a pertinacity that is prophesied by a sheet of five overlapping studies, from 1856, of, presumably, his own left hand. (I'd filch that.) The most enjoyable of the show's conservative works, made in 1867 by Jean-Léon Gérôme, perches Napoleon comfortably on camelback. Others rouse more scholarly than aesthetic interest, though with fealty to the Diamonds' passion for facts, not retroactive opinions, of a century's vogues in figuration.

Then there's the always happy shock of Berthe Morisot, who is represented by a small pencil rendering, *Marthe Givaudan* (circa 1890–91), of a smartly dressed woman which is as economical in form as a calling card. Since seeing a Morisot retrospective at the Barnes Foundation, in Philadelphia, in 2018, I've been in on a widely shared awakening to the singularity of the distaff Impressionist, who subliminally opposed her male peers, and their treatment of women as spectacle, with truths attesting to the inward as well as the outward poetics of female existence. Morisot's perspicacity and unique liberties of brushwork deserve inclusion among the movement's established stylistic repertoires. The sexism of the period had to have been merciless to marginalize her. Observe the impact in the Clark's permanent collection of a Morisot painting, *The Bath* (1885–86), amid several girly Renoirs: it's like a blast of vitality in a wax museum. Renoir's rosy-fleshed models do arbitrarily fussy things with their hands. Morisot's puts up her hair, anchoring in immediate experience the work's lambent lyricism.

What makes anyone draw one line and then add another? How does the second affect the first and determine the character of a third and a fourth? Drawings are commonly understood as process rather than product: things aborning. Do we take a rooting interest in the efforts—binding us to artists as personal heroes of wit and skill, if only for an instant? Or does something rote or predictable in the decisions unfolding on the page bore us? (This, at least, affords us the wan joy of feeling smart.) Context enlivens. The concentration of a show, like the Clark's, on the predilections of specific collectors, committed to specific categories, fosters a conversation that is already under way when we join it. Intimacy reigns: talents are unmasked, social distancing is forgotten.

Published in the September 14, 2020, issue of *The New Yorker*, with the headline "Lineage."

GOYA AND THE ART OF SURVIVAL

A good time for thinking about Francisco Goya is while the world stumbles. Crisis becomes him. *Goya: A Portrait of the Artist* (Princeton), a biography by the American art historian Janis A. Tomlinson, affords me a newly informed chance to reflect on an artist of enigmatic mind and permanent significance. In the tumultuous Spain of the late eighteenth and early nineteenth centuries, Goya worked for three kings—the reformist Carlos III, the dithering Carlos IV, and the reactionary Ferdinand VII—and then for social circles of the French usurper Joseph Bonaparte; for an overoptimistic three-year constitutional government; and, finally, woe to the land, for Ferdinand VII again. Goya kept landing on his feet as cohorts of his friends and patrons toppled from official favor, or worse. His increasingly naturalistic portraits—vivid in characterization and unconventionally flattering, with all but breathable tones and tints in dusky chiaroscuro ignited at times by clarion hues—sustained him at court despite the intrigues of rivals and schemers. It could be argued that the deafness that befell him in 1793 (possibly from lead poisoning), when he was forty-seven, and continued until his death, at eighty-two, in 1828, provided him some diplomatic padding, as he managed his interests with politic correspondence and the support of well-situated admirers. He was firmly prestigious by the time he took to making works of lacerating wit and escalating, ultimately horrific intensity. A stormy petrel skimming waves of change that swamped others, he introduced to history a model of the star artist as an anomalous spirit equipped with social acumen and licensed by genius. His nearest avatar is Andy Warhol.

Tomlinson's dryly written accounts of the Spanish court are no Iberian *Wolf Hall*, but they feature arresting characters, such as the raffish antihero Manuel de Godoy. A twenty-four-year-old military officer when he was elevated by Carlos IV, in 1791, Godoy came to manage Spain's crazily shifting alliances in a war with Revolutionary France and, when that went badly, one in league with France against Portugal, with Godoy promised a personal stake in the spoils. Big mistake. In 1808, Napoleon occupied Spain, made his brother the King, and discarded Godoy, who barely escaped the wrath of his betrayed fellow-citizens. (They made do with destroying nearly every available trace of him, such as portraits by Goya.) Rumored to be the lover of Carlos IV's queen, María Luisa, Godoy may have commissioned, or at least incited, Goya to paint his only erotic nude, *The Naked Maja* (1797–1800). (*Majas* and their male equivalent, *majos*, were flamboyantly cheeky lower-class dandies.) The Inquisition impounded *The Naked Maja* and its clothed counterpart in 1813 and posed stern questions to Goya, which he seems to have successfully ignored. There can be a lucky charm, during treacherous times, in being really, really good at something. Imperilled after the Bourbon restoration of 1814 by a purge of collaborators with the French regime, Goya redeemed a painting that he had made of Joseph I by substituting, or having someone else do so, the face of Ferdinand VII. He was cleared. The country's cultural establishment couldn't spare Goya's gifts, and arrivistes clamored to be portrayed by him.

Tomlinson addresses, with refreshing clarity, a chronic question of just how independent, not to say subversive, Goya was of the powers that employed him. She debunks a common oversimplification of Goya as a committed post-Enlightenment liberal. He was more complicated than that, and ineluctably strange. Uncanniness had to be part of his magnetism. There's often something haunted or haunting in his portraits and in some of his religious and allegorical commissions, though not in the antic cartoons of Spanish life that were destined for tapestries, an irksome duty of his early career. It's as if he always had something up his sleeve. That impression affected me strongly on a visit to the Museo del Prado, in Madrid, last year. Looking at his works can rouse the sensation of an alarm going off nearby, but you can neither understand the reason for its activation nor find it to turn it off.

Goya didn't emerge as a master through a neat evolution of period styles. He can seem at once decadent and innovative, with some lingering tropes of the late Baroque and the rococo and the brassiness of the then fashionable neoclassicism along with utterly original freshets of Romanticism. Spanish art had become provincial. The country's leading art educator was the mediocre German painter Anton Raphael Mengs, who promulgated a sort of housebroken neoclassicism. In 1778, when Goya was thirty-two, he turned to Spain's own lapsed glories, with a set of etched copies of seventeenth-century masterpieces by Velázquez, skeletonizing the art of the painterly demiurge in incised line with washes of aquatint. The hair-shirt exercise puzzled some of his fellow-artists. The renderings are spot on, but their reductions of color to line and shading are like a broadcast of the "Hallelujah Chorus" over a kid's walkie-talkie. I think that Goya sought gains for painting through grasping what had been lost to it. No longer equal to illusions of reality, paintings were fated to become objects, real in themselves, of a certain kind. Rather than forge a signature style, Goya practiced a temperamental abnegation of anything usual. This kept—and keeps—him impossible to pin down: a deserter from the marching ranks of the Old Masters, forever on the loose.

An homage to Velázquez's touchstone *Las Meninas* (1656) figures in perhaps the most beautiful group portrait ever painted. *The Family of Carlos IV* (1800–01) stands out in Goya's portraiture as a one-off masterpiece on purpose, affirming for good the justice of his recent elevation to the first court painter. In the background, the artist gazes out from behind, it would appear, the very canvas that we behold, suggesting that he's working from a mirrored view of the scene—an unlikely conceit that seems meant mainly, and wittily, to recall Velázquez's similar self-portrayal in *Las Meninas*. (The jape amounts to a proto-modernist instance of art about art.) Thirteen lavishly clad persons, from the fifty-two-year-old monarch to a babe in arms, share a room awash in the softly shadowed, caressing light of a golden afternoon. They assume informal attitudes of everyday aplomb, except for a woman who looks away as if distracted in the pictured instant. She represents a princess of Naples who was the bride-to-be of Carlos IV's son Ferdinand VII; her looks weren't yet known in Spain. She faces a muddy painting, on the room's back wall, that made reference to Sodom and Gomorrah. Some modern commentary detects, in her Lot's-wife posture, a critical stab at the corruption of the monarchic state—as if no one at the time could have noticed it. And doesn't Carlos IV look clownish? Your call. The more germane point is that he looks like—because he is—the King.

The tacit sensibilities of a given era tend to elude subsequent generations. I suspect that Goya's sophisticated contemporaries found his occasional mischief chic. Tomlinson writes that to assign personal perspectives to Goya's work for the court "is to impose values that are not of his time"—a familiar defense of historical figures who are judged harshly by present-day standards, but apt, as well, for an ill-fitting halo. When we presume agreement with Goya's supposed politics, we drift afield of his extraordinary complexity. What it was like to be him crouches behind an ineffaceable question mark.

The lower-middle-class son of a gilder, Goya studied painting in his beloved home town of Zaragoza, northeast of Madrid. When he was twenty-three, he went to Italy and spent two knockabout years of which little is known. (But he won second prize in a competition in Parma for a painting of Hannibal crossing the Alps.) In 1773, he married María Josefa Bayeu, a sister of his elder Zaragozan Francisco Bayeu, who was then a court painter to Carlos III. Among several miscarriages, Goya and Josefa had seven children, only one of whom survived childhood. Does that concatenation of tragedies help explain the radical pessimism of Goya's later works—most shocking, the eighty-two engravings assembled as *The Disasters of War* (1810–20), which he made in reaction to the Peninsular War of Bourbon Spain, Portugal, and guerrilla bands, backed by Great Britain, against the French occupation? Other psychic scars may be adduced: Goya's witnessing of public executions by garrote and, in the case of a woman whose face he remembered and drew decades later, a burning at the stake. And sights of inmates from Zaragoza's mental asylum stayed with him. But any traumas hung fire as he launched himself on a professional career with seething ambition, adapting Bayeu's rococo manner, but with a faster, more spontaneous hand.

In 1772, for his first major commission, Goya frescoed a dome in the immense, new Zaragoza basilica of El Pilar. His drawings for the design displeased the local cognoscenti, leading to a suggestion that Bayeu should touch them up in the correct fashion. Having made grudging modifications, Goya completed the project on his own, but he was summarily dismissed from further work at El Pilar. The affront initiated five years of bad blood between the brothers-in-law. (Tomlinson reports that today a visitor to El Pilar can behold the Goya ceiling in full illumination, while a nearby one by Bayeu hovers in gloom.) The humiliation, staining Goya's reputation in his home town, nettled him for most of his life, even after Zaragoza was obliged to embrace him as an illustrious native son. Nothing like it happened again.

What most dramatically did happen, starting in 1793 with the small paintings on tin that he made (and found a market for) of what Tomlinson summarizes as "natural disasters, cannibals, madhouses, and murder," was the emergence of a blistering negativity. The works coincided with spells of freely admitted anxiety and depression—"at times raving in a mood that I myself cannot stand," Goya wrote to a friend—but there's nothing deranged about the paintings. Strongly styled, they process rather than express his disturbances: correlatives set outside himself. They were followed, in 1797, by the start of a series of eighty satirical engravings of Spanish life, *Los Caprichos*, which proved widely popular. (Carlos IV acquired a set in return for granting Goya's son a pension.) He spared no class—O.K., except the titled—in his burlesques of donkey-headed professionals, superstitious peasantry, female and male poseurs, hypocritical clerics, and fools who, perhaps because so lost in delusion, verge on transmogrifying out of human form. In a rare public statement, advertising the series, Goya coolly declared as his targets "the innumerable foibles and follies to be found in any civilized society, and from the common prejudices and deceitful practices which custom, ignorance, or self-interest have made usual." Note the fatalism in that "any civilized society." If buyers of the works fancied themselves superior to the characters depicted, Goya surely didn't mind; but you know he had his doubts.

No public welcome could be counted on for *The Disasters of War*, which weren't published until thirty-five years after Goya's death. He shared them privately, giving a set of proofs to a friend who inscribed it, laconically, "Fatal consequences of Spain's bloody war with Bonaparte, and other emphatic caprices." Understatement! Murder and dismemberment, rape, desecration of corpses, and ghastly tortures multiply. It is natural to assume outrage in the author of visions so terrible. But what freezes my blood is an equanimity that sublimates rage and sorrow at what people can—and will—do to other people when civilization's thin crust fissures.

Visiting war zones around Madrid, Goya witnessed scenes of the carnage; and he was present for the catastrophe, in 1811, of a famine that filled the city with desperate, diseased, and dying refugees from the despoiled countryside. History is replete with war and starvation, but nothing else in art before or since—including, to my mind, photography and film—compares with the *Disasters* for penetrating hurt. The pictures are something more, less, and other than what we think of as protest art. Working up his nightmare scenarios stroke by stroke, as if from the inside out, he vivifies both the suffering of cruelty and the delirium of inflicting it, without any allowance for a rote response. Nor did he affix blame. One of his sardonically bland captions, "Rightly or wrongly," withholds the verdict on a scene of soldiers about to kill two blade-wielding men who, for all we know, may be patriotic guerrillas or mere criminals. Other captions—"There is no one to help them"; "What more is there to do?"—visit contempt on the impotence of the uninvolved. The same petrifying dreadfulness marks those intermittent engravings which impute monstrousness—embodied by eruptive owls or witches—to the dreaming states of the putatively rational. Goya doesn't indict the evils of individuals and groups; he amasses evidence of universal depravity. He added to the series compulsively, using battered, pitted, or otherwise flawed copper plates to etch when good ones fell subject to wartime scarcity. The sublimity of his skill occasions no relief, but, rather, the opposite. The last turn of the screw is your aesthetic delectation.

Goya had been on hand for the French invasion, which, in 1814, informed two astounding paintings of an uprising fomented by the dethroned Ferdinand VII, *The Third of May 1808* and *The Second of May 1808*. I cite the second date first because the image, a massacre of Spanish citizens by a French firing squad, is so routinely regarded as an antiwar icon on a par with *Guernica*. Its central figure, arms raised in hopeless supplication, feels at once a bit Christlike and a lot like a guy who is appalled to find himself in the wrong place at exactly the wrong time. Now consider *The Second of May*, a street scene of citizens frenziedly assaulting French forces. Their targets prominently include Mamluk cavalry from Napoleon's Imperial Guard. Possibly Muslim, do those figures touch a nerve of Spain's expulsion of its Moors two centuries earlier? (Fanatic religious intolerance had been one factor in the nation's decline from a cosmopolitan empire to a chew toy for armies.) We can't know what Goya had in mind for the picture, other than commonplace lunacy. But it wasn't propaganda.

Goya seems to have been a good enough man who led a decorous enough life, though hot-tempered in such practical matters as being paid for his work—reasonably, considering his early memories of poverty and his obligation to support members of an extended family after the death of his intestate father, in 1781. There's a lingering suspicion of homosexuality regarding his primary and, perhaps, only close friend, a never-married Zaragoza businessman named Martín Zapater. When apart, they corresponded constantly and longed for each other's company.

But Zapater fell silent when Goya became hysterical during a case of smallpox in his remaining heir, Javier, and pelted his friend—"oh my soulmate"—with letters of hyperbolic devotion. (Javier survived, and Goya simmered down.) So there was a limit, though a porous one. The pair revelled in bawdry and exchanged drawings of male and female genitalia. Tomlinson discounts a sexual liaison on the ground that the men were too discreet to risk the possible scandal. But she confirms that the darkest turn in Goya's emotional life coincided not with his deafness or any other recorded misfortune but with Zapater's untimely death in 1803. The open-heartedness (exceedingly rare for Goya) in portraits that he made of his friend, which radiate mutual affection and trust, plunges me half into love with the sitter myself. For the record, I doubt a sexual relation, for want of more than speculative evidence. In Goya's one later painting that bespeaks male intimacy, *Self-Portrait with Dr. Arrieta* (1820), we see the artist, drastically enfeebled, being attended to by a doctor who is almost comically virile, competent, and concerned. It's a picture to make you smile through tears.

We come at last to the Black Paintings (untitled by Goya), of which Tomlinson gives a bracingly investigative account: fourteen pictures that Goya painted in oils on the plaster walls of the house in Spain where he lived from 1819 to 1824, before a sojourn in France and his final four years among Spanish exiles in Bordeaux. (His expatriation was elective. He could—and twice did—revisit Spain.) The works vary in size and format, from panel to panorama. Though effectively installed in an oblong room at the Prado, they arouse a retroactive ache to have seen them in situ before they were transferred to canvas, in the nineteenth century, and, judging from early photographs, in some cases coarsened by clumsy restoration.

There's no getting used to the jolts of a darkling procession of the immiserated and the insane: a crazed giant (traditionally assumed to be Saturn, but who knows?) devouring a human body; two men buried to their knees in a barren landscape and fighting to the death with cudgels;

witches and a goat-headed demon in sinister excelsis; a little dog about to perish in what looks to be a tide of shit. Tomlinson surmises that an oddly ladylike giantess is Goya's maid and companion, Leocadia Weiss, whom he met after the death of his wife, in 1812. That image was situated next to the front door of the house, welcoming visitors to a peculiar scheme of interior decoration.

How do we square the courtier artist with the tour guide to Hell? It may be easier than it seems. For starters, what if the Black Paintings are in the nature of a joke? Tomlinson cites the possible influence of contemporaneous horror-mongering entertainments by showmen. And do the grotesqueries fundamentally contradict Goya's prior imaginative process? (I had thought, before my most recent visit to them, that I must be inured to those paintings. But no. Still and again, I cowered.) Mere squeamishness may impede thought on the question. Relative snowflakes that we are today, we can start by adjusting to the thicker skins of the culture that shaped Goya. Think of the cult of the bullfight, which he adored and immortalized in sensationally informative, visceral engravings and technically innovative lithographs that beggar Picasso's superficial homages a century and a half later. Goya was an avid hunter, once apologizing for having missed one shot of nineteen that had brought down two hares, a rabbit, five partridges, and ten quail. Tomlinson hazards that, for a social climber, hunting with aristocrats was that era's version of golfing with C.E.O.s. She admirably keeps the mysteries of Goya's character distinct from its self-serving machinations. He was unremarkably bourgeois, though salaried by royalty. (Payments kept arriving until the end of his life.) The boring parts of his story are salutary, framing the discontinuous dramas.

Goya's relationship with Weiss seems to have been tempestuous, but he was enchanted by her daughter, Rosario, whom he deemed, from the age of eleven, an artistic prodigy and promoted to everyone he knew. He had no other follower in art—unless you count, indirectly, most artists since. With a knack for miniaturist portraits, Rosario set an example for Goya that he took up and, of course, surpassed, with virtuosic miniatures of his own. Competitiveness consumed him. (Rosario went on to a meagre career as a copyist of paintings and was not above the odd forgery.) Ruling him, too, was humor, if that's the right word for sabotaging anyone's presumption to know his mind. I've compared the effect of the Black Paintings to unfriendly laughter coming out of a well. Don't kid yourself that he cares about connecting with you. But the works test, in the depths of the incommunicable, the degree of anyone's courage to envisage the bad in life, the worse, and the almost inconceivably abysmal. Whether he was driven by perversity or by obsession, there's an unholy glee about what Goya watched himself doing in and to his domestic haven. That's what keeps us returning to the works, as sorry as we may feel, yet again, to have come. One thing's for sure: the series marks no mental disintegration. Goya worked at top form, though reduced output, after moving to Bordeaux.

I believe that the Black Paintings distill, to a hundred proof, Goya's singularity. You can perceive tinctures of it in his best portraits, which register personhoods—specific existences—with curious dispassion. They attract obliquely. That's their eeriness. Be the sitter the Duke of Wellington (posing at stately ease while looking a bit tired, after his triumphal entry into Madrid, in 1812) or a gussied-up little boy (Goya was great with children, savoring their innocence of their preassigned social status), you sense him, when done, gathering his brushes and going home. Something has happened—the live capture of a personality, if not a soul—but it was engendered by a job, not by a divination. The quality of a remote regard, transposed from reality to fantasy, extends to even the most bizarre or tragic of his satirical subjects. No other artist possesses such a capacity to feel and to not feel, at a go. The Black Paintings simply—simple for him!—polarize torridity and iciness at simultaneous extremes that we would otherwise not suspect possible. Goya's cynosure is detachment regardless of the degree of pressure, professional or psychological, he may have been under. He leaves his subjects alone, as he was alone, and he leaves us alone with them. Rarely consummate in the ways that we associate with great art—Goya cranked out lots of so-so pictures—he is an outlier's outlier in the canon. His legacy isn't a commanding body of work but a homing beacon for worried people in worlds that are subject to unpredictable changes, perhaps suddenly and soon. Goya knew the problem and let slip the solution, which is to keep in mind that there is no solution, only an immemorial question: Now what?

Published in the September 21, 2020, issue of *The New Yorker*, with the headline "Waves of Change."

PHILIP GUSTON AND THE BOUNDARIES OF ART CULTURE

Art people have been shocked by the postponement, possibly until 2024, of a major exhibition, "Philip Guston Now," by the institutions that were scheduled to mount it: the National Gallery of Art, in Washington; the Tate Modern, in London; the Museum of Fine Arts, Houston; and the Museum of Fine Arts, Boston. I shared the reaction until I thought about it. At issue are some darkly comic paintings by the great American artist which feature cartoonish Ku Klux Klan figures smoking cigars, tootling around in open cars, and generally making fools of themselves. The dark part consists of abject self-portraiture, the focus of works, including the Klan pictures, that dumbfounded the art world when first shown, in 1970. At fifty-seven, Guston had trashed his status as the most sensitive stylist of Abstract Expressionism and unclenched raucous pictorial confessions of fear and loathing. Stricken with such regrets as having, in 1935, disguised his identity as the son of impoverished Jewish immigrants (his father hanged himself in 1923) by changing his name from Goldstein, he presented himself as a sad sack beset by bad habits and bad thoughts.

The subject matter is self-lacerating, albeit antic. The form stuns with visceral color, prehensile line, and the most insinuative brushwork of any modern painter, all indirectly nourished by Guston's passionate reverence for Renaissance masters. He as much as announced that he had nothing going for him except a way with a brush, which he then exalted from a subbasement of the soul. Long resisted by many—I was slow to come around myself, having venerated his abstractions—the body of work has outlasted, in authenticity and quality, that of every other

American painter since. As an inspiration and a challenge, he companions innumerable young painters everywhere, to this day. (He died, of a heart attack, in 1980.) A celebration by leading institutions is entirely in order. As for the Klansmen, they first appeared briefly, as murderous lynchers, in works that Guston, a lifelong leftist, made in the thirties. Do they lurk, repressed, in his abstractions? This would help to explain the mysterious tension in some of even his most elegant Abstract Expressionism, before they resurfaced as psychological cats out of bags.

But . . . the white hoods, icons of evil at the pitch of swastikas. Guston's Klansmen are the first—and likely the last—things that most people will notice in the paintings at a time when it can seem that no symbol is safe from being politicized, let alone one already steeped in politics. What public reception to Klan imagery in a show of a white artist can the museums have expected? (A revolt against it began with staff members at the National Gallery.) Always risky, perhaps, the unintended but inevitably incendiary provocation belongs to a pre-2020 age of educated innocence. Does it now reveal the boundary of an art culture that is maintained by and for members of an élite so confident of virtue—putatively independent of race and class, democratically self-selected, oozing benignity—as to be unconscious of existing as such? Suddenly silhouetted, the faction is made up of a scant minority of citizens who take an active interest in art and espouse cosmopolitan values—the culturally privileged, whom museums represent and serve while, these days, laudably trying to extend their appeal to neglected audiences.

The National Gallery's director, Kaywin Feldman, has said that the postponement—note, not the cancellation—responds to "a tough time in America." That's putting things mildly. The Guston affair is a symptom of a society-wide deterioration of trust in institutions and tolerance for uncongenial expression. Harsh light falls on long-tacit norms. Consider the fact, cited by Feldman as a decisive concern of the museum, that the curators of the show, with its racially charged content, are all white. A time-out to recontextualize does not, contrary to the thrust of an art-world open letter protesting the postponement, first published by the Brooklyn *Rail* and then quoted in the *Times*, constitute cowardice at a national institution. (Feldman now says that the show is likely to open sooner than was initially announced.)

In a small way, the controversy exemplifies divisions that are splintering the United States: votes of no confidence in the good will of contending interests. (Signatories to the letter include Black artists and intellectuals, as the conflict is widely cultural, not narrowly demographic.) Any difference may breed enmity. In our Partisan States of America, we watch our words—or, perversely, don't—for fear of, or with ardent intent of, offending. Offense doesn't spur debate; it replaces it. With apologies for amateur punditry, I doubt that this will stop after the Presidential election even if the conciliatory-minded Biden wins, with liberal unity against Trump fragmenting and rightists incubating ungodly new species of insurrection.

Welcome to an argument with myself, as I risk the appearance of wielding cancel culture against my lifelong allies in the cause of art. Regarding Guston's Klansmen, I'm ambushed by imagining the intractable opposition of people who neither find humor nor seek subtlety in racist symbology. Guston's subject is moral anguish, which, I suspect, increasingly amounts to a thorny luxury for old-fashioned and atomized liberals like me. Am I underrating the comprehension of viewers new to Guston? Do I condescend? I can't rule it out. But what worries me is the assumption by art-world peers of mine that artistic license is an unexceptionable principle, rather than a persuasion of fortune-favored, cultivated liberal sentiment and taste. If I sound populist here, it's because I'm the kind of liberal who is perhaps oversensitive to the feelings of all constituencies. Having, in thought, stepped outside my cohort, I can't with honesty jump back in, however pained I may be that I won't get to see an assuredly wonderful show in the coming months. I remain preoccupied by the sense of a crisis that spills beyond the misapprehension of a should-be canonical artist. The trouble resonates backward as well as forward in time. Indeed, it is endemic to democracy, a seething of differences that now and then boils over.

The cosmopolitan cast of modern art culture has a history. Until almost the middle of the twentieth century, in the United States, it could be popularly associated with urban clusters of bohemian mavericks and eccentric patrons, arguably besieged by yahoos. (From a provincial distance, that myth retained just enough zing in 1962 to make me drop out of college and drive non-stop from Minnesota to New York. Well, first to a job in Jersey City.) The glamorization of modernism owed much to the aura of Allied triumph in the Second World War, which established so many other parameters of national amity that have lately, and rapidly, been crumbling. Pioneering institutions and, this being America, the charisma of inrushing wealth closed the deal, giving pause even to yahoos. (You might think that a Jackson Pollock was something your kid could do, and that Andy Warhol's fame was an emperor's-new-clothes con, but you became less apt to say so in unfamiliar company.) Aggressive innovation remained a punching bag for conservatives, but arguing back was hardly worth the breath. Cosmopolis won, to its own satisfaction and the apathetic disregard of folk at large. After the sensations of Pop art and the jolts of Minimalism, in the sixties, avant-gardist rebellion turned inward with the esoterica of conceptual art and, later, with applications of critical theory, but they served only to shrink rather than to redraw the public profile of new art. A glaring precedent for the Guston affair came about with malice aforethought in 1989, when institutional displays of Robert Mapplethorpe's (excellent) homoerotic photographs and Andres Serrano's (puerile) *Piss Christ* set Senator Jesse Helms, of North Carolina, on a spectacular moralistic crusade. The art world soon recovered its obscurity, except for odd blips, until, as emblematized by the trophy aesthetics of Jeff Koons, its values were transmogrified into the news-making prices paid by a speculative international oligarchy of the ultra-rich.

Art goes on. Art that is transgressive will recur. But it will do so nakedly for anyone who chooses to characterize it, not only for those initiates who congratulate one another on their shared investment in standards of truth, beauty, and good conscience. Cold winds are blowing from the future onto aspirations to provide society, or even segments of society, with a capacity to bridge differences with mutual respect. I've often reflected that uses of "we" in critical writing are unavoidably presumptuous, though they are rhetorically meant only to invite, or perhaps to seduce, agreement. I've never felt less confidence in the pronoun, at a time of alienations that recall what W. B. Yeats perceived in another pandemic year, 1919: "Mere anarchy is loosed upon the world."

Published in the October 19, 2020, issue of *The New Yorker*, with the headline "Us Cosmopolitans."

HOW TO READ SAM GILLIAM'S FORMALISM

A powerful show of new work by the Washington, D.C., artist Sam Gilliam, at Pace, is his first ever with a major New York dealer, despite past recognition of him at the city's chief museums and, among other honors, his representation of the United States at the Venice Biennale of 1972. The commercial lacuna calls for an explanation. Gilliam, who is still productive at the age of eighty-six, is a leading light of what is termed the Washington Color School of abstract painting, which came to public attention around 1960 in thrall to the doctrines of Clement Greenberg, who influenced a generation of D.C. artists, including the highly successful Morris Louis and Kenneth Noland. The critic posited flatness and appeals to eyesight alone as the destiny of new painting, as preordained by modernism. That was nuts, be it noted. But the era was still smitten with myths of formal progress in art, and Greenberg's proposition bore elegant fruit for a while. Gilliam broke ranks with the movement—or extended it—in the mid-sixties, when he began draping vast unstretched paint-stained and -spattered canvases from walls and ceilings, creating undulant environments that drenched the eye in effulgent color. (Dia:Beacon, in the Hudson Valley, has on view a magnificent example, *Double Merge*, from 1968; exploring it is peripatetic bliss.)

Gilliam's qualified apostasy, with a nod to the space-altering aesthetics of Minimalism, was widely noticed but, taking place outside New York, proved poorly situated and timed. Pop art, minimalist sculpture and a proliferation of heterodox manners that came to be called post-Minimalism, and conceptual art were eclipsing anything to do with color-field painting—and often with painting at all—in the big town, and the Washington School could appear to be a provincial rear guard.

Even so, Gilliam's breakthrough and subsequent achievements with his draping method should have loomed large in the moment's hot and heavy discourse. Why didn't they?

Gilliam is Black, which in the art world back then identified an American artist as a special case, so remorseless was the presumed whiteness of "mainstream" Western culture. (An inaudible asterisk long attended mentions of, for example, the sorely underrated, late New York abstractionist Jack Whitten.) Gilliam's reception was dogged by a double bind of unconscious condescension and compensatory indulgence—or so it seemed to me, over the years. This was more than uncommonly distracting in his case. Gilliam's art seemed to make no clear point of his identity apart from the occasional title, such as *Lady Day* for a work in 1971, that signalled his cultural background. He is temperamentally a formalist from tip to toe, stalking meaning in nuances of format, color, texture, and the other technical givens of his medium: mainstream indeed, to ambitious art of the nineteen-sixties and, at intervals, ever since. It's possible to suspect reparative social justice in his renewed eminence, but really it's a chance to abolish one remnant of double-entry accounting of white and minority artists.

Purgative, to this end, is a dazzlingly stylish essay in the Pace catalogue by the extraordinary Black scholar and poet Fred Moten—a literary work of art in itself, ablaze with on-target wordplay—which teases out inconspicuous racial imprints on Gilliam, from the sight (recalled by the artist) of women's washing billowing from clotheslines to the free-jazz innovations of Ornette Coleman and to tropes, in recent works, of African architecture and design. Antically exaggerated, the focus pays off, for me, by illuminating a peculiar psychological intensity in even Gilliam's most circumspect art: an air of taking nothing for granted and of having things to prove, an asperity in the face of felt or imagined resistance, a hint of playing for stakes beyond what's visible. The formalist credo—what you see is what you see—applies, but Moten proves that a racial audit frees up a general appreciation of Gilliam's excellence. It can't explain the art's self-critically disciplined integrity, skill, inventiveness, and abounding beauty. But Moten's audacity relaxes any lingering nervousness on the score of race by letting it rip, affirming Blackness as a regular feature, or quality, in American art, even or especially when it's not overtly at issue.

Gilliam was born in Tupelo, Mississippi, the seventh child of a truck driver and a housewife. The family soon moved to Louisville, Kentucky, where, having wanted to become a cartoonist since childhood, Gilliam plunged into art studies at the University of Louisville. In 1962, after returning from a two-year stint in the Army and earning an M.A. in fine arts, he relocated to the capital. His enthusiasms ranged across modern art, from German Expressionism through Picasso and Braque to Louis and Noland. He took to painting hard-edged stripes and geometric shapes, Washington Schoolishly dead flat. Then he jettisoned concerns with style for a redefinition of what paintings could be and do. His drapings enlist chance operations of pouring and flinging that gradually, as he less directed than monitored them, generate not so random instances of rhythmic snap and chromatic counterpoint. (A watcher as much as a wielder of paint, Gilliam rang a fresh change on Jackson Pollock's drip technique.) Each viewer of the softly hanging canvases comes to a unique experience of their cumulative effects and then, if sticking around, discovers yet another.

Gilliam's quest persisted when he discontinued draping canvases around 1980 and returned to the wall by way of intensively pigmented compositions in types of free-form style, categorized at the time as "lyrical abstraction," often on constructed reliefs of angled and jutting planes—a bit in the manner of contemporaneous works by Frank Stella, but zestier. Circles occurred, oddly portentous. Again, the works' key success is formal, as an effect of obdurate density and jagged animation. But Moten stays on the hunt for racial propensity. He relates Gilliam's affinity for circles to the title of a 1959 track from Ornette Coleman's 1970 album *The Art of the Improvisers*: "The Circle with a Hole in the Middle," which mundanely describes a vinyl record but resonates with hints of a flaw or a void. (Moten upends the suggestion by titling his essay "The Circle with a Whole in the Middle.") Gilliam has embraced the form in recent large wall-mounted wooden doughnut shapes that are dyed, rather than painted, in gorgeous hues. One from this year is titled *Black Mozart / ORNETTE*. Also new are works on sheets, some more than six feet square, of washi, a Japanese paper made from fibres of the inner bark of the gampi tree, the mitsumata shrub, or the paper mulberry. Repeatedly soaked in acrylics, allowed to dry, and then soaked again, the sheets end up not so much covered as replaced by slabs of solid monochrome, their surfaces varied, when you look closely, by traces of the artist's manipulating hand. These are blasts of pure chroma like nothing else I've ever seen: while meltingly beautiful, they are no more passive than the front ends of oncoming trucks.

The show's main news is in sculpture: there are several small pyramids and one immense one, all raised slightly off the floor and built of innumerable horizontal sheets of laminated plywood with regularly spaced bands of aluminum. Gorgeously dyed in sumptuous color—bringing out and celebrating the textures of the wood grain—the blunt structures radiate like light sources. Do they suggest late entries in the repertoire of Minimalism? They do, but with a sense of re-starting the aesthetic from scratch—getting it right, even, at long last. The pieces play a role in another of the show's revelations: a series of large (up to twenty feet wide) neo- or post- or, let's say, para-color-field paintings that owe the ruggedness of their paint surfaces to incorporations of leftover pyramid sawdust. Bevelled edges flirt with object-ness, making the works seem fat material presentations, protuberant from walls, rather than pictures. But, as always with Gilliam, paint wins. Thick grounds in white or black are crazed with specks, splotches, and occasional dragged strokes of varied color. While you feel the weight of the wooden supports, your gaze loses itself in something like starry skies: dizzying impressions of infinite distance in tension with the dense grounds, which are complicated by tiny bits of collaged and overpainted wooden squares. Registering the jittery chromatic harmonies and occasional underlying structures—ghosts of geometry—takes time. Seemingly decorative at first glance, the paintings turn inexhaustibly absorbing and exciting when contemplated. Like everything else in this show of an artist who is old in years, they feel defiantly brand spanking new.

Published in the November 16, 2020, issue of *The New Yorker*, with the headline "Off the Wall."

THE METROPOLITAN MUSEUM AT A HUNDRED AND FIFTY

"Here time becomes space." A famously enigmatic line from Richard Wagner's *Parsifal* toyed with my mind during a recent visit, my first since last winter, to the Metropolitan Museum of Art. It chimed with my experience as I prowled the prodigious institution, which has been celebrating, in a pandemically muted manner, its hundred-and-fiftieth birthday as the world's chief encyclopedic art museum. "Making the Met," a huge show, roughly tracks the sequence of the museum's acquisitions and policies since its founding, in 1870. A hundred and fifty is a lot of years, though a mere flicker compared with the five millennia's worth of objects from the permanent collections that are sampled in the show.

If you're so inclined, there's much to think about when considering the successive mind-sets of patrician New York, from Eurocentric Victorian tastes to universalist ideals—an evolution that has rarely been rapid. Art that the Met deemed "primitive" was initially consigned to the American Museum of Natural History, across Central Park. This gaffe was remedied in the nineteen-seventies with spectacular gifts of African and Polynesian items that Nelson Rockefeller had amassed for his own Museum of Primitive Art. Photography, scorned for decades, arrived with a bang in the twenties and thirties, thanks to the indefatigable lobbying of Alfred Stieglitz. Three exquisite crepuscular prints of the Flatiron Building, by Edward Steichen, from 1904, heralded that breakthrough. But derelictions persist from the starchy conservatism that long retarded the museum's engagement with twentieth-century art, when it lazily let the Museum of Modern Art get the best stuff while the getting was good. Complaints about chronic cluelessness at the Met were once common in the art world, unmitigated by such maladroit stabs at contemporaneity as "New York Painting and Sculpture," a show in 1969 by the putatively hip curator Henry Geldzahler, which mistook abstract painting as the wave of the future and included just one woman, Helen Frankenthaler, and no Black artists. And the less that's remembered the better of a patronizing debacle from the same year, "Harlem on My Mind," which again excluded artists of color. The Met is endeavoring to counter its legacy of benightedness on this score, but, like the turning of a battleship, the process is gradual.

On the other hand, and meanwhile, c'mon. The Met is our Home Depot of the soul. It has just about whatever you want, and it has a lot of it, very largely the harvest of past donations, en masse, of the collections of major benefactors—a New York tradition that, per a bequest in 1969, entitled the banker Robert Lehman to require the construction of a whole new wing, devoted to his gifts. (That was annoying, but the art was worth it.) It needs to be said that recent scholarship has cast shade on the robber-baron and colonialist provenance of many Met treasures—a problem shared by other formerly piratical museums worldwide. But it's hard to gainsay, to start with, the tremendous value of the museum's foundational commitment to ancient Egyptian (hello, Temple of Dendur, 1978), Greek, and Roman treasures, from the Mediterranean cradles of Western tradition, even as it has extended its aegis to Asian, African, and other cultures, most recently with a wondrous refurbishment of the Islamic galleries, completed in 2011.

If there's ever a hitch to enjoying the Met, it's satiety: so much, so all at once. But that keeps us coming back—and the inability to do so for months during the COVID lockdown felt like a spell of localized brain damage. To return now exhilarated me—those marble halls, the noble stairs, the niche concentrations of thises and thats. Time becomes space, indeed, in stilled torrents of forms and epochs that engulf you, wherever you chance to stand. "Making the Met" magnifies the utter variousness of the place. If the effect is disorderly—with a time line cutting across departmental divisions and educational chronologies—so are we these days. I'm for rolling with it.

The show starts with a chapel-like room emphasizing the museum's present collecting goals—a political statement, unavoidably. There's a van Gogh painting, a Rodin sculpture, a sixteenth-century Nepalese mask, a wooden power figure from the Kongo Kingdom, a Greek marble stele, a Surrealist sculpture by Isamu Noguchi, and a Richard Avedon photograph of Marilyn Monroe. Do the juxtapositions disorient? Good. You're primed for a panoply of incongruities with a cumulatively odd effect on aesthetic perception. Anachronism reigns. An early masterpiece by Édouard Manet, *Young Lady in 1866*, predates in the acquisition annals a set of carved stone fragments of an Aramaic palace in what is now Syria (circa the tenth or ninth century B.C.). I think I never looked at those before; they're terrific.

Profiting greatly are items of craft and decoration—keenly selected ceramics, jewelry, armor, furniture, and whatnot—granted solo appearances away from their normally crowded shelves and vitrines. Some startle. A framed swatch of wallpaper, from 1922, by the tragically short-lived Wiener Werkstätte designer Dagobert Peche, ambushed me into rapture: bright leafy and floral accents scattered across a ground of depth-shaded vertical bands of ambrosial color. (I've been a Peche nut since a retrospective of his work at the Neue Galerie in 2002.) The design seemed to essentialize a human will to beauty as a matter of workaday routine: ordinary ecstasy. Come to think of it, almost everything on display in "Making the Met" crowned a good day for someone, craftsman or artist, who was charged with some specific purpose, generating for the viewer a parade of privileged encounters that bestir bygone forms to present-tense eloquence.

The show's strangest effect, for me, was a relative deflation of major art, as a consequence of having been made to compete with a melee of minor but pestering charms. Paintings by Manet, Rembrandt, Vermeer, Chardin, and many another master, popping up unpredictably, felt almost apologetic for diverting toward profundity a general flow of enthusiasm for any and all instances of sufficiently motivated creativity. Those painters are gods to me, and I'll want their works returned to suitably dignified hangings. But it's valuable, as an antidote to excessive piety, to register the raw fact of physical existence that they share with innumerable other made things, each with something or other to say for itself and about the human appetite for betterment, whatever the occasion. The show induces a kind of therapeutic delirium. Aesthetic response rejoices as readily in the eye-catching as in the sublime. The vacation from serious judgment seemed to me serious in itself, a reminder that nothing possesses inherent qualities except by attribution, necessarily ratified in personal experience. (Beauty really is in the eye, among other faculties, of the beholder; that's where it can do the most good.) Putting revered works to hard tests, as "Making the Met" does, disrupts and may thereby reground their wonted hold on us.

Roaming the museum apart from the show, I found the levelling effect hard to shake, tamping down my giddiness at being back in the great building and dispersing my promiscuous surrender to the show's seductive bibelots. Regular stops for me, like *Bather (from a fountain group)*, a fantastically poignant young figure in white marble from 1782 by Jean-Antoine Houdon, felt off duty, as if backstage awaiting a cue. I evaded disappointment by skipping the Renaissance, Mannerist, and Baroque demiurges—Bellini, Tintoretto, Velázquez—who normally rivet me. The reason was a mildly estranging reminder of how artificial the assumptions and protocols of museums tend to be. Like any learned behavior, museumgoing can slip the mind. I had a flash memory of being a bored kid, thrust into a mysterious jumble of things that grownups insisted I like. (I liked some, but sullenly.) That mood befits, I've decided, a thaw of sensibility after a period of benumbing house arrest. I keep noting that the objects are the same, but we who view them are different now: not resuming, rebeginning. Loving art always involves catching up to ourselves. I count on my Met touchstones to be more sociable, and myself to be less self-conscious, when next we meet.

There's looking at art, and then there's thinking about it, which can sprawl without limits across our apprehension of the ways of the world. The Met's anniversary show affords stimulus for a great deal of both, rather bravely inviting skeptical scrutiny of the institution's record of cardinal decisions. Every choice made during the museum's century and a half—what to display, and how, and why—settled an in-house argument that can percolate anew, when confined to aesthetics, or that may run afoul of latter-day cultural and political realities. Most institutions tend to be clumsy beasts in this respect, on the back foot of critical and social changes that may either confirm or trash the wisdom that they presume to embody. I think of a section in the show that celebrates Met personnel who, as "monuments men," rescued Nazi-looted art works during the late stages of the Second World War—a point of pride that touches on discomfiting issues, some not yet resolved, of the works' proper ownership and disposition. (Rounding the stuff up was the easy part.) Most gravely, as an open wound, there's the fact that, until the last two rooms, the show features hardly a Western work that isn't by a white man. The behemoth museum details—and embarrasses—the moral character of what has been mirrored to us as the sum of a comprehensive civilization: a heritage to be lived with and, by the way, lived down.

It's nice to see a painting by Romare Bearden, a consummate artist who was long burdened with token status in the art world. More satisfying still, there's *Street Story Quilt* (1985), an array of three large sewn panels by Faith Ringgold. Formally commanding, the multicolored suite captures in sprightly imagery and describes in demotic words a host of Black citizens—real lives, really led—in windows of tenements along a city street that's past due for intersecting with Fifth Avenue.

Published in the November 30, 2020, issue of *The New Yorker*, with the headline "Happy Returns."

THE MELANCHOLY GESTALT OF ISOLATION

An invitational show of international artists, "100 Drawings from Now," at the Drawing Center, in SoHo, speaks to our lockdown epoch with startling poignancy. All but one of the works have been created since the pandemic's onset. They are mounted on walls with magnets, unframed, and arrayed seemingly helter-skelter. Few are thematic. There are scant visual references to the spiky virus, though there are some good jokes on homebound malaise. Among the better-known artists, Raymond Pettibon pictures himself bingeing on episodes of *The Twilight Zone* and Katherine Bernhardt reports a homeopathic regimen of cigarettes and Xanax. Stylistic commonalities are scarce, aside from a frequent tilt toward wonky figuration. The show confirms a delta-like trend—or anti-trend—of eclectic eccentricities without any discernible mainstream. (Does this signal the end of art history? It can feel that way, absent competitive modes and manners. Anyone today can do anything, which sounds nice but makes for little synergy.) What unites Rashid Johnson's grease-stick abstraction, conjuring a state of alarm in a pigment that he has invented and dubbed Anxious Red; Cecily Brown's pencilled carnage of game animals after a seventeenth-century still-life by Frans Snyders; and a meticulous, strikingly sombre self-portrait by R. Crumb? Isolation. Intended or not in individual cases, the melancholy gestalt is strong, as is its silver-lining irony of satisfying all artists' ruling wish: to be alone in the studio. Alone with themselves. Alone with drawing. I found myself experiencing the works less as calculated images than as prayers.

It's an effect common enough in both art and life: consciousness stumbling upon soulfulness. I think of lines by John Ashbery:

the soul is not a soul,
Has no secret, is small, and it fits
Its hollow perfectly: its room, our moment of attention.

An event rather than an entity, the soul defines our deepest depths, oblivious of sensation, thought, and feeling—touching bottom in our simple existence. Nearly all mystics posit a oneness of attention and worship. This may seem a lot to lay on a group show of overwhelmingly secular and cosmopolitan art, but you know what? I may have a point. Friends agree with me that, for those of us who have been confined to home, these past months of forced lassitude have given rise to moments that are essentially mystical: temporary losses of ourselves, like existential hiccups, that we would likely not have noticed if we were leading full lives. When time is a trackless waste, escapes from the aridity detonate. Gone before we're quite aware of them, they return us to interminable tedium—in which it's easy to brood that the world is full of possibilities, all of them over—but with a lasting glint of resilience. The universe isn't done with us yet. Will we recall our ordeals and their momentary reprieves or expunge them from memory when the vaccines kick in? (The flu of 1918, which resulted in fifty million deaths, seemed to have dropped from the nation's collective mind the instant it ended.) But here we are, and "100 Drawings from Now" vivifies the situation for me.

Drawing seems the most apt medium for expressing the fix we're in. It's quick, and hospitable to surges of soulfulness: the assertion (or insertion) of individual solitudes in shared time. For most artists, perhaps including most of those in the show, drawing is a workaday task central to a process that is destined to yield results in painting, sculpture, installation, or another format. (If a drawing is like a prayer, a completed project is like a Sabbath.) I'm imposing my thesis on a lot of work that, while impressive on its own terms, seems output-as-usual for its creators: a powerfully composed (and plenty timely) protest of institutionalized violence against Black people, by the Bahamas-born Lavar Munroe; an antic scarecrow figure against a geometric ground, by the thirty-one-year-old Walter Price, from Georgia; a congeries of jammed-together gray-and-yellow checkerboard patterns, by Sam Moyer, a promising Brooklynite new to me. But those fine efforts amount to background accompaniment to the show's instances of urgency and agitation. (And who can say what inner pressures attended their making?) Even—or especially—understatement succeeds. I was at first perplexed and then riveted by the contribution from Karen Kilimnik, a rococo visual poet of courtly romance. She sketched only the symbols of the four card suits—heart, spade, diamond, club—in blue, two greens, and red. I take the work as a confession of the inadequacy of art in the face of lived suffering, but also as a log-in for the occasion: another artist is present, making things despite all. Kilimnik's gesture seemed to me the next best thing to Wittgenstein's dictum "Whereof one cannot speak thereof one must be silent." A fluent acrylic of a blooming iris by Amy Sillman evinces similar tact: the artist weighing in with the little, but all of the little, that she can muster amid common distress.

The Drawing Center merits gratitude for the thoughtfulness and nimble timing of the show. It is an exemplary nonprofit that has survived art-world ups and downs since its founding, in 1977, in a disused warehouse on Greene Street and its move, ten years later, to 35 Wooster Street, in what was then a hot zone for galleries but is gelid now. The rationale for its creation was an argument that graphic mediums are too often discounted in assessments of new art. I remember initially doubting the emphasis, which seemed to me a mite precious. (What next? The Macramé Nook?) But the center's exhibition programs, featuring artists both prominent and tyro, have proved invaluable for their sidelights on technical developments and critical issues in art and the wider culture. (There have been tours de force representing tattoo artists, writers, chefs, soldiers, and, last year, prisoners.) The artists in "100 Drawings from Now" were selected by three staff curators of different generations: the boomer Laura Hoptman, the Gen X-er Claire Gilman, and the millennial Rosario Güiraldes—though, again, you wouldn't easily distinguish period styles among their respective cohorts. The works pick no perceptible critical fights with one another. Movements are moot. Romances of avant-gardism have died on the vine. Today, becoming an artist at all has come to seem the limit of an individual's intervention in history. But quality and energy count, as always. You know you're in good hands with brisk portraits that the New Yorkers Sam Messer and Rochelle Feinstein drew of each other, simultaneously, via Zoom. There's refreshment, besides ominousness, in the Chinese artist Cao Fei's realist rendering of a bottle of hand sanitizer and introspective drama in the Hong Kong-born Paul Chan's inky and dense semi-abstract of his studio, drawn with his nondominant left hand.

Silence reigned as, masked and wary, I viewed the show. The space was almost deserted. I might have thought, Where is everybody? But, of course, I knew. The world's population is atomized among the dying, the ill, the quarantined, the sheltered, the heroically imperilled "essential" (never forget!), and, God save the mark, the blinkered fools. None are likely to crowd art shows anytime soon, even as precautionary measures have enabled the reopening of galleries and museums in parts of the country. Do you sometimes imagine that you're getting used to the emergency? I think I can guarantee that you're not, burdened by states of mind that will be comprehensible only retrospectively, when they no longer pertain. The world going on nonetheless, as the world will, feels bizarrely conditional, subject in thought and action to a blanketing subjunctive mood: things as we wish they were. We are waiting this out with nostalgia for lost freedoms, fear and empathy in the present, and, perhaps, vague anticipation of eventual survivor's guilt. Never has social privilege seemed more unfair while being clung to so tenaciously. Some of us—artists—are undergoing the siege in ways that can alert us to the subjective dimensions of an objective calamity. We should want those people to keep it up as best they can.

Published in the December 21, 2020, issue of *The New Yorker*, with the headline "The Fix We're In."

WHAT ARE ARTISTS FOR?

Your first impression of "Engineer, Agitator, Constructor: The Artist Reinvented, 1918–1939," a vast and exciting show, at the Museum of Modern Art, of interwar Soviet and European graphic design, may combine déjà vu and surprise. You likely know the look, loosely termed Constructivist: off-kilter geometric shapes, vectoring diagonals, strident typography (chiefly blocky sans serif), grabby colors (tending to black and orangeish red), and collaged or montaged photography, all in thrall to advanced technology and socialist exhortation, in mediums including architecture, performance, and film. But you won't have seen most of the works here. About two hundred of the roughly three hundred pieces on view were recently acquired by the museum from the collection of Merrill C. Berman, a Wall Street investor and venture capitalist. Fresh images catch the eye, as do unfamiliar names. The scope is encyclopedic, surveying a time of ideological advertisement, when individuals sacrificed their artistic independence to programs of mass appeal.

"The title 'artist' is an insult," the German Communists George Grosz and John Heartfield declared in 1920. Grosz subsided into satirical painting and drawing, but Heartfield became a dedicated propagandist who cast Hitler as a puppet of capitalism and savaged centrist opposition to the tyrant's rise. The cover of the show's catalogue features Heartfield's photograph of a worker's soiled, forward-grasping hand, which was used for a poster promoting the Communist Party in a Weimar election in 1928. The image seems rather more menacing than rallying. It is at an extreme of the era's politically weaponized design, which generally took less inflammatory forms in Germany and other European democracies. These countries incubated movements that are well represented in the exhibition but tangential to its Russian focus—Futurism, Dada, the Bauhaus. In Russia, there was no partisan campaigning because there was only one party. After 1917, it won the ardent allegiance of a generation of creative types who reconceived of the artist as a self-abnegating servant of the masses and the state—or who professed to, whatever their private misgivings. What is an artist, anyway? MOMA's show stalks the question.

The Revolution usurped or bypassed the energies of the Russian Empire's wartime avant-gardes, most prominently the metaphysically spirited Suprematism of Kazimir Malevich, who is allowed a perfunctory cameo in "Engineer, Agitator, Constructor," with one small abstract painting, from 1915. His day was over with the coup of Constructivism. He continued to support the Revolution, but his manner was adjudged too esoteric for proletarian tastes. Central to the new dispensation was the extravagantly gifted Alexander Rodchenko, who was really—almost helplessly—an artist, despite his militant posturing. In 1921, he painted three monochrome canvases—red, yellow, and blue—and announced that that was that for painting, which was henceforth obsolete. He also posed for a chic photograph as a platonic socialist worker, sporting a uniform of his own design and standing amid his own abstract sculptures. The celebrity gesture ran riskily afoul of Soviet impersonality and was not repeated. When, in 1932, he was accused of "bourgeois formalism," he retreated to sports photography, finding a safe harbor that was denied his movement colleague Gustav Klutsis, a master of photomontage whose worshipful imagery of Josef Stalin didn't forestall his execution, on unclear grounds, in 1938. Rodchenko's diminution illustrates the Soviet tragedy of formal and visionary genius that was ground underfoot even before the inception, in 1928, of Stalin's ruinous first Five Year Plan, and of the coerced visual banalities of Socialist Realism. Not that the MOMA show indulges in historical drama. Its focus is scholarly, separately documenting creators who, as one redemptive credit to Soviet social reform of the time, include a great many women. It builds knowledge. Meaning is up to us.

Art happens when someone wants to do it. Advertising and

propaganda start from given ends and work backward to means. There's just enough genuine art in the exhibition to hone this point. The small Malevich, of cockeyed red and black squares on white, elates. Then there's my favorite work, which I'd like to steal: a version of the sublimely sophisticated Liubov Popova's *Production Clothing for Actor No. 7* (1922). A black-caped, robotic figure extends a square red sleeve like a smuggled Suprematist banner. Personal flair and practical use merge. (What would Popova's fate have been if she hadn't died of scarlet fever in 1924, at the age of thirty-five? The Moscow art world adored her.) Among a few other serious gems included for passing reference, the curators Jodi Hauptman, Adrian Sudhalter, and Jane Cavalier hazard a Piet Mondrian from 1921, *Composition with Red, Blue, Black, Yellow, and Gray*. I wonder if the painting will give you, as it does me, a shock of recognition of true artistry: decisions made not for but with a purpose, as captivating in the context of happy workers working, a heroic soldier standing at the ready, and Stalin strolling among his subjects as is Wallace Stevens's jar in Tennessee.

Art unaffected by personality is sterile. That needn't constitute a failure. It may be a clear-eyed choice made on principle. Many things are more important than art. Today, imperatives of racial and social justice preoccupy numerous artists. Hard light is wanted in a crisis; away with moonbeams. What needs saying conditions how it's said, which means accepting the chance that, should conditions change, the work may prove to be ephemeral. No living artist I know of, however fervently activist, is renouncing art as a distraction from moral commitment, as the more extreme Constructivists did. But a good deal of recent polemical art suggests a use-by date that is not far in the future. Aesthetic judgment, based in experience, confirms differences between what is of its time and what, besides being of its time, may prove timeless. I feel that our present moment, marked by imbroglios of art and politics, forces the issue, even in the face of tendencies a century old.

As the exhibition unfolds, artists-penitent, shrinking from the perils of originality, dominate in Russia. Careerist designers teem in the West, with such fecund exceptions as László Moholy-Nagy and Kurt Schwitters. I know that I'm casting a wet blanket on work that might be—and surely will be—enjoyed without prejudice for its formal ingenuity and rhetorical punch. The architectonic and typographical razzmatazz of the Austrian-born American Herbert Bayer, the Dutch Piet Zwart, the Polish Władysław Strzemiński, and the Italian Fortunato Depero afford upbeat pleasures, and a strikingly sensitive Dada collage by the German Hannah Höch feels almost overqualified for its company. Strictly as a phenomenon in design, Constructivism and its offshoots merit celebration. It's just that the historical outcomes of the period get my goat, as does the show's sidelining of first-rate artists. Don't look for anything by Vladimir Tatlin, Malevich's innovational peer in sculpture: not thematic enough, plainly. The show's freest and most prolific stylist is also, for me, the most annoying: El Lissitzky. A star mentee of Malevich's who immigrated to Berlin in 1921, Lissitzky popularized the Constructivist look as an international style that wasn't about anything: jazzy formal clichés that hugely influenced commercial culture. At MOMA, approaches to abstraction—logo-like ciphers by the Hungarian László Peri, and stark geometries by the Polish Henryk Berlewi—deliver bright promise, then evanesce.

The show has a posthumous heart. It is lodged in the remains of the great poet Vladimir Mayakovsky, who put an omnibus ego to work for emancipatory personal and social consciousness. Passionately embracing Bolshevism, he wrote successful plays, delivered stirring speeches, supervised important magazines, and became wildly popular. During the New Economic Policy, instituted by Lenin in 1921, he collaborated with Rodchenko, contributing snappy slogans to advertisements for light bulbs, cocoa, and cigarettes: highlights of the show. Even in love poems, his free-verse style—a sort of machine-tooled lyricism—stuns and arouses. (The American poet James Schuyler deemed the effect an "intimate yell.") Politically, Mayakovsky can seem a fabulously specialized instrument of worldly transformation. In 1926, he called his mouth "the working class's / megaphone." He wrote a three-thousand-line panegyric in praise of Lenin. But by 1930, increasingly subject to hard-line, and official, attacks for "petit bourgeois" subjectivity and other supposed apostasies, he was meekly policing his unauthorized feelings: "stepping / on the throat / of my own song." A tortuous love life may have helped drive him—on April 14, 1930, at the age of thirty-six—to shoot himself. But it's impossible not to think of him as martyred by his own high church: a trashed prototype of the Soviet new man. His funeral was one of the largest in the regime's history.

In the catalogue, the poets Katie Farris and Ilya Kaminsky offer their fine translation of a poem that was found with Mayakovsky's body. It shows what was lost to the world with his suicide. The poem, with its comic and grand interiority, helps me imagine the unexpressed states of mind and soul of so many artists who were inspired and then blighted by a common cause:

ALREADY TWO

It's already two a.m. You're likely asleep.
The Milky Way's a silver river through the
night.
I'm in no hurry; I'll not storm your dreams
with the lightning bolts of telegrams.
"It's not you," as they say. "It's we."
Love's boat has crashed on our lives.
But we've already closed out our tab,
so there's no need to list each
pain, pinprick, pang.
You watch: silence settles on the earth.
The night taxes the sky of its stars.
In such an hour one stands up and speaks
to the ages, to history, and all creation.

Published in the December 28, 2020, issue of *The New Yorker*.

THE REVELATIONS OF AN UNLIKELY PAIRING

Imagine bits of wood trapped in eddies of a stream, going round and round atop the waters that flow beneath them. The image comes to mind in response to a surprising show—surprisingly great, contrary to my skeptical expectation—at David Zwirner's New York gallery. The works on display are by two artists who can seem bizarrely mismatched: Josef Albers, the starchy German-American abstract painter, Yale School of Art professor, and color theorist, who died in 1976, at the age of eighty-eight, and Giorgio Morandi, the seraphic Italian still-life painter of bottles, vases, and other sorts of domestic objects, who died in 1964, at the age of seventy-three.

In 1950, Albers wedded himself to a format of three or four nested, hard-edged squares on square supports—*Homage to the Square,* he called them—centered a bit below the pictures' vertical midpoints. That was it, for him. His occasional departures from the formula in the following years availed little. The point was color, explored through often arcane contrasts between the central squares and the ones that border them. The combinations never feel familiar or predictable, and you would need acres of color charts to denominate Albers's palette.

Morandi spent half a century transfixed by items in his studio, often arranged on a single high tabletop that he had built so he could work standing up. Often woozily drawn and always tenderly brushed in muted colors, the tableaux look but don't feel repetitive. Each could be the first and only one, quietly struggling with the defining problem of pictorial representation—the reduction of three dimensions to two. A fixation on that challenge seemed to bar Morandi (the odd tentative landscape notwithstanding) from extending his scope in either subject or form. It's as if, every day, he had to finally get right something that can't be got at all: reality as it is, at one with our perception of it.

Albers, who spent thirteen years studying and teaching at the Bauhaus, is academic and even pedantic in spirit, easy to admire while hard to like. Morandi is deeply poetic. What does displaying their paintings together accomplish? In terms of formal art history, nothing in itself; they're so different. But then I think of those circling bits of wood. Both artists worked independently of the canons of modern art without being outsiders—they were in the stream but resistant to its direction. They weren't eccentric, even. Rather, their approach proposed artistic visions that deviated from the forward march of modernism: alternative movements of one. The artists' insistence can seem exasperated, as though they were waiting for the world to catch on to truths that were obvious to them. They were brothers in perseverance. To my amazement, viewing them together electrifies, as their works' extremes play off each other. Think of it as a pas de deux of a drill sergeant (Albers) and an enchanter (Morandi). There's a crackle in perception when you turn from works by one artist to those of the other.

The Zwirner show is one of the best installed that I've ever seen. Its four large rooms host rhythmic arrays and alternations that induce that crackle: the soft cosmos of Morandi is both relieved and refreshed by the architectonics of Albers, and vice versa. The artists share an intensity of artistic vocation. Neither looked over his shoulder at trends of the day. Most of the pieces in the show (twenty-three by each artist) are small. This was Morandi's habitual scale and Albers's most successful one. Albers shines when his superimposed squares deliver their color rhymes and clashes at a glance. His strongest proportion is little more than a foot square—head-size. Extended to larger canvases, the dynamic weakens. Having to shift your gaze from one part of a painting by him to another is tedious: no new information awaits you. The ambition implied by bigness—a fashion made almost obligatory by Abstract Expressionism back then—calls unwelcome attention to the arbitrary parameters of Albers's style. You've stopped looking at the work and fallen to only thinking about it. His strong suit was condensation.

Naming the colors that Albers used is a non-starter, even with an allowance for the physiological fact that all of our color perceptions are hopelessly subjective and indescribable—an evolutionarily primitive function of our brains. (Tell me what red is. Take your time. I'll wait.) By wizardly variations of tone and chroma, he explores the secret lives of hues that seem startled to find themselves conjoined. The result is, remarkably, never decorative; Albers may even be at his most compelling when he flirts with ugliness, throwing monkey wrenches into our instinctive quests for harmony. Colors may never be more themselves than when, in juxtaposition, they don't work. A philosophical commitment rules, governing decisions at a high, rather stern pitch of consciousness. This effect can intimidate when it is taken as an indication that someone, the artist, understands phenomena that you and I will always fumble to grasp. Albers exalts expertise. But be brave. You'll be better from having undergone the salutary ordeal.

The only possible impediment to appreciating Morandi is incredulity at the idea of small, grayish, unresolved images of mundane things as major art. But I believe that no one who is sentient can indefinitely discount Morandi. His efforts to negotiate pictorial depth yield one fresh epiphany after another. It feels not quite right to think of the works as pictures. Morandi cares less about *what* his painted objects are than about *where* they are: standing alone or overlapping at variable distances while, of course, occupying the same paint surface. He describes a metaphysical predicament between what's there in the world and what's here in us. This doesn't require precise drawing or balanced composition. He is not a realist. Sometimes the surface of the shelf appears porous, and gives no felt sense of support for the things atop it. At other times, he alters the level of the line that indicates the junction of the shelf and a wall, from one side to the other of what is rendered in front of it. What's a shelf? What's a wall? What's their interrelation? (Both are flat, as is painting.) Morandi drains our seeing of complacency. He occults the obvious. Normal physics of mass and gravity don't apply to adventures of the eye in space that is given material presence.

I'm leaving out the charm and, on occasion, the beauty of Morandi's repertory company of performing objects—a certain fluted white vase wins kudos whenever it is onstage—because they are incidental to a spatial conundrum that is kept in tension by beautiful over-all brushwork. I'm also setting aside the role of color in Morandi: the practically infinite variations of grays and browns, tinted or patched here and there with subtle coloration, often orangeish, that imparts emotional moods to the works, no less affecting for being ungraspable. Morandi painted a zone of reality that is within reach yet cannot be touched, infusing vision with a delicate frustration of tactility. The result is an ontological mystery, confounding sight with touch and both with wonderment at their mutuality.

The Zwirner show provides a capital jump start to sensibilities deadened by nearly a year of scant physical encounters with art. Commercially, the show plainly aims to boost the allure of artists who, while well known, remain at the fringes of major fame. A cynical thought of the marketing motive hardened my heart in advance of my visit. But "money talks" is a vulgarism disarmed when money says something intelligent and exciting. I had forgotten, after previously having taken for granted, the free services to cultivation, and to sociability, of good galleries. Nearly a year of being disheartened by the online garishness and promotional smarm of digitized images has set me up to rediscover the pungency of direct aesthetic experience. There can be no meaningful discourse about art divorced from that. Intellectual appreciation starves for want of it. The less you see, the dumber you get.

I feel passably smarter now, thanks to the Zwirner show, and returned to the flow of sensation and reflection that constitutes a life in art. Mixed feelings about Albers and renewed reverence for Morandi give my lately wandering mind work to do. Not incidentally, I'm reminded to rejoice at being a New Yorker, in (well, nearby—upstate, pending vaccination) the world's premier city of art galleries.

Published in the February 1, 2021, issue of *The New Yorker*, with the headline "Movements of One."

WHEN A MUSEUM FEELS LIKE HOME

"Welcome to my house," I've said more than once while introducing people to the Frick Collection, my favorite museum. I've had to acknowledge an awkward domestic layout, extending to nine stops on the No. 6 train from the East Village. But I've meant it in a way that I share with a lot of art lovers, or even just art likers. The Frick stirs proprietary feelings as, say, the Metropolitan Museum of Art doesn't. Big museums array works by a historical logic that is cold to the eye until thawed by your attention. Everything at the Frick is toasty at first glance. That's an effect of the place's having been a home, the mansion of the coke mogul Henry Clay Frick, and of the somewhat fictive sense of the collection's memorializing one person's passions: pre-loved, call it. Some works and even whole rooms have been added since Frick died, in 1919. The house opened as a museum in 1935. Now we nervously await the collection's temporary move to the Breuer building, on Madison Avenue—formerly the Whitney Museum and currently leased by the Met—during an expansion and renovation of the main digs: the museum has promised to return the mansion and its contents to their long-cherished states. We'll see.

At the Frick, you feel more than welcomed—you feel invited, like a family friend. You needn't be comfortable with the relationship. Frick was a ruthless capitalist, with mines in Pennsylvania and leading roles in the steel industry and railroads. During the Homestead strike, in 1892, he dispatched armed Pinkerton mercenaries. Several workers and a few Pinkertons were killed (accounts of the number of casualties differ). That year, a would-be assassin, the anarchist Emma Goldman's boyfriend, Alexander Berkman, attacked Frick in his Pittsburgh office, shooting him twice and stabbing him repeatedly. Frick, forty-two years old at the time, soon recovered. (Berkman was imprisoned for fourteen years.) An insatiable collector, Frick was one of several Gilded Age magnates who vacuumed great art from Europe when it was financially pinched. A depression in British agricultural income in the last decades of the nineteenth century made country estates target-rich environments for swashbuckling dealers like the Briton Joseph Duveen, who, at one point or another, had his hands on much that ended up in Frick's house. Almost all the amassments were bequeathed by Frick to the public.

Admission was still free when, as a tyro critic ignorant of the Old Masters, I discovered and was transformed by the collection in the late nineteen-sixties. Over the years, I fell in love with specific works one by one—each identified on the walls by little more than the artist's name, so that I learned from my response to the art before knowing much about it. Likewise self-educated are many of the sixty-two culturati—from fields including literature, music, dance, and film—who contribute short personal essays on favorite works in the collection to a slim illustrated anthology, *The Sleeve Should Be Illegal: & Other Reflections on Art at the Frick*. (The title quotes the novelist Jonathan Lethem's stunned wonderment at an expanse of black-shadowed red velvet in a 1527 portrait of Sir Thomas More by Hans Holbein.) It is published by the museum and DelMonico Books with a foreword by Adam Gopnik, one of several authors in the anthology who regularly appear in this magazine. Some of the most appealing contributions are from thunderstruck amateurs. This is a charm of the book. Though now a grizzled professional, I still identify with them in spirit.

My Frick isn't yours, though yours interests me. The place is a Rorschach for personal meanings, unguided by curatorial programs. (I've pitied ambitious curators there, contending with a collection that is both heterogeneous and, as installed, perfect. What needs doing, beyond keeping the lights on?) There's no overriding historical or institutional narrative to come away with. Most museums have works in storage that can reasonably alternate with those on view, at opportune moments. The

Frick boasts no such depth. It is top-heavy with a medley of the simply superb—fantastic icing on not much cake. Its context is itself, occasioning a rat-a-tat of sensations that accumulate but don't add up. They are episodic, guaranteeing a Babel of individual moods and tastes among viewers on any given day. A visit there is a biographical event: who are you this time? Your alertness to some things and indifference to others will tell you. I'm reminded by nearly every page in the book of my own past and ongoing engagement with the collection, not always agreeing with the contributors but stirred by them to recall bits of the discontinuous stories of how the Frick has affected me.

Keeping in mind that an unprejudiced eye should apply as much to one's hundredth encounter with a compelling art work as it does to one's first, I'll try not to be possessive. I can't endorse, but I enjoy, the writer Jerome Charyn's association of Rembrandt's *The Polish Rider* (circa 1655)—a mounted, heavily armed young man, probably at the dawn of a day of battle—with memories of his own boyhood wildness in the South Bronx. He deems the rider "defiant in his orange pants" and "beyond any sense of authority or ownership." I see the picture differently, perceiving the pathos of a youth who is about to change from somebody's son or brother or sweetheart into an annealed killer. His eyes are already hard. His mouth, still boyishly soft, will have a harsher set by the day's end.

Another matter is the best painting in the museum, if not the world: Rembrandt's fathomlessly self-aware *Self-Portrait* of 1658, made when he was fifty-two and sorely beset by personal and professional woes. He knows that he's the leading painter in Amsterdam, but he seems to wonder if that's worth anything. It does nothing for his tiredness. A shadow falls across his eyes. I'm loath to argue with the five contributors who single the work out. It becomes part of each viewer's life: a talisman. I have my ideas on how the artist achieved it. One feature is the odd placement of the throne-like chair in which he sits. The chair's arms end snugged up against the picture plane, leaving no forward space for his knees to occupy; only shapeless paint smears mark that zone. We as much as view the artist from his lap—an intimation of physical intimacy that intensifies the work's psychological amplitude. The late Diana Rigg recalls thinking, when she first saw the picture, "That is how I want to act!" Roz Chast recounts an existential encounter. She writes, "I felt as if he were saying to me: Once I was alive, like you. Sometimes I suffered. Sometimes things seemed funny, or maybe absurd, especially myself. I was a man. I was an artist. I was a great artist. My name was Rembrandt Harmensz. van Rijn. I painted this painting. I lived. I died. Yet here I am. There you are. We are looking at each other."

My other chief touchstone in the collection is Diego Velázquez's *King Philip IV of Spain* (1644), which initiated me into the higher sorceries of the Baroque. The painter George Condo puts the marvellousness well: "There's a majestic presence here; yet it's all just paint"—true of any painting, perhaps, but minus the majesty. Space becomes porous behind, around, and in front of the subject: a revolving-door effect, spinning pictorial depth out into the real world. Passages of visible brushwork snap into verisimilitude at a calculated distance: about thirteen feet, as measured by me with baby steps. What seem, up close, to be slight variants of the same grayed white become, from the proper remove, satin, silver, linen, and lace. Is Philip an inbred Habsburg geek? Never mind. A contrast between his tight grip, with one hand, on a silver mace of military command and his dandling of a hat with the other hand poses your choice of treatment from him. The portrait is a treatise on royalty.

Unlike Velázquez, Rembrandt plumbed the mysteries of individual humanity, observant but dismissive of social status. I've had moments of feeling that painting has been all downhill since that contemporaneity of a Spanish Catholic courtier and a Dutch Protestant entrepreneur. But elsewhere in the galleries wonders ensue—or predate, as with Duccio di Buoninsegna's pre-Renaissance, gold-backed *Temptation of Christ on the Mountain* (1308–11), in which Jesus fends off the blandishments of a monstrous, winged Satan on a rocky prominence above miniaturized kingdoms. Humbly barefoot and calm, the Saviour rejects with a gesture the Evil One's offer of world-ruling power. The choreographer Mark Morris both astutely analyzes the picture and has fun with it: "After those forty terrifying days alone, who wouldn't be tempted to do something desperate and stupid by such a randy and charcoal-black Satan? It happens all the time."

My first Frick crush, some fifty-plus years ago, was Ingres's *Comtesse d'Haussonville* (1845), the lady in blue satin who raises a finger to a pulse point on her throat as if her beauty were a self-charging battery. Since then, I've recognized the work's shameless solecisms, mainly an arm that, when you focus on it, appears to emerge from two or three ribs down the subject's right side, and the longueur of outsize blue eyes that, far from being windows of the soul, suggest top-of-the-line Tiffany accoutrements. There's a chair at the lower left that only a stick figure could fit into. With Ingres, style conquered all, starting with common sense. The Dominican-born artist Firelei Báez nails the signature qualities: "glossy, soft, and cold." The theatre artist Robert Wilson contributes a handwritten Gertrude Steinian rhapsody: "WHAT IT IS IS ALWAYS IS CLASSICAL." Concerning prosperous women, the great cartoonist Chris Ware, having noted that there "are few uncooler-sounding words than 'eighteenth-century marble portraiture,'" pleases me by selecting Jean-Antoine Houdon's complexly personable *Madame His* (1775). From her features and expression, you can tell the very tenor of her thoughts. Houdon is one of those artists whose work you may walk past for years until a day that feels fated when you stop.

Masterpieces command a drawing room that is very much as Frick left it. There are two portraits by Titian, two by Holbein, and a religious vision, Giovanni Bellini's *St. Francis in the Desert*. (There's also a potent El Greco.) Holbein's *Sir Thomas More* is a miracle of elegance and empathy, coming to a point in the sitter's prodigiously intelligent gaze. Holbein must have loved him. With apologies to Hilary Mantel, the novelistic defender of the subject of the room's second Holbein portrait, *Thomas Cromwell* (1532–33), he looks like a thug to me, sullen in profile. But the singer-songwriter and author Rosanne Cash casts a vote for the picture's richness of color and cuts Cromwell some compassionate slack for his future consignment by Henry VIII to a headsman's axe—"on the mountaintop of power until Henry destroys him," she writes. In a theatrical coup of installation, Cromwell and More, enemies who were doomed to the same end, face each other from either side of a grand fireplace, bracketing a colorful, deadly history.

About Titian, what can be said after you say that he is the finest pure painter ever? Susanna Kaysen, the author of *Girl, Interrupted*, surmises that the subject of *Portrait of a Man in a Red Cap* (circa 1510) "looks to the left, into the past." Reading that, I see it. The other Titian portrait is of the artist's best friend and tireless promoter, Pietro Aretino—poet, connoisseur, power broker, feared satirist, author of popular devotional literature and pornography, intimate of rulers including the Holy Roman Emperor Charles V, and altogether one of the most interesting men of the sixteenth century. (I'm acquainted with Aretino from a bounteous 2012 biography, *Titian: His Life*, by Sheila Hale.) Turning to the Bellini (circa 1476–1478), we behold St. Francis standing outside his cave in a rustic landscape with meadowed sheep nearby and mountains and noble buildings in the distance. He looks skyward and holds out his open hands in a conventional posture of receiving the stigmata. But there's no other hint of anything supernatural. The married artists John Currin and Rachel Feinstein report years of concentrating, by turns, on the radiant scene's intricate topographical and botanical details. My favorite element, which mirrors my mystification at the matter-of-factness of the image, is an adorably witless donkey.

I don't regard the Frick's three Vermeers as first-rate—for the premium grade, visit the Met—maybe because I'm not beguiled by their possible narrative content. Parts of the pictures aren't fully integrated and resolved, bespeaking a haste that compromises the artist's usual—and, for him, indispensable—perfectionism. I am persuaded by the critic and author Vivian Gornick's speculative interpretation of *Mistress and Maid* (1666–67), in which a seated lady evinces alarm at the approach of her servant holding a letter. Gornick decides that both women suspect that it announces the discovery of an affair the lady is having. I only wish the whole picture were up to the éclat of the lady's spellbinding yellow dressing gown. Maddeningly, the Frick once passed up a chance to own Vermeer's supreme *The Art of Painting*, which is now owned by Vienna's Kunsthistorisches Museum. What a baffling artist! He was at his most transcendent with his most quotidian subjects. Vermeer could split the difference between fact and fiction with a tronie—the imagined portrait of a type of person—like the *Girl with a Pearl Earring*, at the Mauritshuis, in the Hague. But when he fell to storytelling, the results tend to weirdness. In the Frick's *Officer and Laughing Girl* (circa 1657), a young woman grins with some ratio of ingratiation and fear at a cavalier-ish man, who is seen from the back. The ambiguous drama makes the pictured room, with its open window and map on the wall, feel like an arbitrary stage set.

In another space, we confront Agnolo Bronzino's peak-Mannerist portrait *Lodovico Capponi* (circa 1550–55), of a handsome, arrogant, somehow discontented youth, clad in a gorgeous outfit that features a startlingly projecting codpiece. (That fashion wasn't Bronzino's invention, though he surely didn't mind it. He was notorious for erotic wordplay in his poetry.) The German-born architect Annabelle Selldorf shares her years-long fascination with the painting's "simultaneous quality of utter impenetrability paired with a provocative invitation to enter, to speculate, and to lose oneself in the ambiguity of the portrait." I've been ambivalent about the work, at times deeming it intolerably arch, but Selldorf persuades me to give it another chance, as does the American man of letters Daniel Mendelsohn, who eruditely speculates about the sitter's downcast air. Madly romantic, Capponi famously pined for a reciprocally smitten girl whose stepfather forbade her to see him. I'm not used to detecting emotion in works by the icily stylizing Bronzino. But now I look again, and there it is. Score points for the book, opening my eyes and mind.

Less surprising to me, but gratifying, are accounts by the British artist and writer Edmund de Waal and the American choreographer and dance impresario Bill T. Jones, both of whom zero in on the seemingly humble, but sneakily powerful, small painting *Still Life with Plums* (circa 1730), by Jean-Siméon Chardin. I have urged friends to contemplate it for several minutes. It's less about how a jug, a glass of water, and some fruit appear—the description is perfunctory and the palette drab—than how they are what they are: instances of matter as densely actual as matter can be. The longer you gaze, the more sensitized you'll be to quiddities of painting in relation to the real—and in relation to yourself as a viewer. Jones calls the painting "a peculiar mirror through which to 'watch oneself watching.'" Ordinary things in the world interested Chardin. That doesn't sound rare, but, oh, it is. No other still-life painter until the twentieth century's Giorgio Morandi is so profound.

James McNeill Whistler's full-length *Harmony in Pink and Grey: Portrait of Lady Meux* (1881–82) and *Arrangement in Black and Gold: Comte Robert de Montesquiou-Fezensac* (1891–92) usually hang, with two others, in the Frick's beautiful wood-panelled Oval Room, constituting a decorative scheme that is platonically perfect. I'm always annoyed when some temporary show displaces them. Adam Gopnik writes of the "X-ray of emotion" in Whistler's portraiture. "Anxiety, doubt, self-reflection, sexual ambiguity: we feel it all," Gopnik says of the rendering of the Count. The artist Ida Applebroog admires Lady Meux, a banjo-playing barmaid who married a brewing heir and repeatedly scandalized London high society. Both paintings are about glamour as an ethic and almost a morality, defiantly accepting the attendant psychological strains. Whistler communes with his subjects' audacities of dress as well as attitude—the Count in svelte black and Lady Meux in a dress that looks corseted from the outside. Taste, as taste, had never risen to equivalent eloquence.

My own taste skates past the Frick's abundance of genteel English portraiture—an Anglophilic craze on the part of Gilded Age American collectors who, lacking distinguished ancestry, as much as bought some. Regarding portraits by Gainsborough that line the Frick's dining room, I'm not insensible to the "delicacy, poise, restraint, and a certain kind of cool" that puts the English musician Bryan Ferry in mind of "a Miles Davis trumpet solo." It's just that I find the manner smugly self-congratulatory. But Alexandra Horowitz, a scientist who heads the Horowitz Dog Cognition Lab, arouses my interest in a Gainsborough park scene by identifying three pooches that frisk amid perambulating ladies: a setter mix, a terrier, and a Pomeranian—"the eighteenth-century version, with longer legs and nose, less of a stuffed toy than a vulpine variant of 'dog.'"

We look at paintings, which are specific objects in specific places, as individuals, alone. We may then turn, with excitement or anxiety, to others in the hope of having our responses confirmed. Those conversations are the test of any art's cultural vitality—commonplace regarding books and movies but rarer, and a mite self-consciously special, in cases of visual art, where undertones of rarity and brute expensiveness intrude. *The Sleeve Should Be Illegal* models for us the starts of such invigorating talk. What's nice about the book is the variety of personality, extending to eccentricity, of the voices heard and awaiting rejoinders. A contributor occasionally veers into sentimentality, which is easily understandable. The museum's sacredness to many, including me, can cloy a little. The book could do with more jokes like Mark Morris's. What is at issue, after all, is only art, a holiday of the spirit on the crowded calendar of life lived. Nor is all the art worthy of reverence. Mixed and even negative opinions can serve as control rods for the fission of overly pious engrossment.

I am not a fan of Joseph Mallord William Turner, though I savor Simon Schama's nostalgic affection for the British showoff's relatively muted *Mortlake Terrace: Early Summer Morning* (1826), which, as the critic points out, deploys a watercolor-like use of oils to convey sights along a bank of the Thames. He writes, "The limpid light washing the scene is the light of my memories, the happy ones anyway." I'm distracted by the calculatedness of the work's technique, which counts on an emotional appeal that doesn't strike me as earned. For his big sea and harbor scenes—there are two harbors at the Frick—Turner applied splooshes of paint that we are expected to interpret as an accurate capturing of light and atmosphere. (Contrary to some opinion, these paintings don't anticipate Impressionism, which coheres in the eye; Turner's visual fictions require complicities of the imagination.) Then he drew in paint on top of them, with an occasional effect like that of bathroom-tile decals. I much prefer John Constable. If I were to choose only one painting at the Frick to write about, it might well be *The White Horse* (1819), which gets everything right about a rural setting—meadow, stream, sky, clouds, woods, path, farm buildings—at a time of day that is signalled by the homeward transfer, by raft, of a workhorse. Constable conducts me into a specific part of his world and tactfully leaves me alone there. I like that.

I suppose that I know the paintings at the Frick better than any others (including some that are superior) by the respective artists. The collection anchors my art love as pocket editions of the Constitution can seem to serve certain politicians—except I'm honest. By the way, would I be a collector if I could afford it? You bet. The very few purchases that my wife and I have made instruct me that writing a check is intrinsically more sincere than writing a review, because the expense hurts. I would pass on a big Goya, *The Forge* (1815–20), in which a blacksmith is about to strike an anvil. It excites the American painter, sculptor, author, and photographer Tom Bianchi as "an intensely modern painting, based as it is on a specific, near-photographic moment." The picture seems to me more akin to the artist's anecdotal etchings—unnecessarily large for its content of a discrete muscular action—than to Goya's more complexly inspired oils.

But Goya! The Israeli-born American artist, author, and designer Maira Kalman attributes the haunting—or is it haunted?—mood of his *Portrait of a Lady (María Martínez de Puga?)* (1824) to its slightly elfin subject's "neutral gaze," scalloped hair, and black dress against a taupe background. "Pensive? Uncomfortable? Indifferent?" Kalman can't decide. Nor can I. This example of Goya's unsettling gifts is a minor painting. But sometimes you may be in the mood for inconspicuous works. Thus the photographic artist Duane Michals comes to rest on an uncharacteristic painting by Jean-Antoine Watteau, *The Portal of Valenciennes* (circa 1710–11), of soldiers lounging outside a city or fortress wall. The master of ceremonious Eros is, for once, hanging out with random guys. This testifies to the eighteenth-century France that Watteau actually lived in while he conjured visions of aristocratic dalliance. A bonus of such oddities is that you can usually have them to yourself on days when the museum is crowded with fellow-viewers.

Crowds can't vitiate the almost violent charm of the Frick's Fragonard Room, which incorporates a suite of paintings, *The Progress of Love*, that was commissioned in 1771 by Madame du Barry for a new pavilion outside Paris (she later decided against the paintings, deeming them out of fashion). After the Revolution, the suite, with additions, ended up in the home of a cousin of the artist, in Grasse. The British dealers Agnew's acquired it for J. P. Morgan. Following Morgan's death, in 1913, Joseph Duveen sold it to Frick on behalf of the banker's estate. Duveen arranged for the room's installation, enhanced with gems of furniture, ceramics, and small sculpture. (However you may judge the sly dealer, he merits lasting honor for this tour de force.) In Frick's day, women would gather in the room after dinner while the men consumed cigars in a basement space that is still equipped with a billiard table and bowling alleys.

As a mot juste for *The Progress of Love*, I nominate "silly." Great art essentializes qualities of human experience, of which silliness is a capital instance. The big paintings theatricalize stages of adolescent amour—resisted seduction, furtive intimacy, triumphant union, and subsequent nostalgia—among young people at court who were given nothing to do in life except to dress up and to play at love. At a heroic scale under sumptuously soaring trees, the tableaux both amuse and overwhelm. "It's like being blown away by a French love bomb," the musician Donald Fagen, a co-founder of the band Steely Dan, writes, adding a confessional rue for the common course of romance in real life: "the feverish rush of desire, the euphoric first months when lovers are compelled to idealize each other, followed by the inevitable crash when the levels of serotonin, oxytocin, and dopamine in the brain start to plunge."

Fragonard didn't neglect love's downside. A final addition to the suite—looking unfinished but really made in a late, simplified style—finds a young woman droopingly alone, with one limp hand resting suggestively in her lap. A stone Cupid above her on a pillar regards her indignantly and points a finger horizontally, as if saying, "Girl, stop moping and get out there." Fragonard's rococo gaga-ness is deceptive. He had a subtle, at times almost subliminal narrative imagination. His tones vary from shouts to whispers. No other major period style ended as abruptly as this one, extinguished by the Revolution.

The Progress of Love brings to an extravagant climax the luxuriousness that is implicit, at the Frick, in the ownership of so much extraordinary art. Its showiness departs from the collection's generally sober temperament. Frick had conservative compunctions. He acquired no nudes, for example. He seems to have dreamed less of glory than of dignity, laundering the machinations of his avarice. There was nothing racy beyond the dandyism of Whistler. Frick collected more works of Whistler's than of any other artist, likely because the painter squared his originality with soothingly patrician airs. Frick was reluctant to endorse his era's cascade of Parisian avant-gardes. (An occasionally displayed Monet or Renoir feels positively reckless in context.) He epitomized sensibilities of the time that said "Not so fast!" to modernity in a way that can only be modern in itself, called forth by the pressure of worldly change: reactionary, certainly, with a touch of hysteria in championing prestigious, almost exclusively dead white men. The collection's bias makes it, as a whole, an illustrative historical artifact that happens to be breathtaking in many of its parts. The works may be old, but our experience of them is strictly up to date. More than one contributor to *The Sleeve Should Be Illegal* invokes a sensation of walking on air after a visit to the Frick, a payoff of renewed faith in the powers of art and a forgivable pride in our own perhaps untrained and underused capacities to comprehend the aesthetic and spiritual stakes of a timeless game.

Published in the February 15 & 22, 2021, issue of *The New Yorker*, with the headline "Home Goods."

SORROWS OF BLACK AMERICA

"Grief and Grievance: Art and Mourning in America," which recently opened at the New Museum, is a terrific art show. I might have expected that, given a starry roster that includes Kerry James Marshall, Glenn Ligon, Lorna Simpson, Carrie Mae Weems, and Theaster Gates among its total of thirty-seven contemporary Black artists. But theme exhibitions normally repel me, shoehorning independent talents into curatorial agendas. What a difference in this case! "Grief and Grievance" is a brainchild of the Nigerian curator Okwui Enwezor, who, notably with his curation of the German mega-show Documenta, in 2002, and the Venice Biennale, in 2015, pried the international art world open for new art from Africa and Asia. He died of cancer in March, 2019, at the age of fifty-five, while planning the present show. The New Museum's artistic director, Massimiliano Gioni, aided by Ligon and the curators Naomi Beckwith and Mark Nash, completed the task, faithful to Enwezor's conception, emphasizing interiority and the patterns of feeling that attend Black experience in America. There's grief, which is constant; grievance, which appeals, however futilely, to some or another authority able and willing to right wrongs; and mourning, the fate and recourse of the irreparably wounded. From this description, you might expect a litany of remonstrance. On the contrary, the show celebrates what artists are good at: telling personal truths through aesthetic form. The predominant result is poetic—deeply so—rather than argumentative.

It's worth noting immediately that there's little explicit address to white racism, white guilt, or, really, white anything, except by way of inescapable implication. Ta-Nehisi Coates, in a devastating essay in the show's catalogue, fills in the lacuna with his well-known, scorching pessimism about white mind-sets. What Coates would like from whites, though he does not expect it, is "a resistance intolerant of self-exoneration." The show was originally intended to open in October, amid the furors leading up to the Presidential election. The pandemic scotched that. But "Grief and Grievance" doesn't have a use-by date. It channels emotional tenors, from personal points of view, that are true to the history, and the future, of race in this country.

Begin with two of the exhibition's few jokes, *Presumption of Guilt* (2020) and *7.5'* (2015), by Cameron Rowland. For the first, the front door of the museum has been rigged to set off a *ding* when opened, like that of a convenience store. The second flanks one side of the door with a vertical strip of height measurements—meant to aid in the identification of departing thieves by surveillance cameras. The ruler tops out at seven feet six inches, suggesting an absolutely colossal brigand. Rowland counts on stereotypical associations of Black men with convenience-store robbery, and of large Black men with menace. You admit to recognizing that if you laugh, as I did. Standup comedians push such buttons all the time, but the trope is beyond rare in serious museums. Now proceed to a darkened room nearby and behold *Love Is the Message, the Message Is Death* (2016), Arthur Jafa's much praised video montage with a rhythmic soundtrack of music and voices. It's a masterpiece. Rapid clips from Black history and daily life, ranging from violent scenes of the civil-rights movement to children dancing, possess specific, incantatory powers. Their quantity overloads comprehension—so many summoned memories and reconnected associations, cascading. The experience is like a psychoanalytic unpacking, at warp speed, of a national unconscious regarding race. Irresistibly exciting and profoundly moving, the work will make you gasp, I guarantee, and will induce a heightened state of mind and heart to accompany you throughout the exhibition.

I think of Julie Mehretu and Mark Bradford as neo-Abstract Expressionists, what with her storms of kinetic squiggles in clouded atmospheres and his layered impastos of glowering color, both at majestically large scale. In the case of Mehretu's *See Gold, Cry Black* (2019), the title befits a canvas on which orangeish strokes seem to struggle for traction amid enveloping welters of black. In Bradford's *Untitled* (2020), a brushy zone of red punches in among raddled expanses of less bold hues. This resurgence of American art's modern breakthrough, after six decades in abeyance, was already apparent in the at once witty and volcanic neo-Expressionism of Jean-Michel Basquiat, whose achievement looms ever larger in art of the late twentieth century. He is represented here by *Procession*, a painting from 1986, two years before his death, at twenty-seven. That was a period, for him, of illness and faltering confidence, but his originality still blazed. On a ground of boards painted yellow, four loosey-goosey black figures reel and stumble toward a tall man of undetermined race, dressed in red and blue, who brandishes a skull aloft with a gesture of withholding. The work might be a doom-laden allegory of addiction: junkies drawn to a dealer of, ultimately, death. But you rarely know with Basquiat. His teasing mastery of painterly form—he could seem incapable of making a dull mark—speaks, and sings, for itself.

The Chicagoan Kerry James Marshall has become justly famous as a painter who deploys Blackness as a theme and black as a plangent color—hard to do if you're not a Zurbarán, say, or a Goya. A Black cop seated on the hood of a police car radiates watchfulness. Interiors of middle-class homes feature banal furniture and images of civil-rights-era heroes that either hang on walls, like a portrait of Martin Luther King, Jr., bracketed by John F. Kennedy and his brother Robert, or hover as ghosts. Standing Black matrons include a woman who is equipped with angel wings. Another picture incorporates a list of departed Black luminaries spelled out in glitter. Who told Marshall that you can get away with using glitter in an elegiac painting? It's one of many audacities that ignite his style. One interior is overlaid with vertical gray stripes and more glitter. Everything works. Marshall brings genres of domestic and history painting spankingly up to date, achieving an aesthetic and sociological sublime. His art both stirs and mocks nostalgia, subjecting sincerity to irony in ways that intensify both.

There's a piquant backstory to Ligon's *A Small Band* (2015), which consists of the words "blues blood bruise" displayed in white neon letters high on the front of the museum. In 1964, New York police officers beat two Black teen-agers and then refused them medical attention because they weren't bleeding. One of the boys, Daniel Hamm, squeezed a bruise that he had incurred, forcing blood out. He explained later, with a slip of the tongue, that he'd "let some of the blues blood come out." Thus Ligon's beautiful short poem. "Blues" as a stand-in for "bruise" links Hamm's ordeal to a classically African-American way of processing sorrow. Your mind spirals down from an anecdote of police brutality to a sense of the inner life, the subjectivity, and the acculturated sensibility of a victim who is not reducible to victimhood. Ligon's work previews a psychosocial dynamic that abounds in "Grief and Grievance," which takes consequences of oppression and misfortune—grinding poverty, in the case of photographs by LaToya Ruby Frazier—as occasions for tours de force.

The closest the show comes to protest art is Dawoud Bey's *The Birmingham Project* (2012), large black-and-white photographic diptychs recalling the bomb deaths, in 1963, of four Black girls at a church in the Southern city. Each pair portrays a child, male or female, at the age that one of the girls was on the day she was killed—three were fourteen, one was eleven—and an adult at the age that, had the girl survived, she would have been at the time of Bey's work. My first reaction was bemusement at the pictures' excellence as portraiture, sensitively framed and lighted and vibrant with the personalities of the sitters. How could such elegance serve as a memorial of murder? But gradually my reluctant aesthetic pleasure melted into the work's content, registering the distance between present high artistry and the thought, clawing at my mind, of once and forever destroyed young lives. As tranquil as the images are, the burning pain of the reference persists. I've tried to shake the spell that they cast but haven't yet.

Coming after a year of death and mourning as universal spectres, the show's lessons in strategies and tactics of emotional resilience, necessities for Black lives, resonate broadly. The art touches on shared human needs and capacities. It's a start.

Published in the March 1, 2021, issue of *The New Yorker*, with the headline "Mastering Sorrow."

THE X-ED OUT WORLD OF KAWS

In 1992, a Jersey City graffiti artist named Brian Donnelly adopted KAWS as his nom de spray can, only because, he has said, he liked how the four letters looked together. Nigh on thirty years later, as a phenomenally successful painter and sculptor with lines of toys and other merchandise, he remains pragmatic. "KAWS: WHAT PARTY," at the Brooklyn Museum, is the latest in a globe-trotting series of institutional exhibitions of neon-bright acrylics, antic statuary, and gift-shop-ready tchotchkes that are either based on familiar cartoons and puppets—the Michelin Man, *Peanuts, The Smurfs, Sesame Street*, and, especially, *The Simpsons*—or run changes on such characters of his own devising as Companion, a lonesome sad sack sporting Mickey Mouse-style shorts and gloves.

The figures are jokey-saturnine. They have "X"s for eyes. Many of their heads suggest skulls, with the ends of bulbous crossbones protruding behind them and three quick vertical lines at chin level, a trick that hints at missing lower jaws or sags of decaying flesh. The sizes range from a few inches to more than thirty feet high. All are well made, in materials that include vinyl, fibreglass, wood, and bronze. Donnelly's craft ethic was striking from the start, as seen in photographs of train cars and billboards that he once sumptuously vandalized—returning in the morning to gauge the success of a nocturnal raid before the evidence was defaced or scrubbed away—and original phone-booth and bus-shelter posters that, having learned how to pick locks, he took home, altered, and put back in place. (Many of his augmented posters were stolen and eventually made their way to the art market.) He realized complex, rhythmic, even elegant wonders with variations on his tag. Were there a Royal Academy of Bubble Letters, KAWS would be knighted.

Those ephemeral misdemeanors may well be my favorite things in the show, crackling with precocious virtuosity and renegade drive. Carefully overpainted, they look seamlessly professional, until you register their additions of sinuous shapes and skull heads. Donnelly's work since he went legit lacks any equivalent emotional charge—it is flat in feeling. I marvel that so many people like it. (Why am I reviewing the show? Because it's there, and it invites a diagnosis of certain conditions in the art world—notably, a cheeky, infectious dumbing-down of taste.) At a Sotheby's auction in Hong Kong—KAWS has an immense following in East Asia—in 2019, an anonymous buyer liked Donnelly enough to pay more than fourteen million dollars for *The KAWS Album* (2005), a busy painting of *Simpsons* characters massed in imitation of the teeming album cover for the Beatles' 1967 *Sgt. Pepper's Lonely Hearts Club Band*, designed by Jann Haworth and Peter Blake. Plainly, some gradient of nostalgia factors in the KAWS craze, with its triggering of past enchantments. To avoid sappiness, Donnelly tends to complicate his allusions with willful grotesquerie. In one painting, decapitated members of the Simpson family are seen holding one another's heads—to strictly goofball, anodyne effect. (You can bring the kids.) The impact of another figure that is partly flayed to expose its viscera—a steal from the British sensationalist Damien Hirst, who hasn't achieved much with it himself—is anything but visceral. Blandness reigns.

I do enjoy Donnelly's occasional forays into apparently abstract painting, which frees up his considerable gifts for zippy color and hyperactive composition; he knows his way around the pictorial rectangle. The show's adept curator, Eugenie Tsai, remarked to me that there are trace elements of cartoon imagery in those works, if I would look for them. I replied happily and, I'm afraid, impolitely, "But I don't have to." As a graffiti artist, Donnelly, the scion of a middle-class family, was no up-from-the-streets wild child. In the nineties, he attended New York's School of Visual Arts, worked as an animator, and began visiting Japan, where he encountered that country's *otaku* subcultures of manga and anime—updates of a national tradition that prizes all creative pursuits more or less equally. Donnelly, inspired by the boundary-defying aesthetics, added collectibles to his repertoire in the late nineties and, a few years afterward, opened a boutique for them in Tokyo. While gauche by genteel art-world standards, they sold like hotcakes. His burgeoning fan base came to include movie stars and such musicians and producers as Jay-Z and Pharrell Williams.

Donnelly isn't a Pop artist, exactly, except by way of distant ancestry. Most of his career moves were initiated about six decades ago by Andy Warhol, who had the not inconsiderable advantage of being great. Warhol's conflations of fine art with demotic culture were, and remain, pitch-perfect in all respects, including a candid avarice that kidded, even as it embraced, triumphant American commercialism. Do Donnelly's frisky morbidities emulate Warhol's preoccupation with death? Fatal car crashes, suicides, the electric chair, and Jackie Kennedy in mourning invested Warhol's gorgeous stylings with haunting gravitas. Donnelly's semi-defunct figures generate nothing similarly affecting. Nor is he in a league with Jeff Koons, despite the probability that but for Koons there would be no KAWS. Koons's weddings of banality and beauty, in his sculptures of determinedly kitsch subjects, are formally consummate and—once you recover from their insults to your intelligence—fantastically seductive. Koons anticipated a global hegemony of big money in contemporary art, symbolizing it in advance of its arrival. His works look as expensive as they are, and then some. But he delivered the goods.

Donnelly's statues and figurines swing at a similar mojo of high art crossed with nonchalant vulgarity. They miss. The shortfalls are so routine that futility may be a criterion of his art's anti-glamorous glamour. Like his paintings of the tops of *Simpsons* heads, the objects don't feel motivated as art. Their themes ring hollow. The supposed melancholy of the abundant Companions—often slumping in evident despair—seems as coolly calculated as the burlesques of death with the "X"-eyed figures in the cartoon paintings. Branding has long since siphoned away the passion of the train-yard prodigy. The only palpable carryover from his bygone street work is a ravenous hunger to make himself known. Mission accomplished! As a recent profile in the *Times Magazine* noted, he has more than three million Instagram followers.

The established New York art world was having none of KAWS for several years. Professionals quailed at his formulaic production of luxury goods with a populist veneer. But nothing succeeds like success—KAWS found a rapt audience via entertainment-intensive public works, including the *Holiday* series of enormous Companions. One floated on its back in Hong Kong's Victoria Harbor, others rode weather balloons into the stratosphere, or reclined near the base of Mt. Fuji. Call the mode Koons lite—harmless, really, if you leave out the sensitivities of viewers who pay searching attention. Every KAWS indexes every other KAWS. All partake in one predilection—not kitsch, which debases artistic conventions, but a promiscuity that sails beyond kitsch into a wild blue yonder of self-cannibalizing motifs that excite and, I believe, comfort a loyal constituency.

I fail to detect charm in most anybody's cartoons of cartoons. Anything you do at second hand with that lively art—unless you're Roy Lichtenstein, exercising Mondrian-grade formal rigor—merely churns and inevitably dissipates what it's about. How do you satirize satire, in the capital case of *The Simpsons*? And when is a Simpson not a Simpson? When it's a pastiche. But instant recognizability combined with rousing entrepreneurship, at prices for every above-average wallet, seems key to KAWSism—which is certainly democratic, in the sense of making no demands on anyone. It isn't a taste. It's an illustrated success story—naked ambition as its own reward, with just enough tacit irony to disarm some doubters. To Donnelly's credit, he has shaken up the art world, humbling gatekeepers who would love to keep him out but can't any longer.

Be it noted that there is nothing felonious about Donnelly's manipulations, which vivify a possibility—the erasure of hierarchical distinctions between art and, well, stuff—that someone was bound to grab hold of eventually. I find it depressing, but you would expect that from an élitist art critic, wouldn't you? A chance to snoot highbrows is a bonus for KAWSniks, whose glee might as well be taken in good grace by its targets. See the show, for its lessons in a present psychosociology. I predict that you'll be through it in a jiffy, and that little of it, if any, will stick in your mind a day or even an hour later. There's a certain purity in art that's so aggressively ineloquent. Like a diet of only celery, which is said to consume more calories in the chewing than it provides to digestion, KAWS activates hallucinatory syndromes of spiritual starvation.

Published in the March 15, 2021, issue of *The New Yorker*, with the headline "X-Ed Out."

THE PIONEERING FEMINISM OF NIKI DE SAINT PHALLE

"Niki de Saint Phalle: Structures for Life," at MOMA PS1, is a ravishing and scandalously overdue New York museum show of the French-American avant-gardist, who died at the age of seventy-one, in 2002, of emphysema probably caused by her use of toxic materials. The self-taught Saint Phalle is one of the late twentieth century's great creative personalities, ahead of her time in several respects, with traits that once clouded and now halo her importance. Her career had two chief phases: feminist rage, expressed by way of .22 rifles fired at plaster sculptures inside which she had secreted bags of liquid paint, and feminist celebration of womanhood, through sculptures of female bodies, often immense, in fibreglass and polyester resin. The shooting period lasted from 1961 until about 1963. The bodies consumed the rest of her life. Her masterpiece, the Tarot Garden (1979–2002), is a vast sculpture park in Tuscany filled with twenty-two free-form, monumental women, animals, and figures of fantasy, some the size of houses and made habitable with kitchens and plumbing. She was popular in Europe but, until late in life, cut little ice in transatlantic art circles. The problem tracks to a schism, around 1960, with triumphant American formalist abstraction, Pop art, and Minimalism on one side, and, on the other, European Nouveau Réalisme, a cohort (all male but for Saint Phalle) of provocateurs given to neo-Dadaist stunts: Yves Klein painting with pigment-slathered naked women, Arman amassing collections of identical common objects, Daniel Spoerri gluing down remnants of meals and hanging them vertically, Jacques Villeglé presenting ragged, found street posters.

Saint Phalle's gunplay, realized in Paris in 1961, was a stunt for sure: creation by destruction, theatrically perforating first plaster-covered boards and then figurative plaster sculptures of male subjects—avatars of her hated father, who sexually assaulted her when she was eleven. Some pieces concealed spray cans, for explosive effect when hit. That year, Marcel Duchamp, seventy-four years old, introduced the thirty-year-old Saint Phalle and her friend Jean Tinguely, the Swiss kinetic sculptor, to Salvador Dalí, fifty-seven. In honor of Dalí, they fashioned a full-size bull, which, wheeled out after a bullfight in Catalonia, satisfyingly blew up. Saint Phalle usually performed in fashionable white pants suits. The cultural frisson of a beautiful woman wielding deadly weapons and setting off explosives earned her notoriety in France, but there was scant critical curiosity, anywhere, about the motives of the work: a traumatic personal backstory and a politically edged aspiration to better the world.

Born near Paris in 1930, to a tyrannical French banker father and a suffocatingly pious Roman Catholic American mother, Saint Phalle had a childhood of privilege and of horror, first in France and then, after her father's finance company failed in the Depression, in America. Both parents were violent. Saint Phalle described the homelife as hellish. Two of her siblings committed suicide as adults. She was expelled from two Catholic schools and from the Brearley School, in New York, which booted her for defacing its classical statues by painting their fig leaves red. (Even so, she always praised Brearley for having instilled self-confidence in her as a young woman.) Starting in her late teens, she modelled for *Life*, French *Vogue*, *Elle*, and *Harper's Bazaar*. At one point, Gloria Steinem spotted Saint Phalle walking down Fifty-seventh Street, purseless and in a cowboy getup. In an interview quoted by the show's curator, Ruba Katrib, in the catalogue, Steinem recalled thinking, "That is the first free woman I have ever seen in real life. I want to be just like her."

At the age of eighteen, Saint Phalle married Harry Mathews, a nineteen-year-old American aspiring musician, who became an experimental novelist after the poet John Ashbery introduced him to the charismatically daft early-twentieth-century work of the Frenchman Raymond Roussel. Crosscurrents of creative influence flowed among many of the international bohemians of the period. The couple quickly had a daughter. Then Saint Phalle broke down. She and Mathews were now living in France and both were having affairs. In 1953, after a bout of sexual jealousy compounded by ill health (she suffered from hyperthyroidism), she attempted suicide. For six weeks, she underwent electroshock treatments and psychoanalysis at a clinic in Nice. It seemed to help. Saint Phalle and Mathews had a second child, and the family spent most of the remaining decade moving around Europe. In 1955, in Barcelona, she was flabbergasted by the buildings and the mosaics of Antoni Gaudí. (Gaudí became "my master and my destiny," she said.) Plunging into art, at first with naïve styles of painting and assemblage, she separated from Mathews in 1960. He took the kids, but she stayed close to him, as she tended to do, all her life, with miscellaneous friends and (a great many) ex-lovers.

Indeed, sociability was Saint Phalle's element, to the point of blurring her creative identity. At her first shooting performance, she let the invited guests take turns with the gun that she had rented from a fairgrounds for the occasion, delighting in their cathartic pleasure. As free with giving credit as with claiming it, in the Tarot Garden—which she created on an extensive plot of land donated to her by some wealthy friends—Saint Phalle incorporated homages to the Italian workers who had fashioned the steel armatures for her sculptures, covered them with resin, and helped line the exteriors and interiors with ceramic tiles and shards of mirror. (Videos in the show document the years of exacting labor.) She maintained a productive partnership with Tinguely for years, including throughout an intimate relationship that began in the early sixties and resulted, a decade later, in marriage, with the pair collaborating on works that combine her sensuous sculptures and his wittily racketing machinery.

Until 1963, Saint Phalle continued to create patriarchal icons in plaster and, with bullets, make them bleed paint. Some were relief portraits of leading politicians, whom she loathed as a class—one was of John F. Kennedy, before his assassination. Then, in 1965, after some fetching sculptural works, mostly in soft materials, on themes of melancholy brides and elaborate, not terribly menacing monsters, came the first of what she called Nanas, using the French slang that was the rough equivalent of "broads" or "chicks." The Nanas were inspired by a pregnant friend whose body was very curvy—almost hyperbolically female. (It was Clarice Rivers, wife of the painter Larry Rivers.) Saint Phalle fashioned the shape as a container, hollow but apparently formed of seismic internal forces. Nanas proliferated at sizes small and gigantic, turning dancerly and acrobatic. Saint Phalle mastered gloss techniques for preserving their painted surfaces—in black-and-white and, often, sizzling secondary and tertiary hues—outdoors, in all weather. Nothing about the work jibed with anything then current in art. Most critics, especially American ones, dismissed it. Today, as categorical distinctions among art mediums and styles deliquesce, it comes off as heroic.

There's a playhouse feeling and, in some cases, a function to Saint Phalle's big women and to such occasional monsters as *The Golem* (1972), which occupies a playground in Jerusalem. Three snaking red tongues protrude as slides for kids. (When citizens opposed the commission by the city's mayor, Teddy Kollek, Saint Phalle argued successfully that scary things help children master their fears. It was a big hit.) She brought an unchanging spirit to her public works, occasional architecture (a three-part home in the South of France which nestles children's rooms inside a Nana's breasts), and abundant drawings and handmade books. She never winks to educated taste. There's a frequent tendency to deem Saint Phalle's childlike imagery sentimental, but I don't think it is. No matter how playful, the benign quality of her later work drew on the same fund of contrariness—the proto-feminist animus—that fuelled her early weaponized exhibitionism. (She said that she enjoyed the thought of men looking "very small" next to looming Nanas.) At a time that was biased against figuration and only just becoming alert to feminism, she risked—or perhaps guaranteed—condescension. It didn't faze her at all.

If anything disconcerts about Saint Phalle, it's a steely consistency of tone. As a prolific pamphleteer during the AIDS crisis, in which she lost many friends, she saw no need to darken her bouncily cartoonish graphic style, though she embellished it with language that conscientiously addressed the disaster. Art was a place in her. Any work by her is like a destination that, once reached, lets you go elsewhere only by retracing the way you came. Other artists are like this, notably those who are termed outsider or self-taught: birds with their single songs. Saint Phalle's enthusiasm for Gaudí's sophisticated designs extended to the work of such visionary eccentrics as Ferdinand Cheval, a nineteenth-century French postman and the creator of a surreal imaginary palace; and Simon Rodia, of the Watts Towers, in Los Angeles. This predilection points to a compulsive hold on the life force that had propelled her from the start.

In her later years, Saint Phalle slipped into celebrity. She designed and marketed a perfume, jewelry, and scarves, to finance the protracted construction of the Tarot Garden. ("Why don't I become my own patron?" she asked.) Those commodities look great, by the way—they are continuous with her inventive drive, in an art world that was on its way to welcoming heterodox pursuits including retail commerce and overt politics. She pioneered, as well, an epochal rise of installational and environmental art, though with forms too idiosyncratic to be directly imitable. The PS1 show is a cascade of bedazzlements. Is it lovable? Not quite. Saint Phalle was too guarded—wound too tightly around herself—to vamp for adoration. Attention was enough. Understanding proved more elusive, but was foreordained, eventually, by a fearlessness that sweeps a viewer along from start to finish.

Published in the April 5, 2021, issue of *The New Yorker*, with the headline "Life Force."

THE RETURN OF THE ART FAIR

I quite enjoyed Frieze New York, the recent edition of the annual (except last year) international art fair, housed at the Shed—the arts complex in Hudson Yards, on Manhattan's far West Side—rather than, as in past years, inside a colossal tent on Randall's Island. This was unusual for me, because I hate art fairs: they strike me as upscale bazaars, almost immediately exhausting, that reek of quiet desperation. They are a global phenomenon of the last quarter century, born partly out of the competition that dealers face from auction houses, which have recognized—and juiced—the skyrocketing prices of works that may be more or less fresh from studios. Brick-and-mortar galleries can no longer count on preëminence as the farm system of the art industry. To retain top artists and to preserve their own rank in the art world's marching order, dealers can't not laboriously and expensively schlep their wares and staff around the globe, from fair to fair. The events are schmoozefests for the über-rich and assorted influencers, granted V.I.P. privileges. (Such an ugly term, unctuously elevating an élite to an elect.) But they are popular with some upper-middle hoi polloi as well. Tickets to the Shed sold out well in advance, with general-admission and preview tickets ranging from fifty-five to two hundred and sixty-five dollars a pop. How much is exposure to a hodgepodge of recent art worth to you?

For me, three things made this late-pandemic Frieze a tonic. First was the joy of seeing art in person after fourteen months of nearly total deprivation. It was like being given back a body to go with digital-wearied eyeballs. Even so-so works gladdened me just by being real. Second, only about sixty galleries were represented, as opposed to Frieze's usual coma-inducing tally of a couple of hundred. Finally, there was the relative anonymity bestowed by face masks, which had the effect of reducing instances of unsought conversation. Fairs intensify the social rites that attend the showing and selling of art in New York. My mask could hide my chagrin at failing to recognize people who did address me. ("Good to see you" goes only so far.) Not that these are important disgraces, given my temperamental distance from a wholly commercial ecosystem. I cherish the art world for its steady provision of things to look at—and I respect dealers, who wouldn't be involved in art if they didn't love it, and who have the wisest heads in the game, because they can't afford to be uninformed—but I quail at considering the enterprise a club of mutual interests, least of all in the rise and fall of pecuniary fortunes. The cage matches of Eros and Mammon that are fairs leave me dyspeptic, even as I avail myself of a generously supplied V.I.P. pass because wouldn't you?

The chief distinction of Frieze New York is that it happened at all, unlike the other fairs that usually invade the city this time of year. In terms of the art on display, it was mild to nearly sedate. Dealers seemed reluctant to lead with their best or most challenging stuff, perhaps keeping their powder dry for occasions attracting, as this one largely didn't, the European and Asian collectors who would usually walk the floor. (They were still able to fatten the contemporary trade through the fair's online viewing rooms.) Alert to the present era in racial politics, Frieze paid tribute to the Vision & Justice Project, a program initiated by the Harvard professor Sarah Elizabeth Lewis, in 2016. Billboard-size polemical wall pieces by artists like Carrie Mae Weems, Mel Chin, and Hank Willis Thomas lined the fair's halls, to uneven effect. The gesture felt defensive, as a virtuous fig leaf on the fair's naked avarice.

At the booths, numerous Black artists scored higher, given that so many of them—such as the painters Rashid Johnson, at Hauser & Wirth, with bristling, peculiarly nerve-racked abstraction, and Trenton Doyle Hancock, with a solo show at James Cohan, of cartoonish characters, rendered mostly in white on black, that included a wry reference to the ever-controversial K.K.K. imagery in paintings by Philip Guston—are superb. (Speaking of Guston, a K.K.K.-free gouache sketch by him of an open book, at Hauser & Wirth, sparked consciousness of his immense, undying influence on younger artists.) The quality of the artists' work was in synch with their dealers' eagerness to peddle it. There is just no getting around the art world's alchemy of value becoming price—which I would simply prefer to happen offstage, like murder in Greek theatre.

Painting ruled this Frieze. The appetites that govern today's market explain the flourishing of the old medium, which avant-gardists have declared dead, off and on, for a hundred years. I had an uncanny sense of styles and reputations picking up where they left off in March, 2020. (A visitor this year might have had giddy moments of imagining that the horrendous intervening epoch never happened—fake news.) The dominant mode splits differences between antic figuration and formal order. Surrealism is back, with housebroken manners. The present master is Dana Schutz, whose blazingly colored fantasies of enigmatic violence were on show at David Zwirner's booth. She makes sculpture, too, of rousingly bestial grotesqueries. (Schutz naïvely got into public trouble at the 2017 Whitney Biennial with a presumptuous painting based on the mutilated Emmett Till in his casket. She has since eschewed obvious topicality.) Related younger painters (Schutz is forty-four) included Ivy Haldeman, with Downs & Ross, who composes images of bizarrely animate fashionable clothes and occasional body parts, writhing in space. Narrative? Abstract? Either or both, in key with the present premium on supercharged ambiguity.

A bonus of the fair was a gorgeous mini-retrospective of the fey romanticist Karen Kilimnik—assembled by Galerie Eva Presenhuber and Sprüth Magers—of small, loosely daubed pastiches of vaguely seventeenth- or eighteenth-century pastoral scenes, rosy-cheeked women, and lovable animals, mostly horses. A world of her own, which some disdain but I adore. Since the nineteen-eighties, when Kilimnik made many of the paintings, she has conveyed a quality ever rarer in contemporary art: the expatiation of a personal drive. You feel that she would be making the work if she were the only artist in existence, which, in her heart, she may well be. Similarly take-me-home covetable, at Karma, was a small still-life by Dike Blair, an artist who is little renowned but is passionately esteemed by his fans, including me. Blair has taken various tacks since the seventies, most successfully photo-realist paintings in gouache or oil (from snapshots he takes) of unremarkable domestic and worldly objects and bits of architecture. Flowers feature often. So do fancy cocktails, as at Frieze. Blair's compositions are deadpan and his colors emphatic. A subtle air of ironic detachment pervades his work, as if he were startled by his own temerity in offering pleasures so unprepossessing. But once you start looking at a picture by him it's hard to stop. You almost watch, rather than look, as though some ultimate secret of life and art were in the offing, momentarily out of sight and not to be missed when it reveals itself.

But taking the cake in terms of personal aesthetic audacity was *Untitled* (1990), a pale canvas, at Michael Werner, by the late and, by many of us, still lamented German artist Sigmar Polke, who died in 2010, at the age of sixty-nine. He was a wizard of heterodox materials and an unpredictable humorist with mystical nuances. He created this work in the dark with slathered silver nitrate, silver oxide, silver iodide, and silver bromide. Exposed to light, the strokes resolved into a filmy gestural cadenza: quietly ferocious, if such is imaginable, like superimposed eddies in a whipping windstorm. As often during Polke's career, chance was his sidekick. To view this work is to share in his surprise when it became visible. The painting couldn't have been more remote from the fair's pageant of product lines—not that Polke didn't work in series, but he could be counted on for exhilarating instances of turning the tables on himself.

Either several familiar artists have improved lately or my former resistance to them has expired. So it is with the French multimedia specialist Annette Messager, with two installations at Marian Goodman: a large wall hung with scrolls bearing fluent drawings that are interspersed with small individual figures of uncertain species, and a darkened room containing a heap of taxidermied or toy creatures (rabbit, duck, pigeon, kitten, raccoon, lizard, and more) and sculpted hands with raised fingers, all embedded in a sort of primal crud. Tiny spotlights rotated within the pile, casting on the surrounding walls huge shadows of things near the lights and diminutive ones of those more distant. The flow of the scale shifts mesmerized. A poetry of some organic natural process was suggested—perhaps evolution or, I don't know, devolution, on fast forward. The works' theatrical richness provided an immersive time-out from Frieze's teeming thises and thats.

Contemplation, art's primary exercise of the human mind, is the last thing enabled by art-fair hurly-burly. But it could and did occur at points in Frieze New York, an event marked less by celebration than by gasping relief, like a swimmer saved from drowning.

Published in the May 24, 2021, issue of *The New Yorker*, with the headline "A Trip to the Fair."

MY STRUGGLE WITH CÉZANNE

Some of us don't like the inarguably great artist Paul Cézanne as much as we know we are supposed to. I, for one, have struggled with him all my art-loving life. Others, as I've confirmed in recent conversations with Cézanne devotees, are astonished and appalled to hear anything with even a trace of negativity said about him. "Cézanne Drawing," at the Museum of Modern Art, with some two hundred and eighty works on paper (too many? Not really, because quantity intensifies the works' qualities), has a cumulative impact that is practically theological for both believers and skeptics, akin to a creation story, a Genesis, of modernism.

It's a return to roots for MOMA, which initiated its narrative of modern painting in 1929 with a show that included van Gogh, Seurat, and Gauguin as well as Cézanne, whose broken forms made the others look comparatively conservative as composers of pictures. He stood out then, as he does now, for an asperity of expression that is analytical in form and indifferent to style. The appearance of his works is an effect, not a fulfillment. He revolutionized visual art, changing a practice of rendering illusions to one of aggregating marks that cohere in the mind rather than in the eye of a viewer.

You don't look at a Cézanne, some ravishing late works excepted. You study it, registering how it's done—in the drawings, with tangles of line and, often, patches of watercolor. Each detail conveys the artist's direct gaze at a subject but is rarely at pains to serve an integrated composition. Cézanne was savagely sincere in his ways of looking, true to what he called his "little sensation" in how things, bit by bit, met his regard. He made pictorial vision the exercise of an artist's concerted will and a challenge to a viewer's understanding. The show looks at first glance like an overwhelming ordeal, with its profusion of so many works, mostly small, for you to shuffle around peering at. They seem much the same—as in a real way they are, but with a consistent intensity that refreshes itself from piece to piece. As big as the show is, it can be taken as a mere sampler of prodigious creativity. I usually disdain wall texts, but those here, written by the curators Jodi Hauptman and Samantha Friedman, are soundly spot on and informative. Sanctifying or not, the occasion is richly educational.

Cézanne was personally shy, to the point of being asocial. He was viewed by some in Paris, including Édouard Manet, as something of an uncouth hayseed from the South of France, though he was the scion of a well-to-do family. His often clumsy and weird early works, mostly from the eighteen-sixties and seventies, when he was in his twenties and thirties, seethe with violent imaginings of rape and murder. A man stabs another person on a rural road. An elegant dude evinces surprise upon entering a room heaped with corpses. Naked women figure as objects of hyperbolic sensuality, at times enthroned among lusting male worshippers. He was plainly bent on forcing notice, without much success outside a circle that included his best friend since childhood, Émile Zola.

What ensued next was a remarkable sublimation of unruly emotion into an austere ambition to, as Cézanne formulated it later, "make of Impressionism something as solid and durable as the art of the museums." The catalyst of the change was Camille Pissarro, nine years his senior, who mentored him in Impressionist techniques and remained a close friend until they were estranged by the Dreyfus affair, in which Cézanne passively sided with the outrightly anti-Semitic Renoir and Degas. Pissarro was the subtlest of the leading Impressionists, devising ways of giving distinctive presence to each part of a painting, by, for example, defining the edges of objects with the paint that surrounded them. For him, an edge was a place where paint didn't stop but only changed color. Cézanne, compulsively copying motifs from classical painting and sculpture, gradually forsook Pissarro's fictive unities within the pictorial rectangle in favor of notating rather than reproducing observed reality. His drawings are as likely to leave backgrounds blank as to fill them in. It was a radical shift, scorning both verisimilitude and imagination.

Cézanne was fearless of error. You see that in his figure drawings from sculpture. If a contour isn't quite right, he doesn't correct it (the one drafting tool that he seems never to have employed is the eraser): he multiplies it, with lines on top of lines. (There's accuracy in there somewhere.) His audacious independence was enabled by willful isolation, at his family's Aix-en-Provence estate, far from the competitive milieu of Paris, where even the most adventurous of his contemporaries had to subsist on sales. He attained a degree of fame among fellow-artists and bold collectors, while being repeatedly subject to public ridicule. The full import of his mature art burst upon the world in a retrospective exhibition in 1907, a year after his death, from pneumonia, at the age of sixty-seven. It may be too much to say that he changed everything in the course of art history. But he was bound to make artists whom he didn't directly influence more than a little nervous.

Cézanne drew nearly every day, rehearsing the timeless purpose—and the impossibility—of pictorial art: to reduce three dimensions to two. His greatest works, from late in his life, partly reconstitute visual drama, notably in scenes of bathers in Arcadian settings and (my favorites) still-lifes of fruit and domestic objects which yield a sense of seeing, or, somehow, of feeling, around the summarily represented masses. Apples stay delicious while acquiring the density of cannonballs. The effect holds for portraits of his wife, Hortense, and of his gardener—themselves effectively domestic objects, for all that Cézanne cared about them as living souls. To my eye, the show's only portrait heads that suggest personhood are a couple of his son, Paul, pictured sleeping.

Thingness magnetized him, in tirelessly repetitive renderings of, for example, the nearby Mont Sainte-Victoire, eight barely varying versions of which are in the show. Thereness, too, reigned. You rarely feel any passionate attraction on Cézanne's part to his subjects, but, rather, a stubborn, even obsessive responsiveness to their existence. He couldn't help depicting them, because they couldn't help but be. He seems to have been impervious to boredom. His interest in the visible world was unquenchable. The payoff reminds me of an adage from William Blake: "If the fool would persist in his folly he would become wise." Cézanne's scattershot approach triumphed in his conflations of surface with depth, which abolished perspective by locating the near and the relatively distant with shading and color, perceived all at once in increasingly perfect equipoise. All that remained for Cubism to introduce was the geometric fragmentation of subjects in abstracted, shallow space: a decorative function departing from Cézanne's unshakable loyalty to facts.

So what's my problem? Partly it's an impatience with Cézanne's demands for strenuous looking. I tire of being made to feel smart rather than pleased. (Here I quite favor the optical nourishments of van Gogh, Gauguin, and Seurat.) But my discontent is inseparable from Cézanne's significance as a revolutionary. How good an idea was modernism, all in all? It disintegrated, circa 1960, amid a plurality of new modes while remaining, yes, an art of the museum. It came to emblematize up-to-date sophisticated taste, spawning varieties of abstraction that circle back to Cézanne's innovative interrelations of figure and ground. It also fuelled a yen in some to change the world for the more intelligent, if not always for the better. The world took only specialized notice. Modernism's initially enfevered optimism could not survive the slaughterhouse of the First World War and the political apocalypse of the Russian Revolution, which ate away at myths of progress that had seemed to valorize aesthetic change. Dedicated newness in art devolved from a propelling cause into a rote effect. Lost, to my mind, is the strangeness—which I strive to reimagine—that had to have affected Cézanne's first viewers, as he began to upend traditions that had been more or less continuous since the Renaissance. I have felt this retrospective discomfort in other contexts. It peaks for me in "Cézanne Drawing," even as I join fellow-congregants in genuflecting before the artist's genius.

Published in the June 28, 2021, issue of *The New Yorker*, with the headline "Drawing Conclusions."

THE MEDICI AS ARTISTS SAW THEM

One of the best jokes in movie history is an apologia for evil. Harry Lime, the black-market peddler of diluted penicillin for sick children, indelibly played by Orson Welles in *The Third Man*, trolls a straight-arrow friend with lines scripted by Graham Greene: "Remember what the fella says: in Italy for thirty years under the Borgias, they had warfare, terror, murder, and bloodshed, but they produced Michelangelo, Leonardo da Vinci, and the Renaissance. In Switzerland, they had brotherly love, they had five hundred years of democracy and peace—and what did that produce? The cuckoo clock." That's delectable enough to make up for mangling art history. Among the oligarchic republics and monarchies of Italy in the late fifteenth and early sixteenth centuries, it was the guileful Medici, in Florence—not the irrepressibly corrupt and, yes, betimes homicidal Borgias, mainly in Rome—who nurtured Leonardo and Michelangelo and most fruitfully advanced humanism in all fields of culture. (Niccolò Machiavelli was also a native son.) Unlike Greene and Welles, "The Medici: Portraits and Politics, 1512–1570," at the Metropolitan Museum, assigns credit where it is due.

The banking family rose to govern Florence, nominally a republic, in the fourteen-thirties. After losing power in 1494, they reinstated themselves by force, with support from Pope Julius II, in 1512, the year that the Met show takes as its starting point. A further republican interlude, from 1527 to 1530, was crushed by armies sent by Pope Clement VII (a Medici himself) and the Holy Roman Emperor Charles V. This entailed a devastating ten-month siege that coincided with a plague epidemic and a famine. Disgusted by the Medici's reactionary usurpation, Michelangelo, the city's premier creator, moved to Rome, never again to set foot in

Florence. (Neither he nor Leonardo is represented in the show.) But most other artists fell into line, flattering the regime with masterly portraiture that came to characterize Mannerism—an exaggeration of Renaissance aesthetics which exalted virtuosic artifice. As dukes and grand dukes, eventually extending their domain to all of Tuscany, the Medici held sway for the next two hundred years. It helps to keep in mind the violence of their restoration, which left memories of fearful suffering that could only discourage further opposition. If needful of consolation, the artists took it in beauty.

The Met show focusses narrowly on court culture, mainly through portraiture but also including books, prints, and manuscripts. The highlights are portraits by Jacopo da Pontormo and his student Agnolo Bronzino, two artists whom I have come to love. The warm-blooded Pontormo and the deceptively icy Bronzino developed variants of a style for style's sake that used to be deprecated by art critics and historians as a decadent descent from Renaissance peaks. (Lone paintings by Andrea del Sarto and Raphael, along with one tentatively attributed to Raphael's workshop, stand in for the old school.) Mannerism did indeed lack the gravitas and trailblazing form of the work done by Michelangelo's cohort, but it achieved a sort of glorious sunset sophistication, which the show's curators, Keith Christiansen and Carlo Falciani, and several consulting scholars relate to the politics of the period.

The art is great, the politics abstruse. I found the show fascinating without being terribly interesting. (Good luck keeping the names, dates, and deeds of the players straight. They teem like grasshoppers.) But the connoisseurship dazzles. Exquisitely selected and installed, the portraits, including mighty busts sculpted by Benvenuto Cellini, have no truck with mediocrity, apart from a haplessly overthought, fantasized grouping of historic poets painted by Giorgio Vasari, who, despite being a leading theorist and champion of Florentine *disegno* (design at one with drawing), was blah with a brush. His book *Lives of the Artists* (1550, enlarged in 1568) invented the practice of art history. Literature, notably poetry, obsessed

Florentine artists and intellectuals, who led the consolidation of the turn made by their fellow-citizen Dante, in the fourteenth century, from Latin to the vulgate that became modern Italian. Science, too, had moments of support. A Medici patriarch was an important patron of Galileo's, though the family's next generation, likely deferring to the panicked Vatican, largely condoned his trial for the heresy of demoting Earth from the center of the universe. Flexible if not outright cynical tactics served the clan's long-term strategy: to secure Florence's independent eminence in Italy and beyond.

In a section on literature, the show turns up a poet new to me: Laura Battiferri, a woman who, married to an architect and sculptor, engaged in witty exchanges of poems with the multitalented, reliably sassy Bronzino, who was given to writing riotously homoerotic rhapsodies that were circulated among receptive readers. In 1560 or so, Bronzino portrayed Battiferri in profile—unusual for him—with a long nose and prominent chin cannily recalling those of Dante. Radiating intelligence, she holds open a manuscript volume displaying two sonnets by Petrarch. The friends enjoyed impersonating the fourteenth-century Florentine bard and his idealized ladylove, Laura. They had to have been a lot of fun, ornamenting a milieu of preening style and often freewheeling Eros. Such charms nestled within the scheming ambitions of the Medici state, which loomed large in Italy with its financial clout and a resourceful diplomacy that involved numerous marriages of convenience. The family finagled the installations of four popes (the Borgias managed two) and two queens of France. After the world-changing insurrection of Martin Luther, in 1517, Florence became a stronghold of the Counter-Reformation, although that movement's overbearing piety was slow to affect the city's deluxe tastes.

The best Florentine Mannerist portraiture stands up to the contemporaneous painterly feats of Venetians like Veronese and Tintoretto, whose absence rather haunts the show. But no one anywhere could rival that other Venetian, Titian, whose sensitivity to character, prodigies of color, and preternatural touch make him the greatest of all prior to

Rembrandt. Pontormo comes closest with respect to color. Look long at his works, such as *Portrait of a Young Man* (circa 1525–26) and *Portrait of a Halberdier*, which is dated circa 1529–30—the years of the bloody siege that returned the Medici to power. (The formidably armed young man must have been a defender of the city.) Allow the hues and tones to surprise and absorb your gaze. You might well swoon. Even Pontormo's blacks and grays glow. He was relatively inattentive to personality, but a sitter had to be glad of inclusion in the golden circle of his regard. For individual character, Bronzino rules. For me, Bronzino's cool depiction of court personalities secretes a pathos of emotion held in check by obligatory elegance—an aesthetic of praise fringed with melancholy. Bronzino liked young men in art as in life. New Yorkers will be familiar with his *Lodovico Capponi* (circa 1550–52), a rare loan from the Frick Collection: an adolescent page strives toward arrogance, not quite nailing it, in a getup that features the projecting codpiece (with self-control, you can cease staring at it) that was a cynosure of male fashion at the time. (The equivalent attribute in earlier Italian portraits of men was apt to be a sword.) A wall in the last room of the show, hung with five tip-top Bronzinos, staggered me like a sequence of Sunday punches.

Less persuasive is the curators' insistence on a triumvirate of masters, interspersing works by Pontormo and Bronzino with ones by the eclectic Francesco Salviati. I don't get it. Though plentifully skilled, Salviati strikes me as often wacky, with a caricatural bent that can seem modern in accidentally burlesque ways. Some background elements in his *Portrait of a Man* (1544–45) bring to mind the American cornball regionalist Thomas Hart Benton, and the long-necked youth in his *Portrait of a Young Man with a Dog* (circa 1543–45), oblivious to the flyby of a semi-naked angel, might be something out of *Mad* magazine. The humor feels unintentional, unlike that found in a go-for-broke series by Bronzino of allegorical portraits that render leading lights of the court as figures of theological and mythological pedigree. The long-ruling duke Cosimo I de' Medici becomes Orpheus, nude and wielding a kind of viol while watched by the helldog

Cerberus, and his son Giovanni impersonates John the Baptist. It's hard to imagine the subjects countenancing these antic depictions, but they must have, or we wouldn't have the pictures to look at now.

The elevation even of japes in Medici-sponsored portraiture may induce a certain monotony, pleasurable on the eye but a mite starchy in the mind and conditioned by servitude to despotic patronage. For explosive relief, head just down the hall at the Met to the concurrent, huge retrospective of the bohemian demiurge Alice Neel. Neel, who died in 1984, embraced a raw humanity in her subjects that had only simmered in previous traditions of portraiture. It's remarkable how an artist long classed as an eccentric outlier has come to seem an Old Master for present sensibilities. Her motto could have been an injunction that is associated with the poet Arthur Rimbaud, though likely not written by him: "Take rhetoric and wring its neck." You are immersed at a glance in the untidy livingness, in the flesh, of persons from various strata of society, with a tilt toward the poor and the marginalized who for many years were neighbors of Neel's in Spanish Harlem. A frisson of nakedness infuses even her clothed subjects, whose resilience consists in being fully and, therefore, by Neel's reckoning, lovably human. The predominant feeling is a sort of rugged agape. Now return to the Medici and imagine their fainting fits, were they exposed to Neel's principled gaucherie. Art has many mansions. Today, the most compelling tend to the tumbledown.

Published in the July 12 & 19, 2021, issue of *The New Yorker*, with the headline "Power Players."

HAVE YOU HEARD OF NIKOLAI ASTRUP?

Have you ever heard of a Norwegian artist named Nikolai Astrup, a younger contemporary of Edvard Munch? If so, you're either a rare bird or Norwegian. Astrup is new to me—and I'm of Norwegian descent, with ancestral roots in much the same rugged, sparsely populated, preposterously scenic western region of the country where Astrup, who was born in 1880, spent nearly his entire life. (There's a farming community called Skjeldal.) An enchanting Astrup exhibition at the Clark Art Institute, in Williamstown, Massachusetts, startled me with densely composed, brilliantly colored paintings and wizardly woodcuts, mostly landscapes of mountains, forests, bodies of water, humble farm buildings, and gardens (among other things, the artist was a passionate amateur horticulturalist), with occasional inklings of mysticism relating to native folklore. A receding row of grain poles could be a sinister parade of trolls, and the shape of a pollarded tree in winter evokes a writhing, unhappy supernatural being. I learned that Astrup is, arguably, the most popular artist in Norway—ahead of Munch, who, I've been told, makes schoolchildren sad—while largely unknown beyond its borders. How could that happen?

Astrup was a naturalist, influenced by modernist movements including post-Impressionism and Symbolism, thanks to his early training—with help from a patron's grant—in Paris and Germany. Afterward, he promptly returned to the mountainous municipality of Jølster, and stayed there. But he hardly vegetated. Restlessly inventive, often varying his manner from picture to picture, he is like no one else. He could effectively start from scratch even when repeating such motifs as that of a mountain viewed across a lake: his Nordic Mont Sainte-Victoire. It seems that many houses in Norway display reproductions of his art somewhere on their walls. In a "prelude" to the show's catalogue, the novelist Karl Ove Knausgaard recalls one in his childhood home. For Norwegians, Astrup's appeal was and remains something like patriotic. His fame can seem captive to a sentimental nationalism, which the Clark show, subtitled "Visions of Norway," exacerbates with photographic murals of Jølster that suggest a walk-through travel brochure. O.K., the place is gorgeous. Now, what about the art? Can it be pried from an understandably fond communal embrace?

Astrup painted thickly, with details atop generalized forms. There's an intensity about his process that's hard to explain. Knausgaard asserts that the pictures are "devoid of psychology," and, in comparison with Munch's illustrative poetics, that's certainly the case. But I sense a mental pressure in Astrup's work as a whole: there's something personal that he had to deal with or kept trying to get at, bearing on obsessive memories of his childhood. He was the first of fourteen children of a pietistic Lutheran pastor who opposed his vocation in art. Astrup repeatedly painted taciturn views of the parsonage in which he grew up, as if it possessed some unresolved import. It's a banal building, in the attic of which Astrup and his siblings endured bitter cold on winter nights, the result of splits in the decaying external walls. (The fissures were papered over, but the kids couldn't resist poking holes in the paper.) Still more telling is the point of view in a number of spectacular paintings and woodcuts of midsummer-night frolics around huge bonfires: the spectator stands outside the goings on. Astrup was strictly forbidden by his father to participate in the pagan ritual. Such works echo a predilection that was stated by Munch: "I paint not what I see but what I saw." Knausgaard writes that Astrup recorded features of the landscape that he could see from the parsonage in his notebook, but he omitted the ones that postdated his childhood. For all we know, his apparently more objective pictures secrete early impressions, too.

Astrup could have escaped his exigent native society. By 1902, while still in his early twenties, he was already cosmopolitan in style and collegially esteemed by artistic circles in Kristiania (which was renamed Oslo in 1925). At some point, Munch bought three of his works. But Jølster drew Astrup back and held him fast. One reason may have been his outsider temperament, or the limitation that respiratory ailments put on any travel—he had chronic asthma and survived tuberculosis only to die of pneumonia in 1928, at the age of forty-seven.

He seems to have cherished the company of his wife, Engel Sunde Astrup, a skilled textile printer who had a successful career of her own until her death, in 1966. They had eight children, including two small daughters who, wearing red dresses, are glimpsed picking berries in a forest in a phenomenal woodcut, *Foxgloves* (woodblock, circa 1915–20; print, 1925). Astrup's laborious technique for that medium involved carving congeries of scattered shapes into multiple blocks, each block imprinting a different color. In *Foxgloves*, a trickling watercourse leads the eye from a verdant foreground to the background of a periwinkle mountain and filmy blue skies. The girls provide points of focus, but there's nothing cutesy about them. They inhabit what Knausgaard terms "a parallel universe," as if seen by Astrup "through a windowpane that he was pressing his face against." A use of oil-based inks fortifies colors and textures. The woodcuts are sui generis, in a mode that can seem, befuddlingly, equidistant from prints and paintings. (I want one, and not on account of its country of origin. I have been to Norway and like it fine, as any gadabout New Yorker might. My chief stirring of emotional identity is with North Dakota, where my immigrant people went and I was born. But I recommend the sublime Lofoten Islands, in the Arctic Circle. There, one June night, I watched the sun start to set and then think better of it.)

Getting things right mattered mightily to Astrup, even as he could never be sure he had succeeded. The drama of the work inheres in self-doubt, which tormented him ceaselessly, in the face of a drive that sustained him nonetheless. Each touch of his brush can seem to be a momentary victory against troubling odds. This epitomizes him as modern, making things up as he went along. He lamented in a letter to a friend in 1922, "I ruin practically every serious work that I have made recently. I am so uncertain." In an earlier letter to another friend, he had written, "I no longer know what art is—when it comes to my own pictures." I found myself rooting for this good man in his agon with himself.

Astrup depicted the surrounding mountainscape in different seasons. I was riveted by one moment in time, *Gray Spring Evening* (before 1908), in which a massive, still snowy peak looms beyond a thawing lake. Someone out there is rowing a boat amid ice floes. A line of small, mostly leafless trees laces the foreground, delicately evincing Astrup's love of Japanese prints. The application of that linear influence works well in this case; sometimes the formality jars with his freehand painterliness. But Astrup's intermittent, relative failures to achieve coherence fascinate in their own way, as evidence of a talent incessantly pushing its limits. Scenic beauty is incidental. Unforced, his renderings of natural splendor responded to topographies that were there to be beheld by anyone. The individuality of his decisions sneaks up on you. That its charm took more than a century to be recognized internationally bemuses.

The Clark show, curated by the independent scholar MaryAnne Stevens, insures that, from now on, Astrup must figure in any comprehensive survey of early-twentieth-century European art. One keynote is a mastery of detail, particularly in the characters of plants. Each leaf or flower amounts to a faithful though never photograph-like portrait of its species, rewarding attention that extends beyond an initial error of thinking that you know the kind of thing you are looking at. Swiftly brushed, the accuracy of the botanical elements suggests a shot-from-the-hip deadeye aim. Astrup's artistry keeps getting stranger—and stronger—as you gaze, often triggered by such marvels of color as the blazing red and yellow bonfire flames amid the crepuscular sullen greens and charcoal grays that accompany fleeting solstice sunsets. What might appear, at first glance, eccentric in the art of its era redeems itself with a specificity to a time, a place, and a personality, impelling a period style to extremes of authenticity.

The popular myth of important artists being neglected in their lifetimes is for the most part balderdash. Van Gogh would likely have become a raging success soon enough had he not been so isolated in the South of France and, in 1890, hurrying to be dead. The trope tends to elegize artists who are perceived to be ahead of their time or otherwise inimical to regnant conventions. Astrup's case has me wondering about alternative instances of reputations, ones that are caught in obscure eddies of the art-historical mainstream, relating sideways rather than centrally to hegemonic movements. We are too habituated to the canonical march of modernist progress and a reflex of deeming anything marginal to it "minor." An exploration of hinterlands elsewhere might well foster a category of similarly prepossessing misfits. For a name, consider Astrupism. With apologies to proprietary Norwegians, Nikolai Astrup belongs to all of us now.

Published in the July 26, 2021, issue of *The New Yorker*, with the headline "A Great Unknown."

THE PHOTOGRAPHS THAT WOMEN TOOK

"*LIFE*'S BOURKE-WHITE GOES BOMBING," reads the headline of an article in *Life* from March 1, 1943, with pictures of an airborne B-17 and of the eponymous photographer, Margaret Bourke-White, somehow making a padded flight suit look snazzy as she became the first woman to be allowed on an Air Force combat mission. The breakthrough was bound to be hers. She was made a national celebrity by Henry Luce as the premier photographer for *Fortune*, starting in 1929, and then for the newly founded *Life*, in 1936. Her skill and charisma are among the things that stand out in "The New Woman Behind the Camera," a monumental show, at the Metropolitan Museum, of a hundred and eighty-five works by a hundred and twenty female professionals from more than twenty countries which were made between the nineteen-twenties and the fifties. Crowning years of heroic research by the head curator, Andrea Nelson, an associate at the National Gallery of Art, the show builds a case for the historic contributions of women to a field that, until very recently, was monotonously dominated by men. Most of the artists are unknown to me. Nearly all did tip-top work in genres that include reportage, ethnography, fashion, advertising, and determinedly avant-garde experimentation. Widely recognized names—the Americans Berenice Abbott, Dorothea Lange, and Helen Levitt among them—are few. Only Bourke-White really towered in her time.

The irony of Bourke-White's *Flood Relief, Louisville, Kentucky* (1937), which shows Black victims of a devastating Ohio River flood lined up for aid in front of a huge billboard of a happy (white, of course) family in a car, with the scripted assurance "There's no way like the American Way," bites so hard as to scar the soul. (That it's beautiful amplifies the shock.)

Luce let Bourke-White do that. Liberal sentiment was no hindrance to his avidity for sensation. Lange and Levitt did as well or better as social documentarians, with the former's empathetic coverage of sufferers from the Depression and the latter's breathtakingly affecting shots of slum children. Levitt's *New York* (circa 1942) catches three rapscallion boys joyously play-fighting in a rubble-strewn lot. Two of them wield sticks and the other, the smallest, hefts an immense tree branch. The work is a miracle of observation and timing, as one of the smiling stick-holders takes off at a dead run. For me, the over-all image encapsulates a violent happiness, or a happiness in violence, that resonates with millennia of human experience. I can still see it with my eyes closed.

But here I am singling out classics from a show that, nonjudgmental to a willing fault, blurs discriminations of fame and even of originality. The array, installed by the Met's Mia Fineman, tantalizes to the point of possibly maddening some viewers, with perhaps one or very few prints by photographers who rouse in us a yen to see more of them. In truth, that's a payoff for Nelson, who imposes no unifying aesthetic beyond a general concordance with modernism. She advances just one, foggy thematic idea: "the New Woman," a phrase, or slogan, that was coined by two European writers in the late nineteenth century for rebels against Victorian conformity. I think most of us associate it with bobbed-haired partyers in the twenties and the wisecracking heroines of Hollywood comedies in the thirties. Its vagueness serves Nelson's intent of equalizing all types of photography, without observing a distinction between art and commerce. She and five essayists in the show's catalogue are at pains to avoid essentializing femininity. There's reference, but only slight, to our present-day preoccupation with gender identity. The essayists do little opining; one gives a glancing disapprobation of "colonialism" among European and American photographers in Africa, most of whom are from the thirties—easy to judge now but opaque back then. Only a division of bodies of work by category suggests a critical criterion. The show is less a survey than an index. The effect of heterogeneous images in flashing sequence dizzies—physically so, in my case. At certain points, having heedlessly given myself over to too many compelling items, I had to sit down.

Nelson's catholicity obliges her to include, in a section entitled "Modern Bodies," a spectacular high-angled view of young Germans doing coördinated pushups, by Leni Riefenstahl, in 1936. Countering that totalitarian mystique are horrific shots of recently liberated concentration camps by Bourke-White and Lee Miller, who, formerly a protégée of Man Ray's, was, like Bourke-White, embedded with American forces. Exposing the hell of the camps constituted photography's greatest service to collective memory. Miller's capture of a leather-coated, handsome S.S. guard, dead and adrift under water, grimly satisfies. (Miller went on to be pictured—not in the show—taking a bath in Hitler's tub at his apartment in Munich.) A terrific combat photograph by the Russian Galina Sanko, of two running Soviet soldiers in the act of hurling grenades, raises doubts. Was it staged? Who has the sangfroid to perfectly frame an assault on armed enemies who are near enough to throw things at? Sanko, perhaps. Another photograph by her, of German prisoners being hauled across snow on a sled at Stalingrad, affirms her grit. It is reported that she was injured twice during the war.

Many of the show's motifs—of architectural subjects and street scenes, for example—could imaginably have been taken by talented men. This serves the point of establishing an equality, at least, of professional achievement. Femaleness becomes germane intermittently, as in portraiture and self-portraiture of women at work with their cameras and in a few stabs at Surrealism, a movement that was all but defined by poisoned-sugar male treatments of womanhood. A tour de force from 1938, by the German-born Argentine Annemarie Heinrich in league with her sister Ursula, finds the two reflected in a mirrored orb. In the background—from our point of view—Annemarie grins as she snaps the shutter of a standing camera; Ursula looms gigantically and wildly distorted as she leans forward to grasp the sphere. It takes time, enjoyably, to puzzle out the picture's vertiginous structure. Other works that appeal to me include portraits by Berenice Abbott of her friends Jean Cocteau, aiming a pistol at the viewer, and Janet Flanner, the contributor to this magazine of the Letter from Paris column, who maintains a regal mien despite wearing a funny tall hat with masks attached to it. The show's chief instance of outright feminist agitation is a shot, by Lola Álvarez Bravo, the great Mexican visual poet of her nation, of a melancholy woman leaning out a window and gridded with shadows: *In Her Own Prison* (circa 1950). An uprising of such inmates was a few short years away.

A mood of buoyancy reigns in a section called "Fashion and Advertising." Marketing and magazine content targeting female consumers gave women photographers license and authority. The models' postures took on kinetic vivacity, and jokes became permissible. I only gradually realized that the pert young woman in a 1931 German ad for a hair-styling cream is, in fact, a cunningly made-up mannequin dressed in an old-fashioned blouse. The hand that it appears to extend, presenting the product, is human. Many Weimar fashion photographers were Jewish, finding ways to enter society and to make a living with independent flair. Like every other photographer in the show—however fiercely individualistic—they are implicitly enlisted in a common, retroactive struggle for simple justice.

Now for something that brought tears to my eyes: five shots of an incredible Japanese actress, Yasue Yamamoto, that were taken clandestinely, around 1943 and 1944, after her theatre company was banned by Japan's wartime government. Wearing a kimono, and either seated or kneeling, Yamamoto enacts moments from a play entitled *Elegy for a Woman*, with tiny shifts of facial expression—mouth closed or slightly open, eyes raised a bit or downcast—that speak or, really, sing of muted emotions that are no less moving for being unidentifiable. The performance was a collaboration with a pioneering Japanese photographer, Eiko Yamazawa. Their complementary artistry, exercised in secret under humble circumstances (a paper screen has holes in it), pierces the heart. The style is flatly vernacular, with nothing fancy or overtly dramatizing about it. The results, feeling timelessly here-and-now across a span of sixty-eight years, didn't so much blow my mind as take it away and begin to replace it with a better one.

Published in the August 2, 2021, issue of *The New Yorker*, with the headline "Another Eye."

JASPER JOHNS REMAINS CONTEMPORARY ART'S PHILOSOPHER KING

In sixty-six years of multifarious art works by Jasper Johns, the subject of a huge retrospective that is split between the Whitney Museum, in New York, and the Philadelphia Museum of Art, I can think of only one work that expresses an opinion: *The Critic Sees* (1961), a sculpted relief of eyeglasses with blabbing mouths in place of lenses. (The piece is not in the show.) The image suggests exasperation from a great artist—America's greatest, post-Willem de Kooning, in terms of a capacity to reset formal and semiotic ideals for subsequent striving artists. Johns has often been burdened with overinterpretation despite his stated commitment, early on, to dealing with "things the mind already knows," starting with flags, targets, numbers, and maps, before proceeding to trickier motifs that are nonetheless equally matter-of-fact. Johns's extraordinary virtuosity with line, texture, and color is an adequate hook for any of his works.

It all began in 1955, in a ramshackle building on Pearl Street, in lower Manhattan, that Johns shared with his lover, Robert Rauschenberg. The twenty-five-year-old Johns, a South Carolinian survivor of a broken home whose upbringing was largely farmed out to relatives, had studied at the University of South Carolina and done a stint in the Army. Having had a dream in 1954 of painting the American flag, he did so, employing a technique that was unusual at the time: brushstrokes in pigmented, lumpy encaustic wax that sensitize the deadpan image, such that there is an aura of feeling, though particular to no one. The abrupt gesture—sign painting, essentially, of profound sophistication—ended modern art. It torpedoed the macho existentialism of many Abstract Expressionist stars then on the scene and anticipated Pop art's demotic sources and Minimalism's self-evidence. It put art into the world, and vice versa. Politically, the flag painting was an icon of the Cold War, symbolizing both liberty and coercion. Patriotic or anti-patriotic? Your call. The content is smack on the surface, demanding careful description rather than analytical fuss of a sort that is evident in this show's heady title, "Mind / Mirror." Shut up and look.

Take *False Start* (1959), in Philadelphia, a burlesque of Abstract Expressionism with energetic splotches of mostly primary hues bearing stencilled color names that do or don't match. A blue may be labelled "blue," but so may an orange. The almost incidentally beautiful result is a delirium of significations—and it's thrilling. Or *Watchman* (1964), a mostly gray painting with the attached rugged sculpture of a leg and butt cast in wax in an upside-down upholstered wood chair. There's a sense of some engulfing emergency, no less urgent for being entirely obscure. You are roped in at a glance, blessed with heightened intelligence and fraught with nameless anxiety. Arbitrary blocks of red, yellow, and blue assure you that this is a game local to painting, but it resonates boundlessly.

Johns's famous silence about his art's meanings must be our guide. He heroizes for me a remark of the most vatic of the Abstract Expressionists, Barnett Newman—"The history of modern painting, to label it with a phrase, has been the struggle against the catalogue"—even as catalogues swarm him. Johns has faults: at times, he can be a mite precious, though winningly so, or given to complexities that dilute his powers. In past writing, I've complained about those frailties in the face of pious praise of everything from his hand. I guess I wanted him, great as he is, to be greater still. Now, amid his art's abounding glories, I declare unconditional surrender.

His styles are legion—well organized in this show by the curators Scott Rothkopf, in New York, and Carlos Basualdo, in Philadelphia, with contrasts and echoes that forestall a possibility of feeling overwhelmed. Each place tells a complete story. Regarding early work, New York gets most of the Flags and Philadelphia most of the Numbers. Again, looking rules, as in the case of my favorite paintings of Johns's mid-career phase, spectacular variations on color-field abstraction that present allover clusters of diagonal marks—that is, hatchings. These are often misleadingly termed "cross-hatch," even by Johns himself, but the marks never cross. Each bundle has a zone of the picture plane to itself, to keep his designs stretched flat, while they are supercharged by plays of touch and color and sometimes poeticized with piquant titles: *Corpse and Mirror*, for example, or *Scent*.

Make your own Johns show, as I did. There are major paintings among some that are not so hot, along with terrific drawings and prints that belie the common status of those mediums as "minor." Curatorial eccentricities in Philadelphia include the use of a computer program to select prints for display, in rotation, from the museum's immense collection, and a maddening sound element, in that prints section, of John Cage—a formative early influence on Johns, like Marcel Duchamp, both of whose ideas he thoroughly subsumed—droning through some not very good poems that he wrote in response to words of Johns's. The Whitney display would have profited from being two-thirds its size. Johns stumbled a bit in the nineteen-eighties and early nineties, repeating tropes to diminishing reward, though with intermittent tours de force such as the painting *Racing Thoughts* (1983), an omnibus of affections that includes Johns's paintings of the *Mona Lisa* and a work by Newman. Plumbing fixtures hint that the point of view is from within a bathtub. He then recentered himself, triumphantly, in a poetics of death, the most personal of impersonalities.

Many of the later works take surprising cues from art history, as the hatch paintings do from the bedspread pattern in Edvard Munch's masterpiece of his wizened self, *Between the Clock and the Bed* (1940). The show alludes to that and to Johns's further spiritually symbiotic involvements with the Norwegian, notably with several monotypes of a Savarin coffee can filled with used brushes above a skeletal arm. Other raids on art history include the pilferage of a gawky interstitial passage—a shapeless shape—from Matthias Grünewald's ferocious crucifixion scene in the Isenheim Altarpiece (1512–16). You'd never guess the source without being told. It's like Johns to daintily invoke holy rage. His proliferating skulls and skeletons anchor various of his caprices to comic effect: their subjects are dead, as he is not. Johns taunts the Grim Reaper, putting the "fun" in "funereal" and sailing past the mortal irony of his own advanced age. (He is ninety-one.) He savors losing battles. Speaking of which, his series *Farley Breaks Down*, starting in 2014, rends the heart with adaptations of a photograph of a U.S. soldier in Vietnam weeping at the loss of a comrade—a quintessential evocation of an insane war.

Is there an overriding melancholy about Johns's art? Sure. It is instrumental, forbidding sympathy. He's not selling it—with such rare exceptions as *Skin with O'Hara Poem* (1961), part of a series that salutes the poet Frank O'Hara, one of Johns's most valued friends, with black ink directly imprinting the artist's face and hands. Also compelling to me are renderings of a photograph of the dealer Leo Castelli, whose chance discovery of Johns, in 1958, while on a visit to the celebrated Rauschenberg, initiated a whole new art world. I found a small canvas of the image, overlaid with a pale puzzle-piece grid in pastel colors, at the Whitney, desperately moving. I revered Castelli.

Although Johns is regularly embraced by art institutions, he has suffered spells of relative neglect by working artists, I think owing to intimidation. When you go to his art, you can't sensibly hit on ways to get back out. In his tenth decade, he remains, with disarming modesty, contemporary art's philosopher king—the works are simply his responses to this or that type, aspect, or instance of reality. You can perceive his effects on later magnificent painters of occult subjectivity, including the German Gerhard Richter, the Belgian Luc Tuymans, and the Latvian American Vija Celmins. But none can rival his utter originality and inexhaustible range. You keep coming home to him if you care at all about art's relevance to lived experience. The present show obliterates contexts. It is Jasper Johns from top to bottom of what art can do for us, and from wall to wall of needs that we wouldn't have suspected without the startling satisfactions that he provides.

Published in the October 11, 2021, issue of *The New Yorker*, with the headline "Just Look."

"GREATER NEW YORK" CONFIRMS RATHER THAN SURPRISES

What did I expect of "Greater New York," a show of hundreds of works by forty-seven more or less contemporary artists and collectives at MOMA PS1? I know what I fantasized: the discovery of things that creators hereabouts have been up to during a year and a half in pandemic isolation. This was a foolish mistake on my part, ignoring the fact that the survey—the fifth that PS1 has mounted since 2000—was slated to open in 2020 and necessarily postponed. The result, with the exception of a number of up-to-date entries, amounts to something of a time capsule: a collection of judgments that predate a period so tumultuous it feels like an age. One current trend that is represented, albeit scrappily, is neo-Surrealism: the wild subjectivity of artists turning from outer worlds to inner. But the fundamental mood is external, slanted toward politically charged urgencies and the proclivities of eccentric though not quite outsider talents. A consensus is projected that scants aesthetics.

Abundant artists' photographs document half a century of social activism in New York City, starting with Puerto Rican protests in the sixties and brushing up against the Black Lives Matter demonstrations of 2020. Almost a hundred works, in all mediums, were created before the year 2000. Nine of the artists are deceased. The show's chief appeal is an emphasis on foreign-born residents, historically a cynosure of New York as a bubbling rather than a melting pot. There are contributions by people from Egypt, Iran, Tunisia, Nigeria, Japan, Mexico, Argentina, India, and more. There's also a solid contingent of Native American artists. It is all somewhat blurry, however, in view of preoccupations with the more distant past as much as with what was novel a year or so ago.

Much of the show's painting, sculpture, video, and assemblage, while well crafted and often flashy in terms of production values, preaches to art-school and urban-coterie choirs.

The show's gist could use a watchword related to "avant-garde," perhaps whatever the French for "sideways-garde" might be. A curatorial team led by Ruba Katrib has exercised considerable finesse while tending toward a semi-underground orthodoxy. They give pride of place to a gaudy video installation by the Mohawk artist Alan Michelson, the subject of a recent feature story in the *Times*, that laments the historic collapse of the Lenape people's cultivation of oysters in tributaries of the East River. Go oppose that. Who isn't pro-oyster and regretful of the Lenape's displacement? Less overt assumptions of automatic agreement infect even some surreal and abstract works, or so it seemed to me. Am I overreacting? It's possible, as I scan the show's illustrated checklist for examples that I could deplore. There's an ambient restraint despite predominant agitation. What bugs me is a bent that frustrates delectation.

Exactly one artist really enthralled me: the Japanese-born Yuji Agematsu, who, since the mid-nineties, has fashioned tiny sculptures from detritus that he comes across in New York's streets. Three hundred and sixty-six of these, displayed on shelves in twelve plexiglass cases, memorialize as many recent strolls. Typically snugged into the cellophane wrappers of packs of cigarettes the artist has smoked, they are singly—and all together—exquisite, achieving feats of formal and coloristic lyricism by way of used chewing gum, scraps of fabric, metal fragments, feathers, thread, and very much whatnot. The works convey a homing instinct for beauty in the humblest of materials, and in the most democratic of citizenly activities: walking in the city. It's easy to imagine them as monuments, thirty or so feet high, when you lean in to behold them from low angles. There's inarguably a political vibe about Agematsu's activity, but it's one that is subsumed by personal devotion. The suggestion of an underfoot Utopia is here and now, requiring no reformation of other people's attitudes. The works stand in contrast to many in the show that at least seem to toil backward from rote concluding sentiments, to the detriment of unforced pleasure.

A peculiar highlight, harshly disrupting the show's occasional airs of would-be subversion, is a looped hour-long film by the Swedish artist Marie Karlberg, *The Good Terrorist* (2021), derived from a 1985 novel by Doris Lessing. Squatting in a high-rise New York apartment, ultra-left radicals debate planting a bomb, sure to harm innocents, as a way to dramatize their cause. Some are fanatical, others hesitant. We learn toward the end that the bomb has detonated prematurely, killing the woman who was assigned to place it, in addition to some unlucky bystanders. Hysteria erupts at the squat, shattering the radicals' comity. Both the actors and the production are defiantly amateurish in a way that, if you go with it, invests intimacy in a talky script. The characters' discordant emotions sink in, even when appalling. The scenario unfolds casually on the way to seeming nightmarishly plausible. The work is a fable without a moral, evincing Lessing's uncanny comprehension of twisted humanity. The fidelity of Karlberg and her cast to the integrity of the tale rattles and absorbs. How it befits a show marked by decidedly non-homicidal dissatisfactions hangs in the air. You won't forget it, wish as you might to do so.

The political is more important than the artistic. Using art to advance causes isn't bad; it simply surrenders independent initiative, always a fragile affair, to overbearing powers of worldly argument. There's an ethical heft in the sacrifice, shaming mere aestheticism. I can't defend my wish for autonomous experience in the face of concerns that acknowledge the real suffering of real people. But I find myself clinging to instances of creativity that eschew rhetoric. At PS1, some very odd sculptures by the young American Kristi Cavataro stumble toward bliss. Gamily geometric configurations of colorful stained glass are mounted on walls or stand knee-high on the floor. There's a whiff of nostalgia for Art Deco, but the pieces are subject to unprecedented ingenuities of form and mysterious pressures of feeling. Only the artist's desire justifies them.

Full disclosure: this is vaccinated me speaking, art-starved during my ongoing exile from the city since 2019, when my wife and I had to retreat upstate after a fire in our apartment building (still under repair). We thus missed New York's share in the pandemic, its summer of protests, and first-hand contact with fellow-culturati. Now my pent-up craving for gratuitous transcendence disgruntles me at the PS1 show. I want a reëngagement with art history that speaks to personal drives rather than to programmatic discontents. The show's neo-Surrealists and abstractionists are too miscellaneous and hermetic to do more than gesture in a compensatory direction.

Must ideology define us? Can we demur from one extreme without implicitly being lumped in with its opposite? The art world has become an aviary of miners' canaries in this respect; there is a near-certainty, whatever you do, of offending—or, anyway, disappointing—somebody. The PS1 show takes what has seemed the safest position, one that identifies cultural legitimacy with obeisance to supposedly unexceptionable opinions. The introductory text asserts that "we must push against colonial borders and address Indigenous geographies." Who, pray tell, is this mighty "we"? Strong, historically grounded works of authentic complaint by the Seneca artist G. Peter Jemison prove plenty entitled to the first-person plural. Beyond that, however, the curators' presumption of in-group prerogative edits not the panoply of current art but the makeup of its audience. (Don't like it? Get lost.) Can we do better by accepting art's limits as a force in the world?

"Poetry makes nothing happen," W. H. Auden observed, but life without poetry is apt to be pretty bleak. How about basing value in joy and letting agreement and disagreement see to themselves? In the short term, seeking disapproval, as *The Good Terrorist* does, would seem to be the most availing escape hatch to freedom. Only doing things that one is not supposed to do and saying things that one is not supposed to say promise relief from a climate of stagnating sensibility. Being disreputable beckons. Open up. Reinstate surprise.

Published in the October 25, 2021, issue of *The New Yorker*, with the headline "Who's We?"

THE INSURRECTION OF SURREALISM

"Surrealism Beyond Borders," at the Metropolitan Museum, is a huge, deliriously entertaining survey of the transnational spread of a movement that was codified by the poet and polemicist André Breton in 1924, in Paris. It had roots in Dada, which emerged in Zurich, in 1916, in infuriated, tactically clownish reaction to the pointlessly murderous First World War. Most of the show's hundreds of works—and nearly all of the best—date from the next twenty or so years. As you would expect, there's the lobster-topped telephone by Salvador Dalí and the locomotive emerging from a fireplace by René Magritte, both from 1938 and crowd-pleasers to this day, smoothly blending into popular culture. But the show's superb curators, Stephanie D'Alessandro and Matthew Gale, prove that the craze for Surrealism surged like a prairie fire independently in individuals and groups around the world. The tinder was an insurrectionary spirit, disgusted with establishments. Not that the revolt required much personal valor: you couldn't be prosecuted for your dreams. The formula looked easy. There were no rules or hierarchies, despite Breton's efforts to police the ranks. Anyone could play, and for a while many sorts of people did.

The show tracks eruptions in about forty-five countries. Painting and photography dominate, though magazines, texts, and films explore certain scenes, such as a late efflorescence of politically militant turbulence in Chicago in the nineteen-sixties. By then, what had passed for the aesthetic sorcery of the movement had petered out. But it didn't die. Today, there's a surprising revival, unacknowledged at the Met, among younger artists who, like the movement's founders, have turned inward from worldly imperatives to plumb the so-called unconscious, presumably a timelessly real realm that is superior to reason. Sigmund Freud, without meaning to, had inspired the lively delusion that the fracture of rationality (he was plenty rational himself) was a royal road to universal truth, rather than, as often seemed to be the case, a repertory of clichés.

Birds always meant sex for the German Max Ernst, although you can't fail to adore his delicate construction of little figures, *Two Children Are Threatened by a Nightingale* (1924). The vivacity of the movement frequently ran to miniature scale, as with the poetic box constructions of Joseph Cornell, which the American artist began making in the thirties, and to such epiphenomena as the party game exquisite corpse, in which players take turns drawing parts of figures on folded paper and leaving traces of outline for others to continue. The show features an accordion-like version thirty-six feet long that the American poet Ted Joans took along to encounters with cultural luminaries until his death, in 2003.

Surrealism began in literature, though with impetus from the haunting cityscapes that the Italian Giorgio de Chirico had been painting since 1909. It rapidly infected artists worldwide, acting in opposition to arguably bourgeois modernisms including Cubism and Constructivism, albeit cribbing forms from them now and then. The movement was essentially conservative, rejecting engagement with external modernity despite such wishful identification with radical causes as that of a magazine edited by Breton between 1930 and 1933, *Le Surréalisme au Service de la Révolution*. (The Soviet Union would have none of this.) The association persists in the anti-colonial sentiments of several non-European artists. In fact, in addition to being a taste favored by educated élites, Surrealism was colonialist in its own way. Nearly interchangeable dream images popped up everywhere. A doctrinaire rejection of nationalism fostered a sense that the adherents stemmed from nowhere in particular. Surrealism was individualist Romanticism on steroids. I know the magnetism and its limitations well.

I was a Surrealist poet at the age of twenty in 1962, intoxicated but not terribly well informed at my small Midwestern college. Though hobbled by having next to no French, I struggled to translate a section of *Les Chants de Maldoror* (1868–69)—a proto-Surrealist text by the short-lived Uruguayan-born Frenchman Isidore Ducasse, who styled himself the Comte de Lautréamont—in which the hero joins a female shark in slaughtering seaborne rivals and then has rapturous sex with her. Extravagant grotesquerie in many flavors was all the rage. Evil excited certain Surrealists who, for instance, celebrated the predatory libertinism of the Marquis de Sade. (I quailed at that.) Breton's 1928 novel, *Nadja*, about his brief affair with a young, waiflike possible clairvoyant, was Biblical to me; I failed to register that Breton's attitude toward the girl was exploitative. He stepped away when she received a diagnosis of clinical insanity.

For me, much of the movement's allure involved glamorized maleness, with the likes of the poets Paul Éluard, Robert Desnos, and close to a dozen others modelling a sexy cool in which I was sorely deficient. Marcel Duchamp and Man Ray figured as genius associates, and the darkling anthropologist and philosopher Georges Bataille provided intellectual ballast laced with pornography. Women were sex objects or muses, with rare exceptions such as the British-born Mexican Leonora Carrington, the German Meret Oppenheim, the American Dorothea Tanning, and the infallibly amazing Frida Kahlo. Breton, no slouch as a critic and in this instance just mildly sexist, termed Kahlo's typical self-portrait "a ribbon around a bomb."

I missed the fact that, by the time I stumbled across it, Surrealism was out of date from a Western point of view, its influence having been plowed under by formally rigorous painters like Joan Miró and Arshile Gorky, who are in the show, and, decisively, Jackson Pollock, who is not, and by laconic poets like John Ashbery and Frank O'Hara. It dawned on me that Pablo Picasso had, from the start, made the very most of Surrealism's Dionysian audacity by combining it with his own Apollonian aplomb: one-stop shopping in erotic and perceptual revelation. After I fled East by stages and, in 1964–65, spent a disillusioning year in Paris, I became embarrassed by the longueurs of latter-day Surrealists. I think I can trace an aspect of my style to prior exercises in the Surrealist shibboleth of unguided "automatic writing," hellbent on insulting the commonplace. It didn't have to make sense. Maybe best if it didn't. But I came around to concluding that the conscious mind, that flickering spark in cosmic obscurity, is the indispensable site of mysteries that matter.

The rest is charm, which abounds at the Met with particular élan from the border-crossing variants headlined by the show. Divisions into multinational cohorts, organized by theme, constitute a world tour with local nuances that modify a collective fervor. The variety of discoveries, detailed with exceptional scholarship in a ravishing keeper of a catalogue, defeat generalization, with such one-off, tonic shocks, new to me, as a hyperactive tangle of abstract shapes, *Baton Blows* (1937), by the French-Egyptian Mayo; *The Sea* (1929), a fantasia by the Japanese Koga Harue that displays, among other things, a bathing beauty, a zeppelin, many swimming fish, and a flayed submarine; and *Untitled* (1967), a weaponized throng of human and animal faces and figures, by the Mozambican Malangatana Ngwenya. Certainly, the show's range satisfies an aim to pry the movement's history from the grip of its would-be Mecca in Paris, where Breton devolved into a parochial tyrant whose powers of excommunication could descend without mercy even on Alberto Giacometti, in 1935, after the greatest of related sculptors dared to essay some relatively objective figuration.

It's rare to have a conscientiously ordered overview teem with unfamiliar seductive delights, like a suite of uncanny photographs mostly of enigmatic women outdoors, from 1958, by the Colombian Cecilia Porras. The perspective applied to twentieth-century art will stay with you, as a standing challenge to modern art's dominant march of formal avant-gardes. Man Ray idealized original art as "a creation motivated by desire." That, for me, is the keynote of Surrealism, which was dedicated to anarchic motives that brooked no institutional authority. Each work is a jailbreak, successful or not, from a civilization that could be held responsible for spirit-crushing conformity and, in the annals of war and injustice, systemic lunacy. In the end, Surrealism came down to gamy incoherence. But its gospel of liberty encourages a rethink, even now, of what cultural adventure is all about.

Published in the November 1, 2021, issue of *The New Yorker*, with the headline "Far Out."

CHOOSE YOUR OWN KANDINSKY ADVENTURE AT THE GUGGENHEIM

Choose a direction for your perusal of "Vasily Kandinsky: Around the Circle," a retrospective that lines the upper three-fifths of the Guggenheim Museum's ramp with some eighty paintings, drawings, and woodcuts by the Russian hierophant of abstraction, who died in France in 1944, at the age of seventy-seven. The show's curator, Megan Fontanella, recommends starting at the bottom, with the overwrought works of the artist's final phase, and proceeding upward, back to the simpler Expressionist landscapes and horsemen of his early career. This course is canny in terms of your enjoyment, which increases as you go. The teeming complexities of the enigmatic glyphs and contradictory techniques that mark Kandinsky's late phase defeat my comprehension: they are numbingly hermetic. A middle range, from about 1910 to the early twenties, seethes with the artist's excitement as he abandons figuration to let freely brushed, spontaneously symphonic forms, intended as visual equivalents of music, enthrall on their own. He became a devoted fan and friend of the atonal composer Arnold Schoenberg.

Finally—that is, primarily—we are engulfed in cadenzas of hue that have come to impress me as the strongest art of their kind and their time, relatively crude but more vigorous than the contemporaneous feats of Matisse, Derain, Braque, and other Parisians whose Fauvism anchors standard accounts of modernism. There's much to be said for Der Blaue Reiter—a movement, centered in Munich, where Kandinsky had moved to study art, and which shares a name with one of his paintings, from 1903. It enlisted such colleagues of Kandinsky's as Franz Marc and Alexei Jawlensky in the project of rendering nature with chromatic audacities.

Seen from the bottom up, the show progressively dispenses with arid affectation on the way to freshets of inspiration. I took it from the top, beginning in joy and ending in downbeat perplexity, then returned upward to assess what had happened to a visionary who had been onto something epochal.

Kandinsky was right on time when he published the eloquent book *On the Spiritual in Art*, in 1911. It called for artists to reject materialism—a soul-crushing evil—in favor of, ideally, a worldwide spiritual awakening. He graphed artistic intention as a triangle with gross materiality at the bottom and perfect transcendence, true to inward experience, at the peak. He located previous artists at points in the ascent. His exhortation bore fruit in subsequent work that included the Orphism of the French painter Robert Delaunay, for one, who was shown with him in the vastly influential 1913 Armory Show, in New York. However, the drive for enlightenment would ultimately fall prey to self-seductions that led Kandinsky up desultory paths.

Kandinsky was born in Moscow in 1866. The son of a prosperous tea merchant, he moved to Odessa as a child, and then returned to Moscow to study law and economics. Smitten with a haystack painting by Monet and an intuition, from Richard Wagner's opera *Lohengrin*, of synesthesia—sounds seen, colors heard—he began to paint, with a bang, at the age of thirty, on folkloric themes that were infused with the quasi-religious tenets of Theosophy. As he would write in the 1911 book, "Color is the keyboard. The eye is the hammer, while the soul is a piano of many strings. The artist is the hand through which the medium of different keys causes the human soul to vibrate." His initial variations on nature gave way to spontaneous gestures and energized shards of geometric form. Some intoxicating breakthrough paintings include *Black Lines* and *Light Picture* (both from December, 1913), which stage dances of liberated line atop passages of effulgent color.

Kandinsky hit on a symbiosis of mysticism and geometry that had affected religious traditions (the European Gothic, the Indian tantra) since well before its ancient Greek codification, notably by Pythagoras:

a force field in which the least rational of entities, the soul, meshes with the utter rationality of mathematical design—the latter subliminal but still present in Kandinsky's brushy manner. The conjunction had never before been consistently addressed in fine art. And Kandinsky wasn't alone in seizing on it in the early years of the twentieth century, as a wildly and justly popular show in 2018, also at the Guggenheim, of the all but unknown (partly because she was secretive, surely because she was female) Swedish painter Hilma af Klint (1862–1944) proved. Af Klint, for those keeping score, seems to have beaten Kandinsky to the punch of modern abstraction by five years. She did so most dramatically with a suite of huge, stunning floral and geometric paintings, begun in 1906, whose genesis she attributed to dictation from named supernatural beings.

Kandinsky was no Spiritualist of af Klint's table-rapping-séance type, but he shared an affinity for the occult which was rife among otherwise levelheaded intelligentsia before the First World War. Kandinsky held back from the ghostlier variants of Spiritualism but was in key with the anti-worldly tendencies of a period that has long embarrassed art historians. Many still skate past the mystic roots of the formally reductive painters Piet Mondrian and Kazimir Malevich. That scanted tradition is up for rediscovery. I sense stirrings of a renewed interest in spiritual motives today, primarily among young artists who are fed up with postmodernist irony. If I'm right, I sort of empathize with the urge as a matter of speculative faith, albeit one short of conviction. You can't gainsay results, however peculiar their premises.

Staked to wealth by the inheritance from an uncle of a building in Moscow, in 1901, Kandinsky lit out for a bohemian existence in Germany, abandoning a wife for a partnership with the dashing German painter Gabriele Münter. They travelled widely, including to Tunisia. Kandinsky, determined to counter French aestheticism with modes that were both earthier and less tied to observation, quickly attracted allies and followers. Owing to his classification in Germany as an enemy alien, he returned to Russia at the onset of the First World War and was trapped there by the

Revolution, which expropriated his property, and which he toiled to serve as an educator and an administrator until, with difficulty, he managed to leave, in 1921. He did so with a new wife, Nina Andreevskaya, who may still have been a teen-ager when she married the fifty-year-old Kandinsky, in 1917. He taught at the Bauhaus, where he pursued his commitment to abstraction alongside valued friends and rivals, mainly Paul Klee, who maintained tenuous links to real or imagined reality. After 1933, when the school closed under pressure from the Nazis, the Kandinskys took refuge in Paris. Vasily came to know practically everyone associated with Surrealism and abstract art while solidifying his chief dogma, "inner necessity"—a motive that was his to know and baffling to anyone else. But the impenetrable puzzle of a painting like *Around the Circle* (1940), a riot of heterogeneous whatsit shapes—whimsies, really, adrift in zero gravity—acquired a fashionable sort of prestige, as emblematic of far-out modernity. Didn't get it? That was the point. You weren't supposed to.

The mining heir and mogul Solomon R. Guggenheim met Kandinsky in 1930 and began collecting him in bulk. The two men were connected by a mediocre German painter, Rudolf Bauer, who further ingratiated himself as the boyfriend of Guggenheim's principal adviser, the enthusiastic German baroness Hilla Rebay. (Pastiches by Bauer lurk in the institution's deep storage.) Rebay styled Guggenheim's emerging public profile and the midtown quarters of his collection, the Museum of Non-Objective Painting—a solecism, given that all paintings are objects with subjective content—mounting shows on velour-covered walls and piping in classical music. She merits credit for recommending Frank Lloyd Wright as the architect of the museum's hypermodern whorl, which opened in 1959, though she resigned amid controversy in 1952, three years after Solomon's death. Her devotion to Kandinsky lingers in the ancestral DNA of the museum. Even absent works by Kandinsky, his equivocal majesty haunts every visit to a building that cannot cease to amaze.

Published in the November 15, 2021, issue of *The New Yorker*, with the headline "Anti-Material."

SOPHIE TAEUBER-ARP'S CRAFTING OF ABSTRACTION

My first-ever solid take on Sophie Taeuber-Arp, the subject of a wonderful retrospective at the Museum of Modern Art, occurred nine years ago, by way of a survey, also at MOMA, of the genesis of abstract art, circa 1910–25. Until then, I had regarded the Swiss virtuoso of many crafts lightly. But on that occasion, which featured such heavy hitters of the aesthetic revolution as Kandinsky, Mondrian, and Malevich, I kept coming back to a smallish wool embroidery of rectangular forms, *Vertical-Horizontal Composition* (1916), by Taeuber-Arp. Beautiful, utterly assured, and ineffably heartfelt, it made the artist's associates, nearly all male, seem relative louts, worked up about innovations that were a breeze for her. That the medium was "woman's work" by the standards of the time added to my startlement, upending the lazy pejorative. No doubt feminism's revaluing of historic values had sensitized me. Good is good whether accomplished with a brush or with a needle.

Now here the embroidery is again, like an old friend, in "Sophie Taeuber-Arp: Living Abstraction." The show tracks the artist's multifarious achievements, under the radar of ruling styles, until her death, in 1943, when she was fifty-three years old. The work's nubbly, asymmetrically structured bars and swatches in white, black, red, blue, gray, and two browns generate a seemingly effortless majesty. The execution secretes bits of fun that I hadn't noticed before: a minuscule, eccentric off-colored shape in a brown field; an almost imperceptible checkerboard pattern of alternating horizontal and vertical stitches in a black area (prophetic of the black-on-black paintings of Ad Reinhardt); and a small lump of congested yarn that would seem to be a flaw if it did not so candidly emphasize the work's tactility. No matter how committed she could be to geometric order, Taeuber-Arp communicated her freedom.

Sophie Taeuber was the fourth child of a pharmacist father and a mother who ran a linen-goods store in Davos. After her father died, of tuberculosis, when she was two, her mother boarded students at their home in the mostly German-speaking town of Trogen. Taeuber studied fine and applied art at schools in Switzerland and Germany. In 1915, at an art show in Zurich, she met the Alsatian sculptor and poet Arp, who used Jean as his first name in France and Hans everywhere else. They were among the early members of Dada, which centered on a night club in the city, the Cabaret Voltaire, and convened artists and writers in revolt against anything that could be associated with the obscenity of the First World War. Others on the galvanic scene included the Romanian poet Tristan Tzara and the German Hugo Ball. The multitalented, routinely daring Taeuber fit right in.

The Dadaists, deprecating museum-worthy art, devoted their self-defining energies to evenings marked by such high jinks as improvisations of willfully incomprehensible poetry. They conceived of their activities as the termination—a sardonic swan song—of a disgraced Western civilization. Taeuber, elaborately costumed, would dance in a manner that, in 1917, Ball described as "full of spikes and fishbones." Only one blurry photograph documents that phase. Also scantily recorded, with set designs and a few photographs, is her hectic three-act marionette show of 1918, an adaptation of an eighteenth-century commedia-dell'arte play, *King Stag*. The production closed after three performances, amid the perils of that year's deadly flu pandemic. The marionettes survived and are on view at MOMA—astonishingly inventive human, animal, and fantastical figures, such as a several-sword-wielding whirling dervish of a gizmo—in brightly painted, metal-hinged wood. Clips from a speculative re-creation, which was filmed in 1993, stir a longing in the viewer to have attended the original show. You don't *have* to have been there, but what bliss if you were.

Largely inspired by Taeuber's tours de force of design, experiments in nonfigurative art took hold in the Dada circle. Further embroideries and gouaches of hers, also entitled *Vertical-Horizontal Composition*, develop a language of form so fluent that she could seem to have been born to it: intricately balanced, invariably surprising. She extended the mode to involve triangles and then curvilinear or patchy, scattered shapes, all vivacious and, such is the intimacy of her surfaces, begging to be touched. She often detoured from two dimensions, painting wooden heads with irrational abstract patterns, as if cogitating some superior realm of the psyche. Asked by Tzara in 1920 to supply a photograph of her face, she had several taken in which she peeks out, smiling, from behind one of the *Dada Heads*.

Taeuber and Arp married in 1922, and she joined his name to her own. They travelled widely among the hot spots of the European avant-garde before settling in France, in 1929. Her repertoire included some staggeringly labor-intensive beading, which she deployed in jewelry and small purses that she could sell commercially. She also made delicately woven tablecloths that you wouldn't dream of setting a coffee cup on. Her devotion to crafts can seem strategic, allowing her to evade comparison with the big-time fine-art styles of the era—in which, nonetheless, she was fully versed. An inveterate joiner, she enhanced group shows of numerous tendencies, including Surrealism. People liked having her around.

Starting in 1930, Taeuber-Arp concentrated on oil painting. She proved a topnotch contributor to the movements Cercle et Carré and Abstraction-Création—both of which were organized to promote geometric abstraction—at a certain loss of charisma. Another painter. But look closely. She exercised such technical subtleties as building up what appear to be freehand flurries of curling lines with tiny, almost undetectable strokes to give them subliminal physical mass. Whatever she did, including incursions in stained glass and designs for architecture and interior-decoration projects, acquired mystique from how she did it.

In 1940, Taeuber-Arp and Arp fled their home, outside Paris, for the Unoccupied Zone of southern France, shortly before German troops entered the city. The couple contemplated but stalled a possible immigration to the United States (they had visas) before taking refuge back in neutral Switzerland. In January of 1943, Taeuber-Arp spent a night at a friend's house. She lit a woodstove in the guest room but, having inexplicably neglected to open the flue, died in her sleep of carbon-monoxide poisoning. The calamity persists as a rankling hurt.

A friend has suggested to me that the Taeuber-Arp show exemplifies what he calls "the MOMA apology tour." Having promulgated a canon of modernist masters and movements since its earliest days, under the direction of Alfred H. Barr, Jr., in recent years the museum has taken to celebrating past talents and phenomena that it once consigned, when considering them at all, to marginal status. A concurrent show at the museum, "Joseph E. Yoakum: What I Saw," presents works by a Chicagoan outsider artist who died in 1972. Yoakum began painting at the age of seventy-one, toward the end of an obscure, knockabout life, and was warmly embraced by a cohort of wackily figurative Chicago artists who, flipping off New York influences, dubbed themselves the Hairy Who; they have lately been coming in for recuperative justice themselves. Yoakum's landscapes of sensuously swollen forms, seething with visceral imagination, fill one blank in MOMA's narrative of twentieth-century art.

But Taeuber-Arp's case goes beyond a gesture of belated catholicity. Her elevation revises what is understood as "major" in modern art. Far from incidental in her epoch, she was integral to the wholesale expansion of what art could be and how it could alter the world at large. The show recasts assumptions of value that were long held hostage to hierarchies of medium and that were dominated, with rare exceptions, by men. The story it tells liberates thinking about what has mattered—and still does, and henceforth will—in our cultural annals of consequential genius.

Published in the December 6, 2021, issue of *The New Yorker*, with the headline "A Woman's Work."

WHEN POP CULTURE RAIDS ART – AND THE REVERSE

What explains the lasting wonderment of French rococo, the theatrically frivolous, flauntingly costly mode in art, ceramics, furniture, décor, and fashion that flourished in mid-eighteenth-century aristocratic circles before, having gradually given way to sober neoclassicism, being squelched utterly by the Revolution of 1789? And why did that bedazzling visual repertoire recur in twentieth-century America as a species of imitation art—kitsch, in a word, although managed with undoubtable genius—in animated films branded by Walt Disney? "Inspiring Walt Disney: The Animation of French Decorative Arts," a fun show at the Metropolitan Museum, answers the question by conjoining the pleasures of authentically froufrou historical objects, mostly from the museum's collection, with their style's application in production drawings and video clips from Disney movies. The films include an early short, from 1934, called *The China Shop,* in which porcelain figurines have come to life and are prettily dancing minuets; two classics of the nineteen-fifties, *Cinderella*, released at the beginning of the decade, and *Sleeping Beauty*, which came out at the end of it; and, forming the pièce de résistance, an extravaganza in which atavistic pottery and candlesticks and clocks athletically celebrate a romance for their owner in *Beauty and the Beast*, from 1991.

Walt Disney himself had admired the look from early on—as witness amateur footage in the show of him with his family prowling Versailles in 1935—and he came, shrewdly, to grasp its viability for his coming revolution in popular culture. At the age of twenty, in 1922, Disney had founded a studio called Laugh-O-Gram Films, in Kansas City, with aid from the artist Ub Iwerks. It soon went bankrupt. Within a year, he started up again in Los Angeles. Brief comic animations that came to star Mickey Mouse, who first appeared in 1928, and the growing cast of the amiable rodent's animal pals delighted moviegoers worldwide. But Disney aspired beyond that rudimentary success and began to produce feature-length narratives of folklore provenance, often with grippingly sinister elements. I believe that his breakthrough in this regard, *Snow White and the Seven Dwarfs* (1937), was the first movie I ever saw. I was told that I screamed at the first appearance of the witch-queen and kept it up until my removal from the theatre. (And don't get me started on the trauma, shared with other former tykes of my generation, of the killed-off mother in *Bambi*, from my birth year of 1942.) The Germanic source and pictured artifacts of *Snow White* would eventually be displaced by more reassuring enchantments of French origin, with an instinct that was sagely politic.

Disney steered his studio to exploit rococo's gratuitous swank, emulating the feckless hedonism of the court of Louis XV while chastely suppressing its frequent eroticism. The language of antic curlicues, increasingly abstracted from film to film, blended smoothly into the insouciance of Disney's fairyland fantasies: escapist worlds, complete in themselves. Though thoroughly secular, like his nostalgic evocations of circa-1900 America, the pastiche has something churchy about it. Under the pretense of entertaining children (if childless, borrow one), I have enjoyed visits to the consummately engineered Disneyland and Walt Disney World while noting a peculiar solemnity in their transports of innocence. The impunity of a justly doomed French regime (not our problem!) translated perfectly to fabricated realms that are carefully alien to anyone's troubling reality. Cinderella's castle, at Disney World, is modelled on Versailles, among other French châteaux. Centering Disneyland is a materialization of a related, crowning folly, the mad German king Ludwig II's fantastical Neuschwanstein Castle (1868–92), which Disney adopted as the template for his studio's logo. Nightly, Tinker Bell descends on a wire from its peak.

The Met show is replete with demonstrations of wizardly animation techniques, pre-digitally antique now, that take a viewer from sketch to cel to excerpted film. Notably transfixing is a pencilled sequence of the Beast's physical transformation—airborne, cyclonic, a claw becoming a hand—into a dashing prince in the 1991 movie. But the keynote is industrial. A few eccentricities briefly beguiled Disney, such as gloomily stylized settings for *Sleeping Beauty*, by one Eyvind Earle, which distressed some fellow-animators with backgrounds that distracted from their characters. More typically, Disney subsumed the talents of his crews within uniformly anodyne schemas, where they register, if at all, like bumps under a blanket.

The sameness of calculation wearies after a while. This redounds to the comparative advantage of such juxtaposed French authenticities as a Sèvres vase, made in 1758, with handles in the shape of elephant heads. Sconces make a very big deal of hoisting candles aloft, and furniture hardware ennobles the act of opening drawers. In no milieu before or since have accoutrements of daily life, for those who could glory in affording them, been so systemically saturated with beauty. Rococo design complemented figurative, architectural, and vegetal allusions with gorgeously lapidary patterning, slipping between representation and abstraction in ways that, as we experience them, are a joy forever.

Stylistic excess, wretched or otherwise, comes and goes in art history, almost always in periods of complacent political stability. This is no paradox. Worldly crisis tends to foster disciplined expression. Relative tranquillity tasks artists with reminding people, for their amusement, if not as a moral caution, of the ineluctable chaos of human nature. The show, as organized by Wolf Burchard, who oversees British decorative art at the museum, adduces prior examples of determinedly over-the-top seductiveness as old as an early-sixteenth-century, amorous tapestry, *Shepherd and Shepherdess Making Music*, that was probably designed in France and woven in the southern Netherlands. Disney and his staff funnelled centuries of serious artistic precedent into their rote stylings.

Flowing out, the results were—and remain—fleetingly delectable mush.

Before seeing the show, I'd had misgivings about the august Met's hosting of what boded to be cynically corny corporate artifice. These faded, so engaging is the installation—and far be it from me to snoot a dreamy concept rendering, by the designer Mary Blair, of Cinderella's pumpkin carriage—but the qualms reinfected me in the end. While we have grown used to crossovers of "high" and "low" in contemporary taste, the difference isn't meaningless when any use of the past not only sterilizes its original import but makes a fetish of doing so. The payoff is diverting and may seem funny. But it lacks fundamental humor, which can't do without at least a whisper of irony. We aren't party to the Disney creative sorcery but only passive consumers of it. More humanly complex long-form animation arrived with the ongoing triumphs of Pixar, which the Walt Disney Company had the timely wit, in 2006, to acquire from Steve Jobs as a subsidiary.

How come I had never before now heard of the commercial poster designer E. McKnight Kauffer, the subject of a startlingly spectacular show, "Underground Modernist," at the Cooper Hewitt, the Smithsonian Design Museum? I guess it's because I'm used to tracking raids by art on popular culture but less so the other way around. Kauffer, who died in 1954, was a magus of boundless resourcefulness in the nineteen-twenties and thirties. With assistance from his second wife, Marion V. Dorn, a master of fabric design who survived him by ten years, he mined—and evangelized for—adventurous aesthetics to change the street-level look of cities, invigorate book-cover design, and inflect theatre sets and interior decoration. He insisted on working directly with clients, intent on persuading them to take risks in far-out geometric and surreally contorted imagery. His influence proved so infectious that it was swallowed up by successive generations in a profession whose manufacture is inherently ephemeral.

Starting as a restless lad from Montana, where he was born, in 1890, the then named Edward Kauffer spent his childhood in Evansville,

Indiana. He dropped out of school at twelve or thirteen with aspirations to paint and, while still a teen-ager, went West, working odd jobs—bouncing from a travelling theatre company to a fruit ranch. Then, in San Francisco, he began an education in advanced art while working at a bookstore. His work caught the attention of a regular customer, Joseph E. McKnight, who so believed in Kauffer's abilities that he offered to sponsor the young artist's studies in Paris. Kauffer altered his name in homage to his benefactor. He furthered his schooling in Chicago (where he was exposed to the avant-garde marvels of the 1913 Armory Show, after its New York unveiling), and then Munich, before arriving in Paris. Based in England from 1915 to 1940, he became a live-wire cosmopolitan. A vast chart spanning a wall of the Cooper Hewitt show amounts to a name-drop constellation, with lines of association that radiate from a portrayal of his handsome face to the likes of, among other starry personages, Alfred Hitchcock, T. S. Eliot, Aldous Huxley, Wyndham Lewis, Virginia Woolf, Langston Hughes, Man Ray, and Sir Kenneth Clark.

Another factor obscuring Kauffer's reputation is his practically exotic integrity, public-spirited in service to civic and political causes and holding that a proper designer "must remain an artist." Working mainly with small agencies, though winning commissions including the creation of some hundred and twenty-five posters for the London Underground, he denounced, in a lecture at New York's Museum of Modern Art in 1948, the recourse of the dominant firms to the "usual methods of appeal through sex, snobbism, fear and corruptive sentimentality." Never settling on a signature style, he said that his criteria for posters were "attraction, interest, and stimulation," deeming "no means too arbitrary or too classical"—Apollonian values.

Moving with Dorn to New York in 1940, he had intermittent success with campaigns for such businesses as American Airlines and with distinctive cover designs for modern classics published by Alfred A. Knopf, Random House, and Pantheon, including James Joyce's *Ulysses* (the fat white "U" and the skinny blue "l," both radically elongated, seize attention) and Ralph Ellison's *Invisible Man* (a shadowed face crossed by white lines and granted one staring eye). But he suffered declines in both his health and his productiveness. He never felt at home in his native land, he said. Sorely missing his overseas friends, estranged from Dorn, and alcoholic, he came to a sad end. Even then, his prestige among colleagues who had known his work lived on long afterward. You will see why if you attend this show.

Published in the December 27, 2021, issue of *The New Yorker*, with the headline "Pleasure Principles."

THE UNCANNY IMPACT OF CHARLES RAY'S SCULPTURES

"Charles Ray: Figure Ground," at the Metropolitan Museum, is a succinct retrospective of nineteen works from the more than five-decade-long career of America's most enthralling contemporary sculptor. Ray is an artistic and philosophical provocateur whose ever-startling creations look back in spirit, if rarely in appearance, to the sublimity of ancient Greek art. Labor-intensive recent works—often figurative pieces that he develops in clay before they are machined from single blocks of aluminum or stainless steel, or carved in solid cypress by Japanese woodworkers under his direction—rivet and bemuse. Take *Mime* (2014), a life-size aluminum representation of an eponymous male performer lying supine on a cot and, with eyes closed, pretending (one may assume) to be asleep or dead. The work isn't a description. It's a thing, splitting a stylistic difference between realism and abstraction. Just to begin comprehending it you must walk around to absorb, from several angles, aspects of its resistantly gleaming, reflective surface.

"Space is the sculptor's primary medium," Ray once said. The point is emphasized at the Met by the dispersal of individual pieces in two cavernous rooms. The prevalent emptiness becomes an aesthetic stimulus in itself, as you wander the installation. Each item, sampling Ray's multifarious subjects and means, scores a discrete shock. *Family Romance* (1993), in painted fibreglass and synthetic hair, depicts a dad, a mom, a young son, and a toddler daughter, lined up with hands joined. All are naked and exactly the same height, scaled to the average stature of a child eight or so years old. The piece is fraught with inexplicable emotion and, once seen, apt to take up permanent residence in your memory.

Family Romance stands in for other works, not in the show, with which Ray has returned to the vulnerabilities and fascinations of boyhood—sometimes uncannily Oedipal in implication. *The New Beetle* (2006), in white-painted steel, portrays a nude boy who is transfixed as he plays with a large toy car, likely fancying himself grownup and masterly. Reversing that power dynamic, *Father Figure* (2007) is an intimidatingly colossal derivation, in solid steel painted green, black, and silver, of an antique toy farm tractor with a beefy bloke at the wheel. It weighs eighteen and a half tons.

Ray was born in 1953, in Chicago, to parents who ran a commercial-art school. Studying at the University of Iowa and at Rutgers University, he was inspired by the formalist mode in assembled abstract sculpture which was prominent then, practiced most notably by the British artist Anthony Caro. Around the same time, Ray was alert to emergent trends in post-minimalist performance art. He added the human body to his materials, starting with the one that he occupied. Photographs in the Met show, taken in 1973, find him, hippie-haired, held aloft against a studio wall by a leaning wooden plank from which he passively dangles, bent at his waist or his knees. The effect is at once borderline hilarious and eerily elegant: truly sculptural, albeit temporary.

Ray continued to pursue gamy self-portraiture, always enigmatic, as when he modified a commercial male mannequin by inserting a sculpted set of his own genitals. He designed clothes for other mannequins, which, mostly larger than life, he acquired or fabricated: somewhat terrifyingly imperious businesswomen, for example, or, as in the show, a fatuously beaming boy in cute suspender shorts. (Does this 1992 piece, *Boy*, enact mockery or self-mockery? Both, I reckon.) Along the way, Ray veered for a spell into abstracted still-life. The plexiglass top of *Table* (1990) and its visually continuous supported objects in clear acrylic, lacking bottoms, generate a dizzying oneness of space and light.

Early on, Ray could seem a merry misanthrope, with a baited animus that, as I think back, puts me in mind of Voltaire, say: attractive in tone, mordant in payoff. The first work by Ray that I ever encountered, thirty-some years ago, at an out-of-the-way Los Angeles gallery, is not in the show. It looked to be a midsize minimalist cube painted with glossy black enamel. Don't touch art works? Really, don't. Likely oblivious of the title, *Ink Box* (1986), some miscreant viewers had discovered the hard way that the cube's top was brimful of printer's ink, one of the world's filthiest substances. When I visited the gallery, its white walls were streaked with the hysterical smears of soiled fingers.

The Met show features another Ray booby trap from that period, *Rotating Circle* (1988), which appears to be a circle drawn on a wall but is the edge of an embedded disk that, motorized, spins imperceptibly at a fantastic speed. Touch that and your fingertip would have cause for complaint. When I first saw the piece, at a Whitney Biennial, I furtively experimented with cellophane from a cigarette pack: *brrrp!*

Many if not most ambitious young creative folk bear the world a grudge for having failed to note their genius from the get-go. Ray's tyro aggressiveness certainly signalled an impatience to make an immediate mark—or dent—in art history. The attitude soon stabilized as a principled boldness, impelling him to do things that were spectacularly hard to pull off and predictable only in triggering surprises.

These have included *Hinoki* (2007), which is modelled on an immense, hollow, drastically rotted oak log, more than thirty feet long, that Ray came across near a rural roadside. Ray has said that it took some ten years of concerted toil to yield a fanatically faithful cypress effigy. Why? More to the point, why not? All art-making is gratuitous. *Hinoki*, owned by the Art Institute of Chicago and not present at the Met, essentializes passionate uselessness—something you would have to do only because you had thought of it and then need never do again—for its own daft sake, and, by the by, looks terrific.

Ray has risked controversy in recent years with two monumental stainless-steel renditions of incidents from *Adventures of Huckleberry Finn*, Mark Twain's classic tale of the pre-Civil War South. The Whitney

Museum had commissioned *Huck and Jim* (2014) as a sculpture for its plaza. The figures are nude. The runaway boy bends to scoop something, not represented, from the ground. (The piece was initially conceived as a fountain, with the figures in shallow water and the unseen element a sculpted bunch of frog's eggs.) The adult fugitive slave stands behind him, watchfully gazing into the distance and extending a hand palm down in a gesture that, hovering above Huck, seems protective. Homoerotic, too? Your call.

Sarah Williams (2021) finds Jim clothed and kneeling behind a standing Huck, but only to fashion the boy's expedient disguise as a girl to research home-town opinions of his delinquency. The pose ironizes a trope of master and servant. Jim is in charge. Both works reek of ambiguity, reflecting on a nation that was, as it remains, riddled with racism. Twain's fable of a redemptive bond, at once antic and desperately moving, didn't let either himself or his readers off the hook of that entrenched obscenity. (The contrary, rather.) Nor does Ray when it comes to both himself and the sculptures' viewers.

Fears of protest, perhaps as reactive to Twain's novel as to Ray's emulative audacity, aborted the Whitney's plan for *Huck and Jim*. A version of the piece, waterless and white, débuted, indoors, at the Art Institute of Chicago, in 2015. Such, now, is a peril in American art of any racial symbolism, unless managed to authentic ends by certain Black artists. Still a formalist at root, Ray has cruised for a bruising when, however tactfully, he touches on social relevance. I would not have imagined him going too far in that vein, but one work in the show troubles me: *Archangel* (2021), a huge wooden carving identified as Gabriel—revered alike in Jewish, Christian, and Muslim religious lore—appearing to alight from Heaven.

Ray says that he updated the seraph, sensuously handsome and clothed only in rolled-up jeans and flip-flops, in response to terrorist atrocities in France, such as the *Charlie Hebdo* massacre, in 2015. Though beautiful, the result strikes me as well-meaning to a fault—we-are-the-world sentimental, unlike the cryptic embodiments of Huck and Jim.

Who is Ray, or any one person, to presume a universally healing mission in torturously complicated times? I hope that *Archangel* proves to be a passing tour de force among a tremendous artist's disciplined sallies, reliably multivalent in meaning, across aesthetic and thematic frontiers that, but for him, we wouldn't know existed.

Published in the February 14 & 21, 2022, issue of *The New Yorker*, with the headline "Shocks of the Sublime."

THE DAZZLING PORTRAITURE OF HOLBEIN

There's a new old painter in town: Hans Holbein the Younger, the dazzling Renaissance German specialist in portraiture, with his first major American show of paintings, "Holbein: Capturing Character," at the Morgan Library & Museum. It has been a long wait since 1543, when the artist died, at about the age of forty-five (his birth year is uncertain), probably of the plague, while in service to England's Henry VIII. Why? Holbein is an awkward fit in art history—overqualified, in a way, for the sixteenth century's march of eclectic Mannerist styles toward the aesthetic revolution of the Baroque. He is familiar hereabouts mainly from two portraits in the Frick Collection: *Sir Thomas More* (1527), a hands-down masterpiece of the great humanist whom Henry had recently appointed the Chancellor of the Duchy of Lancaster and would soon elevate to Lord High Chancellor of England, and *Thomas Cromwell* (1532–33), a rather sullen depiction of the King's chief power broker. (The More is in the Morgan show; the Cromwell isn't.) That both men would have their heads lopped off to Henry's satisfaction—More's in 1535, for objecting to Henry's religious policies, and Cromwell's in 1540, on rumored suspicions that he was plotting to usurp the throne—is an incidental piquancy. Those were treacherous times, fomented by Martin Luther's theological revolt, beginning in 1517, against the universal sway of Roman Catholicism in Europe and racked by sporadic, bloody warfare.

You can't deduce much about the period's upheavals, except obliquely, from Holbein's career as a hired-gun celebrant of whoever employed him, most decisively Henry. Holbein can appear ideological only by glancing association with Christian humanists in the circle of Erasmus of Rotterdam, the illegitimate son of a priest and a towering intellectual who strove to refine rather than to upend Catholic doctrine and bitterly contested the more radical Luther. Testifying to flexible convictions, the Morgan show includes a rondel painting by Holbein, circa 1532, of Erasmus's thin-faced, pointy-nosed mien, and also a small portrayal, circa 1535, of Luther's most efficacious disciple, Philipp Melanchthon. Holbein left no telltale writings and evinced no view of Henry VIII's rupture with Rome and his founding of the Church of England, with himself as its "Supreme Head," in the aftermath of Pope Clement VII's refusal to annul his first marriage, to Catherine of Aragon. (It was never a smart move to exasperate Henry.)

Holbein's relation to contemporaneous religious and political trends might have developed in any number of ways after his early years of precocious and remunerative celebrity in the Swiss city of Basel, a thriving center of artistic patronage and publishing. A son of a late-Gothic painter, he had arrived from his native Bavaria while a teen-ager. Tantalizing hints of unfulfilled potential attend much of his tyro work, notably one of the most indelibly shocking images of all time, *The Dead Christ in the Tomb* (1521–22). The painting, measuring a foot high and six and a half feet wide, depicts a gruesomely putrefying corpse that, if unearthed, could present only a sanitation problem. Famously, Dostoyevsky's encounter with the picture, in 1867, shook his Christian faith and obsessed him thereafter, figuring as a philosophical provocation a year or so later in his novel *The Idiot*. (The work is not in the Morgan show, but I will not forget, no matter how hard I try, my own first look, in the Kunstmuseum Basel, at that . . . what? That *thing*.) Of related fascination are *Images of Death*, gleeful woodcuts that Holbein worked on in the fifteen-twenties, which illustrate all manner of personages being interrupted by skeletons: surprise, surprise.

Holbein left Basel for London in 1532, likely impelled by a terror of rampaging iconoclasm—the wholesale destruction of religious imagery and artifacts by overenthusiastic Protestants in the Swiss city. Might Holbein have continued to evolve as, temperamentally, a visual bard of mortality had he stayed? Perhaps. But Basel's formerly open mind had snapped shut. A sepulchral penchant resurfaced, briefly, in *The Ambassadors* (1533), a double full-length portrait of French agents with a horizontal smear across it in white and gray which, when viewed at angles from the sides of the work, resolves into the apparition of a skull. (That marvel hasn't travelled to the Morgan from its home, in Britain's National Gallery.) Such audacities were otherwise quashed in Holbein's supervening duties to phlegmatic patrons. He had already spent two productive years in London between 1526 and 1528, lodging with Thomas More. Among his first commissions on his return were portraits of Hanseatic merchants—contented but hard men (you would dread having one as your father) thrust forward from flattish grounds, often blankly green or blue. Then he became effectively—and soon officially—the premier artist in Henry VIII's court.

Holbein proved very, very good at modernizing the kicked-up realism of Northern Renaissance styles, routinely executed in oils on wood panels, that dated from Jan van Eyck, a century earlier. Consider, and be wowed by, Holbein's renderings of skin, reminiscent of Hans Memling: aglow with light that can appear, ambiguously, either to fall upon or to radiate from within a subject, if not somehow both at once. His virtuosity with fabrics and heraldic ornament stuns, preternaturally. Holbein abridged Netherlandish portraiture's typically fancy compositions by centering his sitters, either more or less head on or in closeup profile. The Morgan show's proposition that Holbein "captured character" seems a bit of a stretch. The subjects register more in terms of assigned or attained public distinction than of interior lives. They project secular prestige. But their singular physiognomies go bang at a glance.

The charming subject of the earliest really striking portrait in the show, *A Lady with a Squirrel and a Starling* (circa 1526–28), may have been Anne Lovell, the wealthy wife of a functionary in Henry VIII's court. Holbein was sensitive but cautiously unerotic in picturing women, who are usually sombre. (You get a sense that female vivacity was rarely countenanced.) Forensic analysis has revealed that the pictured animal and bird were added later, probably as requested symbols of the woman's family traditions. Holbein was not averse to pandering. Eventually, he ran into trouble with Henry by overdoing it. Ordered, in 1539, to scout the German Anne of Cleves as a possible next bride for the King, he produced a ravishing likeness. Thereby initially excited, Henry had the consequent marriage annulled in short order. Still, Holbein retained his official position at court.

Are you game for further grisly data? Two other men, subjects of excellent Holbein drawings in the show, would keep appointments with the headsman. We can only wonder about the artist's own fortunes had he survived the three or so years between his demise and Henry's, in 1547. There had been about their situation a strange symbiosis, I feel, of royal tyranny and artistic discipline. A formulaic fealty, enforced by reasonable jitters, seems to me part of what isolates Holbein in comparison with rangier, more historically mainstream peers such as Pontormo and Bronzino, in Medici Florence. Could Holbein have been a greater artist if he'd been granted imaginative license? Maybe and maybe not. He would be different, and we would both know a lot more about him as a man and miss the monumentality of his definitive achievement.

Enriching "Holbein: Capturing Character" are somewhat less strong though rather livelier works by his Netherlandish near-predecessors Jan Gossaert and Quentin Matsys. Those artists demonstrate complexities of busy settings and picture-window deep space that Holbein eliminated from their shared genre. In addition, examples of illustration and decorative design by Holbein and others illumine the varied functions of a sixteenth-century court vocation. The show, despite not being large, immerses us in the creative climate of the time, in this case at its icy English extreme. I came away at once thrilled and frustrated by the legacy of a flabbergasting talent.

Published in the February 28, 2022, issue of *The New Yorker*, with the headline "Head On."

MAKING WAY FOR FAITH RINGGOLD

The most provocative curatorial coup in the Museum of Modern Art's recent series of rehangings of its permanent collection has been the placement of a mural-size painting of an apparent, sanguinary race war, *American People Series #20: Die*, by the veteran American artist and, at times, political activist Faith Ringgold, alongside works by Pablo Picasso. For a museum that had long championed a teleological account of the development of twentieth-century aesthetics, this startled, especially by having the Ringgold displayed near Picasso's touchstone of modernism *Les Demoiselles d'Avignon*, with which the Spaniard introduced plangent allusions to tribal African masks to European art. The two pictures were made exactly sixty years apart: *Demoiselles* in 1907, while Picasso was living in Paris, and *Die* in New York in 1967, a year of eruptive racial and political violence in America.

The Ringgold and the Picasso have cohabited surprisingly well, bracketing a complex civilizational if not stylistic history. Contrasting but similarly terrific energies—clenched in *Demoiselles*, explosive in *Die*—generate meanings that are subtler than their initial shocks imply. The pairing substantiates lately prevalent revisionist considerations of what matters, for what reasons and to what ends, in past and present visual culture. Does the Ringgold hold up? It holds forth, for sure, and you won't forget it as long as you live, nor will you settle, if you're open-minded, on any unambiguous interpretation of what it symbolizes.

On loan from MOMA, *Die* appears in *Faith Ringgold: American People*, an overwhelming six-decade retrospective at the New Museum, which consists of more than a hundred works by an artist, now ninety-one years old, who is sorely overdue for canonical status after a protracted defiance of art-world fashion. First came her stubborn fidelity to figuration in times favoring abstraction, and then her eschewal of Pop and postmodernist irony—as opposed to humor, a wellspring of her creativity. (Those tendencies toward representation and sincerity happen to triumph, retroactively, in the penchant of many younger contemporary artists today.) An intermittently active participation in feminist and identity politics has also caused Ringgold to be embraced in some circles and discounted in others. Both estimations obscure the truth of her personal authenticity and artistic originality, which register powerfully in the New Museum show with effects that can be deeply moving and that feel as fresh as this morning.

I single out *Die*—in which blood-spattered Black and white characters suffer impartially while doing scant depicted harm to one another (a gun and a knife intensify the drama but appear to menace no one in particular)—for the recuperative prominence that it grants Ringgold and because it represents an extreme instance of her forte of truth-telling from a fundamentally humane point of view. The picture's furor is atypical of Ringgold's generally ingratiating narrative and decorative qualities, as witnessed by abundant pieces in the show that incorporate ingeniously quilted, colorful fabric and celebrate Black lives, including her own. Notable are such mixed-media depictions as *Street Story Quilt, Parts I–III: The Accident, the Fire, and the Homecoming* (1985), featuring tenements with distinctive characters in nearly every window and passages of hand-lettered expository and diaristic prose.

As effective a writer as an artist, Ringgold is justly known for elating children's books like *Tar Beach* (1991), which memorializes practical pleasures and inspiriting fantasies of a childhood in Harlem, as remembered from her own. Those infectious volumes, sampled in the show, disdain formulaic sentimentality or exhortation, as do Ringgold's propagandistic works from the sixties and early seventies—posters demanding freedom for Angela Davis, for example, and collages endorsing the Black Panthers. No matter how polemical their purposes, such works employ inventive, elegant designs that are ever more striking as their occasions recede in time. Ringgold has extended some of the poster forms to purely abstract pattern, usually gridded diamond shapes, in paintings that are bordered with quilted, woven, or dangling fabric fringes: sheer delight.

Born in 1930 and raised in a middle-class home in Harlem, Ringgold is a driven, true artist of independent mind. Her mother, the fashion designer Madame Willi Posey, taught her needlework and took her on the first of her museum-haunting trips to Europe. Ringgold has said, "If I had to cite the single artist who inspired me the most, I would name Picasso." She acknowledges his 1937 blockbuster *Guernica* as a particular influence on *Die*. But fandom hasn't prevented her from kidding the master in a suite of big, gorgeous, hilarious canvases, from 1991, that convene women, mostly Black, and occasionally children amid cunning pastiches of famous paintings. As a detail in one of these, Picasso apes a pose from Édouard Manet's *Luncheon on the Grass* while clad only in a hat. Ringgold's irreverence can serve as an equal-opportunity instrument.

Racial causes are a given for Ringgold, but they are nuanced by a wisdom in matters of class, which are often a sticking point for would-be radicals. She has stayed candidly true to her own conditioning in a solidly prosperous family. (The men in *Die* wear ties and the women dresses.) But a special historical value in her evocations of cross-cultural alliances and even friendships is a sensitivity to their endemic tensions. She has testified to the experience of often having been the only—or nearly only—person of color in rooms filled with well-heeled liberal whites who, as written in an introduction to the show's catalogue by the pioneering feminist art critic Lucy R. Lippard, tended to be "merely well-intentioned and hoping for sisterhood." Being politically correct doesn't automatically instill political, let alone interpersonal, savvy. Ringgold was not about to be a token ornament to naïve idealisms.

A profound personal essay in the show's catalogue by Michele Wallace, an important critic and one of Ringgold's two daughters, expertly tracks her mother's full-on mergers of racial content and art history, both African and European. These culminate in such pictorial epics as *We Came to America: The American Collection #1* (1997). Black survivors of a distant, burning slave ship swim in seething waters toward a Black Statue of Liberty who is cradling a Black child. Victimhood is rarely at issue in Ringgold's work, however awful the circumstances; irrepressible vitality always is. A party scene from the same year shows guests of various races at what looks to be a Parisian performance by jazz musicians and, repeated in five dancerly poses, Josephine Baker, who is nude but for a skirt of bananas that has to strike us as demeaning but that also comes off as a teasingly barbed comment on the clueless terms of her Continental celebrity. Baker figures elsewhere as a cheerful odalisque, eloquently emulating a motif from Matisse.

In *The Sunflowers Quilting Bee at Arles: The French Collection Part I, #4* (1991), eight Black women produce schematic sunflower designs while in a field of sunflowers, with the skyline of Arles in the background, as Vincent van Gogh arrives with a superfluous bouquet of the same blooms. Subjects drawn from Ringgold's own complicated family history, three generations on from slavery, are more often upbeat than not. African-styled, stuffed-cloth sculptures of hieratic or comic personages pepper the show. Ringgold doesn't so much elide ethnic boundaries as electrify them. They constitute gifts, to her, of surefire imaginative potency.

I had a moment at the museum of wondering whether some viewers might decide that Ringgold's aesthetic flair and emotional buoyancy, exercised with such independence, vitiate her progressive bona fides. Just another artist after all? Then it sank in that Ringgold's confident peculiarities point toward a vibrant pluralism of minds and hearts within and between divided acculturations. Let everyone speak, with neither rancor nor apology, as what and most significantly who they are. That's a standard liberal hope, of course, against the grain of our incurably churlish country. But Ringgold conveys what it might be like if it came to be fulfilled as a matter of course. "It must needs be that offenses come," Abraham Lincoln acknowledged. Here and there, so may remedial sophistications, which, by making offenses more unbearable in the present, dilute their virulence bit by bit in times ahead.

Published in the March 7, 2022, issue of *The New Yorker*, with the headline "Holding Forth."

THE INFLUENCERS OF THEIR DAY

The word "salon," for a starry convocation of creative types, intelligentsia, and patrons, has never firmly penetrated English. It retains a pair of transatlantic wet feet from the phenomenon's storied annals, chiefly in France, since the eighteenth century. So it was that the all-time most glamorous and consequential American instance, thriving in New York between 1915 and 1920, centered on Europeans in temporary flight from the miseries of the First World War. Their hosts were Walter Arensberg, a Pittsburgh steel heir, and his wife, Louise Stevens, an even wealthier Massachusetts textile-industry legatee. The couple had been thunderstruck by the 1913 Armory Show of international contemporary art, which exposed Americans to Pablo Picasso, Henri Matisse, and, in particular, Marcel Duchamp. Made the previous year, his painting *Nude Descending a Staircase (No. 2)*, a cunning mashup of Cubism and Futurism, with its title hand-lettered along the bottom, was the event's prime sensation: at once insinuating indecency and making it hard to perceive, what with the image's scalloped planes, which a *Times* critic jovially likened to "an explosion in a shingle factory."

The Arensbergs' salon, which convened nightly at their spacious apartment on West Sixty-seventh Street, was supercharged in June, 1915, by the twenty-seven-year-old Duchamp's arrival in New York, where, to his astonishment, he was greeted at the dock by a horde of journalists alert to his notoriety and to the public's appetite for news of exotic foreigners. His charisma concentrated and accelerated a ferment in sophisticated American knowledge, creativity, and taste. How would the modernizing New York art world have evolved had the Arensbergs not existed—or if Duchamp hadn't made his way to their door? Differently, for sure, and with considerably less social synergy. One participant, the rich and flamboyant mondaine Louise Norton (who was soon to be a sometime lover of Duchamp's), proposed a collective credo as "Beauty for the eye, satire for the mind, depravity for the senses!" Attendance was nonexclusive; friends of friends were welcomed.

The Arensbergs nourished local modernist talents (not least with free food and drink) like Charles Demuth, Joseph Stella, Charles Sheeler, John Covert, and, fatefully, Man Ray, who became a boon friend and lifelong ally of Duchamp's on both sides of the Atlantic. Other frequenters included the writer, photographer, and promoter of the Harlem Renaissance Carl Van Vechten; the poets William Carlos Williams and Wallace Stevens; and a remarkable roster of such formidable women as the dance artist Isadora Duncan; the ardent promoter of modern art Katherine S. Dreier; the multitalented British-born radical Mina Loy; the wealthy faux-naïf painter and intentional spinster Florine Stettheimer, along with her two likewise chaste and endearing sisters; the all-around outrageous German proto-performance artist Baroness Elsa von Freytag-Loringhoven; and the rebellious daughter of straitlaced New York socialites named Beatrice Wood.

Wood, while by any canonical measure a lesser figure on the scene, is effectively the protagonist and certainly the most appealing subject of *Spellbound by Marcel: Duchamp, Love, and Art*, a gossipy account of the period by the cultural historian and novelist Ruth Brandon. What is left for a writer to explore about the Arensberg group, which has been anatomized by critics, curators, biographers, and memoirists, especially during recent decades in which Duchamp rose to touchstone status in the legacy of modern art, rivalling Picasso? His cachet has ebbed a bit lately, as new artists, critics, and the art market go big for resurgent painting and sculpture, but there's no shaking off his inception of what amounted to a Copernican revolution in art, from a secure set of disciplines to an unmoored category of anything an artist might say it is.

Brandon's recourse is sex, substantiated by relatively unmined archives of diaries, journals, and letters linking mostly French males to mostly American women. The emphasis may add little to art history, but it contributes a fair amount to what the milieu was like for a shifting cast of characters who, as a self-aware constituency of what we now call influencers, focussed and intensified a transformative Zeitgeist. Glimpses into their romantic entanglements provide a flickering, you-are-there perspective that is more entertaining, at least, than academic analyses of their artistic bents and ramifications.

Wood met Duchamp by chance in 1916, in New York, while on a visit to the hospital room of the French avant-garde composer Edgard Varèse, who was recuperating from a broken foot. (Varèse later married Louise Norton.) Wood had been invited along by a journalist, Alissa Franc, whom, naïvely as it would turn out, she regarded as a loyal friend. Wood was twenty-three and, after two years of studying acting and art in prewar Paris, desperate for a life in the arts, or perhaps for any life not reliant on her hovering parents. Her élan is legendary. James Cameron has said that he based Rose, the heroine of his movie *Titanic*, partly on her. Wood's age, social class, and attitude all fitted the character, although she travelled on more fortunate liners. When I imagine her in a peopled room, she is in Technicolor, and the others, Duchamp included, run to tones of gray.

There is something allegorical as well as touching about Wood's self-willed activities as regards certain haps and mishaps of an American élite that strove to become cosmopolitan by welcoming foreign avant-garde sensibilities to these arguably benighted shores. But her story is more than simply illustrative. Hellbent on breaking free of the expectations of her upbringing, Wood seems to me a singular, wild-card creative personality of the twentieth century.

Duchamp was enchanted but without romantic intent. He introduced Wood to the Arensberg group, where she was an immediate hit. He gave her the use of his studio, which the Arensbergs had rented to him on a promise of first dibs on future works of his. There she made deft, witty drawings undisturbed by the relentless hysterics of her mother, who counted on proper upper-crust matrimony, loathed bohemians, and was only further alarmed by Duchamp's disarming suavity when Wood brought him home for dinner. Poor mom. Whatever she urged upon her daughter, Wood predictably did the opposite. Falling into bed with Duchamp, she later recalled their first encounter, cited in *Duchamp: A Biography*, by Calvin Tomkins, as having come about "in the most natural way. . . . He was gentle in that as he was in everything else." But, for the Arensberg chronicle, the cardinal point is their friendship—the French magus and the gamier avatar of Henry James's Daisy Miller.

Wood posed a problem for Duchamp by falling deeply in love with him. She was hardly alone in this among the women he met throughout his life, but the relationship was complicated by his particular and even avuncular fondness for her and by his shyness of commitments. He successfully engineered a transferal of her affections to a French writer friend who was also in New York, Henri-Pierre Roché, whom Brandon succinctly describes as an "artistic hanger-on and compulsive womanizer" with a recurring interest in the wives and mistresses of other men. Roché and Wood kept daily diaries, yielding abundant grist for Brandon. Duchamp, idolized by both of them, registers as the fulcrum of their affair, exemplifying his impact on the lives and, to varying degrees, the art of the many people whom he amazed.

In New York, Duchamp emerged as the Olympian antihero of modernism whom we salute today. Still, he haunts rather than advances Brandon's narrative, as an unfailingly charming, fun-loving presence, but not as a man so much as a shadowy affect. He grew up in a richly cultured family. Two older brothers became prominent artists: the painter Jacques Villon and the extraordinary sculptor, who died too young, Raymond Duchamp-Villon. A younger sister whom he adored, Suzanne Duchamp-Crotti, also took up art, as a Dadaist in several mediums. Ever cerebral—his strongest subject at school was math, and he delighted in games, puzzles, and ribald humor—Duchamp was educated in art but, after tentative stabs at painting, took no interest in rivalling his brothers. *Nude Descending*, instantly an icon of modernist chic, was one of his last canvases. Renouncing painting as a tired medium that was trivially "retinal," he embarked on startling mind games, notably by presenting common objects as art—"readymades," he dubbed them.

The most famous of those is *Fountain*, an inverted store-bought urinal, crudely signed "R. Mutt 1917," that Duchamp submitted to a show at the Society of Independent Artists. Recent scholarship indicates that he may have got the idea from von Freytag-Loringhoven, who had emigrated from Germany in 1910 and acquired her title from her third marriage. (Later a collaborator and lover of Djuna Barnes, the Baroness had many outré, mostly exhibitionist impulses, such as being filmed by Duchamp and Man Ray shaving her pubic hair.) The *Fountain* that you see at the Museum of Modern Art is not the original, if that designation for an infinitely repeatable jape even counts for anything. Duchamp took no pains to preserve the first iteration. He enjoyed and encouraged the furor that resulted, but said that he expected it to be fleeting, destined for oblivion. He may have been as slow as others were to realize that he had lit a long fuse for concatenating detonations in future artistic and intellectual culture.

Fountain was turned down by the show's organizers despite a stated policy of accepting submissions from anyone, for a fee of six dollars. Among the blackballers was Katherine Dreier, who rued the decision when she learned of the work's author. In 1920, Dreier collaborated with Duchamp and Man Ray in the formation, in New York, of a modernism-evangelizing organization, dubbed the Société Anonyme. Duchamp supported himself, when necessary, by giving French lessons and serving as a private art dealer, primarily in sculptures by Constantin Brancusi that became costly catnip for daring collectors. A growing demand for the far-out and, in Brancusi's case, the transcendently beautiful, capitalized inventory. But the Arensbergs served as Duchamp's default sponsors.

The rejection of *Fountain* confirmed Duchamp's already temperamental disdain for artists' groups. He parodied them, in league with his bosom crony the Cuban French painter Francis Picabia (given to "fast cars, opium, and drink," Brandon writes), by initiating a facetious movement—New York Dada, alluding to the artistic insurrection that had erupted in Zurich in 1916. Never conspicuously serious, Duchamp cultivated a novel tone for art: call it seriously unserious. He had been inspired by the methodical nonsense of the French literary renegade Raymond Roussel, who built lengthy novels and plays around arbitrary puns. Duchamp's modus operandi was to be recognized without being understood—impenetrably deadpan. He required an audience, positing that art works, hazarded by artists, are completed in the perception of viewers. Americans supplied him with something like a focus group for that premise.

Brandon dutifully hits familiar high points of the Arensberg saga. Walter, a likable eccentric, spent his life endeavoring to prove, by way of cryptic codes, that Francis Bacon had written the works of Shakespeare. Louise, musically talented and given to entertaining her guests at the piano but averse to performing in public, was the perfect doyenne for spirited conversation and inevitable dalliances. Duchamp's arcane intellect enthralled Walter. Having bid just too late to acquire *Nude Descending*, he bought it years later from the San Francisco lawyer who had beaten him to the punch. And he didn't miss much of the artist's sporadic later works, as Duchamp almost kept his famous pledge to give up on art altogether in favor of chess (at which he came to rate as a master, short of grandmaster status).

The Arensberg collection was eventually donated to the Philadelphia Museum of Art. The museum also holds the laborious project that preoccupied Duchamp throughout his New York years, *The Bride Stripped Bare by Her Bachelors, Even*—a large, fearsomely recondite standing array of gnomic images in various materials, mainly lead wire between panes of glass. Picabia's wife, the writer Gabrièle Buffet-Picabia, described it as a work in which, without touching one another, "machine organisms have extremely human adventures." Subsequent efforts to interpret the piece, consulting a wealth of enigmatic notes and diagrams that Duchamp made while conceiving it, have roiled scholars ever since. In my experience, it is more to be gawked at than quite relished, but it remains epically unusual.

Beatrice Wood, who was bilingual and a willing diplomat, actively collaborated in New York Dada. In Brandon's book, she glows from a gem of a photograph, sporting a broad-brimmed hat, with Duchamp and Picabia on an outing to Coney Island in 1917. That year, she was listed as an editor, along with Louise Norton and Duchamp, of little magazines advancing the conceit, *The Blind Man* and *Rongwrong*, which were supported by the major photographer, sage art dealer, and champion of all things modern, Alfred Stieglitz. In the second issue of *Blind Man*, Wood defended *Fountain* by penning—or perhaps translating from Duchamp—an immortal witticism: "As for plumbing, that is absurd. The only works of art America has given are plumbing and her bridges." Also in 1917, Duchamp enhanced a drawing by Wood, of a woman bathing, by gluing a bar of soap atop the crotch. Shown publicly, the work precipitated a flurry of satisfying indignation. Outraging or, at least, tantalizing American art folk was like shooting fish in a barrel.

I am not a Marcel Duchamp enthusiast, though I'm forever in awe of his cast of mind and, oh my, his cleverness. His sparse production can't contain him. Ad-hoc ideas that for him were amusing, sneakily hostile, and attended by a stubborn indifference to their meaning, if any, aren't fungible. They evoke a hobby more than a vocation. The practically scientific detachment that was his second nature became a posture for subsequent artists who kept—and still keep—taking cues from him, the most profoundly comprehending of whom has been the protean painter, sculptor, and printmaker Jasper Johns. Others, termed conceptualists, have drawn on his authority for varieties of art that are more or less used up in thinking about them, whatever their material trappings.

I am partial to the retinal. Duchamp's disdain for painting came to be weaponized by university-trained artists and theorists who took being as blind as bats to be a good thing. But give me anything by Matisse—or by Johns, who never subordinates the visual beauty of things to the ideas that inform them—in favor of any readymade, even the most beguiling, such as a dangling snow shovel entitled *In Advance of the Broken Arm* (1915), which Duchamp created during his first winter in New York. Pairing banal objects with poetic captions, he activated polar extremes of objectivity and subjectivity with nothing in the middle. The trope became a standing test case of what is required to qualify anything as "art," which turns out to be no more or less than its acceptance as such by one or another institutional agency—a designated burr under the saddle of traditional connoisseurship.

Members of the Arensberg circle found Duchamp's subversive jeux d'esprit a capital diversion. Their affection for him shines in a jolly painting by Florine Stettheimer, reproduced in Brandon's book, that memorializes a picnic for his thirtieth birthday, in 1917. Everybody is on hand—except Wood. Perhaps still bruised from the humiliating end, the previous year, of her affair with Roché and touchy about the group's knowledge of it, she spent the day at the country home of other friends. Duchamp arrived late, in a red roadster driven by Picabia. He stands alone in the picture, the tall and taciturn cynosure of the occasion.

Duchamp's love life, gamely traced by Brandon before, during, and after the Arensberg days, was low key, bracketed by an unrequited passion for Buffet-Picabia early on and, four decades later, by a consuming affair with Maria Martins, a sculptor and the wife of the Brazilian Ambassador to the United States. That ardor also came to naught, despite his pleas. In between, declaring himself "antimarriage but not antiwomen," he radiated an air of gallant reserve in romance as in art. For a spell, in New York, he came to prefer the company of the Stettheimer sisters and other undemanding older women. His favorite, Ettie Stettheimer, detected loneliness beneath his aplomb: "poor little floating atom," she characterized him, tenderly.

As reported by Brandon in an epilogue to her book, Duchamp married an unprepossessing rich woman in 1927, in Paris, with Picabia as best man. The union reads cynically, as a financial stopgap. It lasted six months. For part of his time in New York, he inhabited an apartment on Fourteenth Street furnished with little more than a chair and a chessboard. His final years were enriched by a mutually happy marriage with Alexina (Teeny) Matisse, the smart, vivacious ex-wife of Henri Matisse's youngest son. Duchamp had taken U.S. citizenship. He and Teeny lived on West Twelfth Street, bordering Greenwich Village. He was hospitable though scarcely informative—a courteous sphinx—to inquisitive callers.

When Duchamp died, in 1968, while visiting a second home in France, he left behind as a parting shot a final magnum opus, on which he had worked in secret for twenty years: *Given: 1. The Waterfall, 2. The Illuminating Gas*. This piece is also in Philadelphia now. You peer through a set of peepholes in a decrepit brick-framed door at a realistically sculpted, legs-spread naked woman without pubic hair, her face not visible, holding a lighted gas lamp aloft as a motorized artificial waterfall pours forth in the background. The work eludes pornography with characteristic sang-froid, evoking sex in a vein that is more forensic than lubricious.

As with his earlier cross-dressings as a female alter ego, Rrose Sélavy—sumptuously photographed by Man Ray—Duchamp's own sexuality could seem as much a readymade for him as any material object. I don't know that this penchant quite comes through in his pair of would-be masterworks, *Bride* and *Given*. They are so strange in so many ways as to paralyze exegesis. Duchamp's popular prestige resides in the bare thought of him, known for being unknowable. His life and his art chase each other around a mulberry bush of bestirred, never satiated curiosity. His reticence inconveniences Brandon's soap-operatic preoccupation with romantic and sexual matters.

We learn more from Brandon than we might like of Henri-Pierre Roché, whose one claim to fame is the novel *Jules et Jim* (1953), about two friends in love with an impulsive woman who, liking them both, resolves the imbroglio by killing herself along with one of the pair. François

Truffaut adapted the book for his ravishing film, in 1962. Brandon debunks an apparently frequent speculation that Roché based the tale on his relations with Wood and Duchamp (which he did set out to recast in a novel, *Victor*, that was left incomplete upon his death, in 1959). In truth, *Jules et Jim* drew on another erotic triangle that involved a German poet friend and, off and on for thirteen years until 1933, the poet's wife. Brandon opines that in each case the prevailing love—if not sexual—interest for Roché was the man.

Roché's liaison with Wood was torrid but short-lived, lasting about two months in 1916. It was corrupted by Roché's regular betrayals with Louise Arensberg, who took license from Walter's concurrent peccadilloes, and with Wood's journalist intimate Alissa Franc, who seems to have harbored a festering envy of her more magnetic friend. Franc dropped hints of the situation to Wood, but it isn't clear how Wood finally wised up. Brandon's documentation of the goings on is so replete, and she is so eager to show it off, that the brief episode dominates *Spellbound by Marcel*. Still, Roché was an avid tourist, and he and Wood made a wondrous toy of the city with such outings as a round trip on the Staten Island Ferry. Dates and places of their assignations cascade.

In 1919, Wood married a Belgian theatre manager in Montreal. She had gone there in pursuit of an acting career that then fizzled. She performed, she said, strictly for money to escape dependence on her parents. The groom turned out to be a bigamist, with a wife and child in Brussels, who repeatedly borrowed from the ever-obliging Arensbergs, behind Wood's back, with lies about an incipient business windfall that concealed his disastrous gambles on the New York Stock Exchange. The already tepid marriage, having been undertaken at least partly because Wood's mother deplored it, was annulled.

Did Wood have snakebit taste in men? Evidently, but in a way that was consistent with her homing instinct for the improbable in all of her life-changing decisions, which ultimately enhanced rather than vitiated her fate. Wood was a vegetarian and neither drank nor smoked. She never had a child. To live freely and yet remain at once autarkic and socially viable was no cinch for a single woman at the time. For Wood, there was the way of the world and then there was her way.

With the war's end, the European expatriates dispersed. After travels that included a nine-month sojourn in Buenos Aires, Duchamp resettled in Paris in 1919. The Arensbergs moved to Hollywood, abandoning an increasingly crowded, commercialized, and, for them, tame New York art world. One of Brandon's epilogues is crowned by Wood's late-life triumph as a celebrated ceramicist. After living for seven years with an English actor named Reginald Pole, who then threw her over for a younger woman, Wood decamped to California in 1928. She was lured there by a zeal for the spiritual doctrines of the Indian-born seer Krishnamurti, who was headquartered in the bohemian haven of Ojai.

In 1933, still casting about for a rewarding occupation, Wood took an adult-education class in ceramics at Hollywood High School. The training blossomed into a substantial career. She perfected a technique of lustrous glazing: forcing salts to the surface by starving kilns of oxygen. She had a solo show at the Metropolitan Museum of Art in 1940. Typical vessels of hers, employing various patinas, include vase forms with ascending multiple swellings, each with its own set of handles. The present market for them, though active, is less than robust, judging by prices—in the mere thousands—that I have found cited online. This signals a lingering, blinkered bias of art collectors against craft mediums. Those things are terrific.

Wood stayed friendly with the others in the Arensberg orbit—even Roché, to whom she sent food packets in Paris during the Second World War and later hosted, with his companion at the time, in California. It was like her not to let emotional wounds, which she absorbed as stinging but salutary life lessons, foster grudges. Invincibly openhearted, she continued to regard the Arensbergs as a second family. A photograph, taken by Wood in 1936, shows Duchamp and the Arensbergs, all at ease in one another's company.

I recall from somewhere an anecdote, unmentioned by Brandon, of a busybody who, after seeing work by Wood, warned a friend of Wood's that she risked an early death from her use of toxic chemicals. Having produced, at the urging of friends, an insouciantly unreliable autobiography, *I Shock Myself*, in 1985, Wood expired thirteen years later, at the age of a hundred and five. She attributed her longevity, she once said, to "young men and chocolate." She never ceased to look girlish. After two gratifying trips to India, she took to turning out in saris, with her long hair plaited. Friends and students flocked to her.

Wood entrances me as the Arensberg circle's most outstanding echt American, other than Man Ray. Her untrammelled appetite for experience complemented Duchamp's strategic hermeticism, to their mutual pleasure. Setting her apart from others in the group was an idiosyncratic rather than a vicarious motive for rising to the bait of a bedazzling newness. Her involvement personalizes developments that are otherwise divided in collective memory between arid art history and fatuous mythologizing. Sometimes the marginal witness to an epoch defines it more vividly than its supposed leading lights. I like thinking about Beatrice Wood.

Published in the March 14, 2022, issue of *The New Yorker*, with the headline "In Orbit."

ART IN A TIME OF WAR

War is the worst evil that people have inflicted upon one another, at costs to themselves, since some hominid discovered the lethal efficacy of rocks. It is waged continually somewhere or other in every generation, furiously now, in Ukraine, and fitfully in the Middle East and Africa. The recurring horror has paused on a global scale—holding its breath, you may feel—only because, post-Hiroshima, nuclear weaponry bodes suicide for the next power to use it. Or so we have thought, and perhaps still think, but with shaken complacency. What never ends is the primordial emotional tug toward organized mayhem, which is playing out, yet again, in Eastern Europe in the face of widespread revulsion. Putin: Monster! But a madman? Diagnosing him as such assumes that sanity is the normative state of people with power.

By an unforeseen coincidence, the Clark Art Institute, in Williamstown, Massachusetts, has opened a show, "As They Saw It: Artists Witnessing War," that consists of archival prints, drawings, and photographs that historicize war's sick seductiveness. The images are displayed chronologically, focussed by turns on the Napoleonic Wars, the Crimean War, the American Civil War, the Siege of Paris in 1870–71, and the First World War. The ensemble is a small, smattery affair that nonetheless concentrates the mind on past, present, and, ineluctably, future calamity. At its core is a slide show of Francisco Goya's eighty intaglio prints, *The Disasters of War* (1810–20). For fear of censorship, the works were first published in 1863, as an album, thirty-five years after the artist's death. The Clark owns a copy.

The *Disasters* are philosophically dire like nothing else in art history. Derived partly from Goya's personal observation of battlefields, they begin soon after the onset of the Peninsular War, launched by Napoleon in 1808 with a misbegotten invasion of Spain, and proceed to gruesome renderings of war-induced famine and subsequent collisions of Royalist and liberal Spanish factions. They include instances of torture that make death seem merciful. Each of the plates zooms in on what the artist deemed an innate human capacity for savagery that never expires, persisting at a simmer in peacetime. What is it like to suffer atrocity and, alternatively, to perpetrate it? Goya generally plays no favorites among the parties to his nightmarish scenarios.

Jumping out at me is the twelfth plate, captioned "This is what you were born for," in which a man vomits at the sight of heaped corpses. Though ugly, the man's reaction is a rare hint, in the series, of compassionate feeling. He could be anyone civilized (that is, with inborn instincts inhibited) who comes upon carnage. By comparison, most of the other items in the show, with the exception of a sobering print by Édouard Manet, are banally or viciously propagandistic, demonizing enemies, or else remaining professionally detached—in either case, rhetorically akin to genres of spectator sport. Photographs can't help spectacularizing violence, given that a disinterested object, the camera, is interposed between the viewer and the viewed. While perhaps stirring emotion, they are chiefly informational.

The same goes, in the show, for the rote thrills and martial sentiments of gaudy late-Baroque battle scenes; fetishized military garb and accoutrements that were popular magazine fare in the nineteenth century; and laconic reportage by the likes of Winslow Homer and Mathew Brady. All set us at a distance. Coping intimately with the truths of war requires either firsthand experience or, if one has blessedly been spared it, introspection, which Goya exercised in abyssal depth and which the news of our day might kindle in us.

In 1966, when my draft number came up, I presented myself at the Army Induction Center on Whitehall Street in Manhattan. I did so in a condition that was curatorially drug-addled, sleepless, and unwashed. Already

underweight, more weak than strong, and chronically nerve-racked—I was not someone whose comradeship you'd want in your foxhole—I probably could have done without the frills, but fright drove me to load the odds in my salvific disfavor. Briskly rejected, I was giddy with relief.

Then shame set in. Another guy would have to go in what might, after all, have been my place. In addition, there was the betrayal of my youthful conviction that of course I would serve someday, as the firstborn son of a father who had won a medal during the Second World War, in the Battle of the Bulge. Only much later did I understand that he had probably incurred lifelong psychic hurt from the ordeal, which may have explained his jumpy elusiveness as a dad. Even now, at the Clark, I can summon tingles of the vicarious bloody glamour that, as a boy, I felt when I imagined my father's war.

Wisdom came later, albeit incompletely. I am a frequent reader of military histories. I swear, especially, by the work of the late John Keegan, who is at once humane in his focus on the fates of common soldiers—in his breakthrough book, *The Face of Battle* (1976), he details the specific vicissitudes of those who fought at Agincourt, Waterloo, and the Somme—and unillusioned about the justifications, however compelling, that sent men into harm's way and kept them there, whether from incentives of patriotism or, failing that, remorseless coercion.

Keegan, like Goya, leaves you with the belief that he sees war-making as hardwired in humanity. In *A History of Warfare* (1993), he noted that when the natives of Easter Island, after more than a millennium in isolation, fell to fighting over dwindling resources, they spontaneously hit upon two of the three classic means of defensive strategy: reinforced refuges and a huge ditch. (The island was too tiny to warrant the third expedient: regional fortresses.) Nor did the combatants need to consult the Iliad, say, to grasp what they were about. Havoc with obsidian spearheads developed naturally.

Do wars start with reasons? Always, and they accumulate supplementary imperatives from the first shot onward. You know that life is hell,

someone once remarked, when you reflect that everyone has reasons, albeit often delusory. Keegan recalled that the deciders on all sides of the First World War, having been schooled in the Clausewitzian dogma that war is the continuation of politics by other means, directed a catastrophe that made practically no political sense whatsoever. Cause or no cause, war is something that people do because they can: it "reaches into the most secret places of the human heart," Keegan wrote. Set aside for a moment the fact that the conduct of a war can ennoble even when the outcome is likely doomed, as is generally believed of the Ukrainians, led by the astonishing Volodymyr Zelensky.

Inevitably, one takes sides. I keep replaying the video of a Russian helicopter gunship being shot down with, I assume, a Western-gifted Stinger missile. I don't like to think of the men who perished in that ball of fire. Instead, I contemplate the event as something cartoonishly abstract: the copter *Russia*, the missile *Ukraine*. It counts for something that the crew died while on a death-dealing mission, but they were fellow human beings. Simply, there's no getting around the moral repercussions of a rooting interest once a conflict has been internalized.

Manet updated Goya in a modernizing, strangely urbane manner. He made his lithograph *The Barricade* in 1871, the same year as the deadly suppression of the Paris Commune, which he had witnessed. Soldiers let loose a volley at defenders of a street obstacle. We see only one victim distinctly, in a sophisticated composition that is largely obscured and formally flattened by a cloud of smoke, which effectively eliminates a middle ground between the shooters and the shot.

Had the scene's passionate Communards been properly armed, they might have reversed their encounter with the dutiful soldiery, piling up uniformed bodies. They weren't, and therefore couldn't. Manet, for all his temperamental sympathy with the rebels, doesn't dramatize the slaughter. He fatalistically records it. Whatever uncertainty attends a war's commencement, each conflict ends with facts. Artists have no say

in the matter, but, if they are honest about a phenomenon that makes a treason of honesty, they can at least disabuse us of naïve projections.

Goya's penultimate *Disaster* depicts a glowing female figure supine, and apparently lifeless, amid a mob of standing monsters. The caption reads, "Truth has died." The following, final image, "Will she rise again?," repeats the same composition. The woman's posture and hopeless situation are unchanged. Only, in this one, she has opened her eyes.

Published in the March 21, 2022, issue of *The New Yorker*, with the headline "Facing War."

A COHERENT AND BOLD WHITNEY BIENNIAL

The startlingly coherent and bold Whitney Biennial is a material manifesto of late-pandemic institutional culture. Long on installations and videos and short on painting, conventional sculpture, and straight photography, it is exciting without being especially pleasurable—geared toward thought. The innovative, intimately collaborative curators David Breslin and Adrienne Edwards ignore rather than oppose pressures of the ever-romping art market, which can see to itself. (The hundreds of contemporary works that are always on view in commercial galleries constitute what might be described as a permanent floating Diurnal.) Delayed for a year by COVID-19, the show consolidates a trend that many of us haven't suspected: a sort of fortuitously shared conceptual sensibility that suggests an in-group but is open to all who care about art's relations to the wide world. Even the most expressive of the artists who were selected by Breslin and Edwards seem oriented not to personal feelings but to hard facts of common experience. Away with moonbeams. Does the outward-looking spirit serendipitously coincide with the emotional convulsions occasioned by the war in Ukraine? It does for me.

Any concentration on specific works, many of which require lengthy explanation regarding their motives and nuances, should await registration of the show's collective potency. (I suggest walking through the whole thing quickly, then doubling back to contemplate individual exhibits.) The effect is less cumulative than immediate in each of two main component sections. The museum's vast, sunny fifth floor has been stripped of interior walls to become an open labyrinth of freestanding sculptures and white-painted wooden frameworks that display smaller pieces. The airy structures, in themselves sculptural, are deleterious to paintings and to anything else pictorial, which crave the serenity of flat walls. But the inconvenience to pictures is justifiable by a one-off (not fungible, I hope), terrific curatorial expedient. The gist is an orderly tumult of sensations fed by, and feeding, an impression of besetting emergency.

The Whitney's sixth floor hosts a warren of black-walled spaces that allow for a viewer's immersion in gnomic creations, several of which function in service to the show's most overt embrace of identity politics, keyed to the past and present ordeals of Native Americans in (let's admit it) settler society, and to some of their enduring folkways and evolving artistic preoccupations. In addition to this focus, there's an omnipresence on both floors—sometimes pointedly so, but in general matter-of-factly—of artists who define themselves as anything other than heterosexual white males, indicating a potential climax after years of strident agitation for diversity. Provisional togetherness reigns. If that seems utopian, so do the frail but stubborn wishes of many of us for a redemption of our multiply fractured America. We needn't stop dreaming even when jarred alert by assaultive realities.

Don't necessarily expect to understand much at a glance. A piece by Rebecca Belmore, an Anishinaabe artist from Canada, *ishkode (fire)* (2021), centers on a representation of a sleeping bag, cast in clay, that appears to cocoon a standing figure not otherwise in evidence. Surrounding it, on the floor, are thousands of small-calibre bullet casings intermixed with copper wire. It is beautiful both before you speculate on its thematic aim and after. I single it out for the glory of painstaking design that typifies scores of works in the show. I fancy that pandemic isolation, at once depriving and disburdening artists of career exigencies, has fostered lonely cultivations of perfection. The Biennial's title this year, "Quiet as It's Kept," is that of a 1960 Max Roach album, and was subsequently employed in Toni Morrison's novel *The Bluest Eye*, in 1970, and for a show that was curated in 2002 by David Hammons, the New York provocateur in many mediums. The phrase befits art that, emerging from a spell of obscurity, is as insistent as an unexpected tap on the shoulder.

Perfect, as a matter of course, are figures, placed outdoors on a fifth-floor terrace, by the commanding Californian sculptor Charles Ray. Hand-formed and then cast or machined in metal, three outsized, seated men—unprepossessing, regular guys, by the look of them—impose a force field of held-breath aesthetic tension and laconic pathos. A few other established stars on hand and in good form include Alfredo Jaar, Ellen Gallagher, Jane Dickson, Nayland Blake, and the late Jason Rhoades. But the bulk of the Biennial is devoted to artists unfamiliar to me, whose outputs run the gamut from hanging fabrics to compact narratives. Of incidental note is proof that video art, after nearly half a century of self-conscious experimentation, has come of age: a camera is as second-nature and ready to hand for many artists now as a pencil or a paintbrush. The scant paintings on view reverse an emphasis on figurative imagery in the 2019 Biennial, tilting toward a lately prevalent revival of abstraction in perfervid styles that have yet to demonstrate staying power.

A collection of photographic works by the Laos-born artist Pao Houa Her both document and poeticize her Hmong family and community in North America. There are fifty-two of the images, and none too many. The sense of an intricately braided history, unfolding in the present while irradiated by memory, left me with an appetite for still more. Such gestation in personal testimony, distanced aesthetically, is another frequent tone of the show. It infuses a poem by the mystically inclined N. H. Pritchard, a Caribbean-parented New Yorker who was steeped in art history, and was a member of the Umbra Poets Workshop, a group of Black writers who met on the Lower East Side in the nineteen-sixties. He died in 1996, at the age of fifty-six. *Red Abstract / fragment* (1968–69) is a lyrical verse text typewritten on a brushy red ground and scribbled with restive cross-outs, revisions, and notes. Its meanings dance at the edge of comprehension, but with infectious improvisatory rhythms.

The quality of personhood turned inside out sings in a poignant film by the South Korean-born Berkeley graduate Theresa Hak Kyung Cha, which is projected on translucent cloth and includes haunting portraits—eyes closed alternating with eyes open—of the artist and of a sister of hers. In 1982, at the age of thirty-one, Cha, a tremendously erudite linguistics philosopher (concerned, she wrote, with "the roots of the language before it is born on the tip of the tongue") and novelist as well as artist, was raped and murdered in New York, at the Puck Building, by a security guard. She figures in the Biennial as a too-little-recognized progenitor of ideas and forms that are still in play for art and nowhere near exhausted.

It's not new for the Biennial to include deceased artists who seem relevant to present creative tendencies. The show has served, traditionally, not only to update the public on the state of contemporary art—mostly American, of course, that being a mandate emblazoned in the museum's name—but also to propose benchmarks and challenges for upcoming generations, even by welcoming some foreign talents of local note. What sets this edition apart, for me, is the determined consistency of its taste in this respect, which avoids the baggy eclecticism that has enfeebled some years' exhibitions. (Will our city's art people love the result? Nah. Hating the Biennial is practically a civic duty, or a pledge of un-allegiance, for cognoscenti hereabouts—and bless us for that, as it fuels the contrarian passion that makes New Yorkers crave to be better than . . . well, whatever you've got.) I won't forget the shock of learning Cha's terrible fate. I was assailed by it, having first discovered and savored her work—stumbling from delight to horror in a few minutes. But the delight abides. Where art is concerned, death need be no more than an inconvenience, and, as in the case of Pritchard, being all but invisible may turn out to have been merely a speed bump.

Even among the living, death broods here and there in the catacomb-like sixth-floor rooms, where it finds explicit reference in my favorite work in the show. Indelibly disturbing and enthralling, *Your Eyes Will Be an Empty Word* (2021), by the veteran Cuban American artist and singularly plainspoken social activist Coco Fusco, is a gorgeous twelve-minute video exploration of Hart Island—New York's potter's field for unidentified or unclaimed corpses. Shots of the artist laboring in a rowboat along its shores are intercut with drone overviews of a really quite lovely place where rows of small stone markers perfunctorily memorialize innumerable lost lives. Beauty stands in for unconsummated mourning. The work can seem to invoke the cascading fatalities of the COVID pandemic and, by chance, the remorseless current carnage in Ukraine, whereby the destruction of so many people occasions news headlines as sullen as those stones. To be alive now is to be overwhelmed by a consciousness of the untimely dead, who, in Ukraine, have resigned their parts in a drama of ever more urgent military, political, and humanitarian imperatives. Their silence roars.

On a far less dire but, in itself, weirdly elegiac note is *64,000 Attempts at Circulation* (2021), by the young Queens artist Rose Salane. It consists of tables heaped with incredibly various slugs—metal washers, casino and arcade tokens, religious medals, play money, and what all—that were used as counterfeit bus fare in New York between 2017 and 2019. (Salane acquired them at a Metropolitan Transit Authority auction of unwanted assets.) Call the content misdemeanor populism, representing in each instance the recourse of someone motivated by need or only petty cupidity. Most of those folks, if not including (shh!) ourselves, still walk among us, mute testifiers to the cussedness of humanity chafing at the constraints of law. The disconcertingly handsome ensemble drolly epitomizes this Biennial's predominant detour, for now, from exalting autonomous art to braving the routine chaos of a world where no kind of comfort or conviction can be sure to persist from one day to the next.

Published in the April 11, 2022, issue of *The New Yorker*, with the headline "All Together Now."

THE IMMERSIVE THRILL OF MATISSE'S *THE RED STUDIO*

Henri Matisse's large painting *The Red Studio* (1911) is so familiar an icon of modern art that you may wonder what remains to be said—or even noticed—about it. Quite a lot, as a jewel box of a show at the Museum of Modern Art proves. The exhibition surrounds the eponymous rendering of the artist's studio with most of the eleven earlier works of his that, in free-hand copy, pepper the painting's uniform ground of potent Venetian red. (Some of the original pieces are on loan from institutions in Europe and North America.) In addition, there are related later paintings, drawings, and prints, along with abundant documentary materials. The ensemble, eloquently mounted by the curators Ann Temkin, of MOMA, and Dorthe Aagesen, of the National Gallery of Denmark, immerses a viewer in the marvels of an artistic revolution that resonates to this day.

Gorgeous? Oh, yeah. Aesthetic bliss saturates—radically, to a degree still apt to startle when you pause to reflect on it—the means, ends, and very soul of a style that was so far ahead of its time that its full influence took decades to kick in. It did so decisively in paintings by Mark Rothko and other American Abstract Expressionists in the years after MOMA's mid-century acquisition of *The Red Studio*, which had, until then, languished in obscurity. The works that are visually quoted in the piece—seven paintings, three sculptures, and a decorated ceramic plate—cohabit with furniture and still-life elements. Contours tend to be summarily indicated by thin yellow lines. Part of a pale-blue window obtrudes. But nothing disrupts the composition's essential harmony, the details striking the eye all at once, with a concerted bang.

There's no possibility of entering the portrayed corner space, even by way of imagination. Only certain subtle contrasts of warm and cool hues, pushing and pulling at a viewer's gaze, hint at anything like pictorial depth. Not for Matisse the retention of visually advancing and receding forms, as in the contemporaneous Cubism of his towering frenemy Picasso. (Who wins their lifelong agon? The question is moot. They are like boxing champions who can't tag each other because they're in separate rings.) Even the vaguely Cézanne-esque *Bathers* (1907), picturing a nude couple in a grassy landscape—one of the paintings in *The Red Studio* whose original is on hand for the show—reads democratically. Swift strokes jostle forward in a single, albeit rumpled, optical plane. See if this isn't so, as your gaze segues smoothly across black outlines among greenery, blue water and sky, and orangeish flesh.

In 1907, when Picasso painted his insurrectionary touchstone *Les Demoiselles d'Avignon*, the Spaniard commented acerbically on Matisse's breakthrough canvas from the same year, *Blue Nude (Souvenir of Biskra)*: "If he wants to make a woman, let him make a woman. If he wants to make a design, let him make a design." In truth, Matisse did both at once, integrating painting's two primordial functions—illustration and decoration. *Blue Nude* is absent from *The Red Studio* and from the present show, but its spirit persists in the three sculptures on display, which extend, in the round, the painterly touch in Matisse's flat pictorial figuration. They nearly equal, for me, the twentieth-century feats in three dimensions of Brancusi and Giacometti.

The inception of *The Red Studio* came by way of a decorative commission from the Muscovite textile tycoon Sergei Ivanovich Shchukin, a preëminent collector of European innovations, from Impressionist to post-Impressionist to some on which the paint was barely dry. His holdings, which were impounded by the Bolsheviks in 1918, are now glories of the State Hermitage Museum, in St. Petersburg, and the Pushkin State Museum of Fine Arts, in Moscow. They include an absolute stunner of Matisse's, *The Conversation* (1908–12), which I encountered at the Hermitage in 1989. A wry air of domestic comedy inflects the work's dominant, intense blue and ravishing floral window view. The artist, looking mild-mannered and standing in pajamas, confronts his seated wife, the formidable Amélie, whom I can't help but imagine telling him to get his own breakfast. (Matisse is almost never pointedly witty, but a sort of spectral humor, redolent of sheer audacity, flows through just about everything from his hand.) That picture is also not in the present show, but it is tattooed on my memory.

Shchukin's lavish patronage of Matisse, which began in 1906, relieved the artist and his family from years of penury. It enabled a move to a comfortable home in Issy-les-Moulineaux, four miles outside Paris, and the construction there, in 1909, of the spacious studio that became the site and ofttimes subject of nearly all of Matisse's works until he decamped to Nice, in 1917. In January, 1911, the collector requested a trio of same-size paintings, each about six by seven feet, leaving their subject matter up to Matisse. Shchukin acquired the first, the relatively sedate *Pink Studio*, but, on receiving a watercolor copy of what Matisse entitled *Red Panel*, he politely declined the design.

Shchukin explained that he preferred pictures with people in them, ignoring the presence of figures aplenty in the visual citation of previous works, such as the robustly appealing *Young Sailor II* (1906), the original of which is on loan for the show from the Metropolitan Museum, and the violently bold *Nude with White Scarf* (1909), provided by the National Gallery of Denmark. Or did even the gamely indulgent Russian, though too tactful to say so, balk at the image's molten energy? Matisse remained singularly controversial in art circles at that time, even as Picasso's preternatural draftsmanship disarmed many.

Still called *Red Panel*, the work appeared in 1912 in the Second Post-Impressionist Exhibition, in London, and the next year in the Armory Show, in New York and Chicago, yet neither it nor anything else by Matisse sold. (In a *Times* interview with the artist in France, in March, 1913, the critic Clara T. MacChesney bristled with condescending resistance in face of gracious comments from Matisse, who was at pains to convey that he was a "normal" family man rather than the unkempt holy terror whom she had anticipated.) The painting then remained in the artist's possession and out of public sight until it was bought, in 1927, as a chic bibelot for a swanky members-only social club in London. After a spell of private ownership, it was purchased, enthusiastically, by MOMA, in 1949—right on time for its charismatic relevance to artists in New York and ultimately around the world.

In my opinion, there are three differently instructive failures among the works in the present show. *Le Luxe II* (1907–08) depicts three monumental seaside nudes, oddly rendered in distemper (rabbit-skin glue) rather than in sensuous oils, to a dryly static effect. But it was plainly worth the try for Matisse and takes its place in *The Red Studio*. Nostalgia may have motivated him to incorporate a diminutive clunker, *Corsica, the Old Mill*, painted in 1898, when he was twenty-eight years old, fresh out of art school and newly married. Its conventional motif displays an irresolute miscellany of post-Impressionist and incipiently Fauvist techniques—a ticking time bomb, as it would turn out.

It took me a while to cool on the initially impressive *Large Red Interior* (1948), which closes the show as a bookend to *The Red Studio*. Extravagantly praised at the time by the formalist critic Clement Greenberg, it is masterly, to be sure, with virtuosic representations of previous pictures and lots of flowers in vases. But I find the work vitiated by a quality—tastefulness—that Matisse had sometimes risked but reliably sidestepped throughout most of his career. It feels *unmeant*—passionless, strictly professional. Soon after completing that work, Matisse, ever self-aware, put down his brushes, picked up a pair of scissors, and commenced the sensational improvisations in cut colored paper that absorbed him until his death, in 1954. Yet again, he found his way to an inward imperative that, with typical nonchalance, precipitated deathless outward consequences.

Published in the May 16, 2022, issue of *The New Yorker*, with the headline "Going Flat Out."

THE IMPORTANCE OF SCALE

I relish the abundance of relatively—and poignantly—dud paintings in "At the Dawn of a New Age: Early Twentieth-Century American Modernism," at the Whitney Museum. With an emphasis on abstraction, the show features a number of rarely exhibited works, most owned by the museum, that were made during the learning-curve years—at full tilt by 1912—of artists on these shores who strove to absorb the revolutionary innovations that had originated in Europe. Occupying the museum's eighth floor, the array provides a sidelight (or prequel) to the Whitney's selection of touchstone pieces from its collection, dating from 1900 to 1965, on the seventh floor. That long-running installation parades feats by American adepts—Edward Hopper, Alexander Calder, Jacob Lawrence, Willem de Kooning—along various routes, with propitious detours toward world-beating Abstract Expressionism, Pop art, and Minimalism.

"At the Dawn," organized by the curator Barbara Haskell, samples provincial talents who had plenty of moxie but remained shallowly rooted in the dashing radicality with which Europeans eclipsed embedded traditions. The aspiring Americans thrilled to the explosion but tended to be hazy on exactly what, in prior art history, was being blown up. Their frequent ingenuousness tantalizes. It is a fact of the art-loving experience that serious but failed ambitions teach more about the tenor of their times than contemporaneous successes, which freeze us in particular, awed fascination.

When something doesn't quite cohere, you can see what it's made of. Sources and intentions glare from the canvases. Historical museums should incorporate more of such stuff, to contextualize the happy shocks of excellence, which, on the two floors of the Whitney, include hits in almost their initial at-bats by John Marin, Arthur Dove, Stuart Davis, Georgia O'Keeffe, Florine Stettheimer, and the ever-amazing Marsden Hartley, whose powers of emblematic abstraction peaked in 1914 in Berlin, during a sojourn from his native Maine, and persisted sub rosa throughout his later Southwestern and New England landscapes and homoerotic figurations. Those artists promulgated authentic declarations of independence.

The distinguishing test, for me, is scale, irrespective of size: all a work's elements and qualities (even including negative space) must be snugged into its framing edges to consolidate a specific, integral object—present to us, making us present to itself—rather than a more or less diverting handmade picture. Among the painters in "At the Dawn," that sort of resolution eluded the likes of the Chicagoan Manierre Dawson, America's first true abstractionist and a highly promising artist until, in 1914, he withdrew to run a farm in Michigan; the color stylists Stanton Macdonald-Wright and Patrick Henry Bruce, whose lastingly seductive but fitful beauties went pretty much nowhere; and the Russian-born Max Weber, whose extraordinary *Chinese Restaurant* (1915) mashes up, at a go, assorted tactics of Cubism and never fails to beguile me even as it doesn't really work at all.

Sculptures by Elie Nadelman, who was born in Poland, and Gaston Lachaise, who emigrated from France, memorialize a New York-based, sensuously decorative modernist chic. Many other artists in the show were immigrants, too: German, Italian, Polish, Ukrainian, Lithuanian, Japanese, Chinese, and British (does Canadian count?), flavoring a cosmopolitan melting pot. Works by several of the newcomers are close calls in terms of quality. Visual rhapsodies by the Italian-born Joseph Stella include a game attempt to represent music with the frenetic *Der Rosenkavalier* (1913–14). Plangent landscapes by the German-born Oscar Bluemner, influenced by the Blue Rider movement (which had convened German and Russian avant-gardists in Munich), suffer from a certain cautiousness. A Ukrainian unfamiliar to me, Ben Benn, went native with a creditably sombre abstraction, *Cowboy and Horse* (1917). In general, though, engagements with American subject matter are rare in the show. Imported internationalism reigns.

Of passing reward are stabs at mysticism by lately rediscovered mavericks, including the German-born Californian Agnes Pelton, the subject of a delightful but not entirely convincing retrospective at the Whitney in 2020. Pelton's richly hued, luminous *Ahmi in Egypt* (1931), which depicts a swan beneath cascading abstract symbols against a black ground, anticipates a penchant among some present-day painters for themes of the otherworldly. (This penchant was given a boost in 2018 by a sensational show, at the Guggenheim, of immense proto-abstractions by the early-twentieth-century Swedish spiritualist Hilma af Klint, who had long been all but forgotten.) *Ahmi in Egypt* is lovely but verges, to my eye, on suggesting an overqualified greeting card. Of related relevance is a watercolor with pencil drawing by the chronically underrated Charles Burchfield, *Sunlight in Forest* (1916)—dark trees pierced vertically by a tonguelike shaft of white sunlight—which heralds the soulful idiosyncrasy of Burchfield, a Lutheran mystagogue of small-town and rural epiphanies who was close friends with Hopper. His enraptured art keeps looking stronger, in hindsight.

In addition, room is made for excitingly Expressionist woodcuts from the mid-twenties by the Black artist Aaron Douglas, which include a jagged response to Paul Robeson's performance in the Eugene O'Neill play *The Emperor Jones*, and for a piquantly Symbolist tarot deck that was designed by the American-educated British illustrator Pamela Colman Smith in 1909 but that remained unpublished until more than a decade later. Such items plunge us into a bygone cultural ferment whose paladins may have sputtered in their aims but who pitched into them enthusiastically. Though they were only sometimes personally allied, they evoke, en masse, a national team effort.

The show occasions time-travelling connoisseurship, to sort out instances of brilliance from more prevalent disappointments. You are there, immersed in peaks and valleys of an effervescent day and age. I don't expect your judgments to match mine. I recommend attending with an argumentative companion. The very unevenness of the offerings makes for fine sport. When you think about it, art appreciation parallels all manner of games that people play—not least baseball, the individualistic American invention that has just lost its Homeric bard, Roger Angell, to unexpectedly devastating effect for some of us—with the pesky difference that art does so without a scoreboard and, eschewing inning breaks, never ends.

Several younger painters today play at hybridizing representation and abstraction. It's a mode of have-it-all eclecticism that is frequently redolent of the wishful artists' statements that art schools require their students to write—a godforsaken prose genre that is, at best, wholesomely cynical. (Graduates in literature aren't obliged to supplement their theses with paintings.) But here I am, wowed by "Pearl Lines," a large show at Greene Naftali of paintings and drawings by Walter Price, thirty-three years old, who deploys just such crossover stratagems with sterling discipline and untrammelled liberty. The forms of his eloquently colorful art, which mingles imagery of banal manufactured objects with evocations of fire and water, can seem at once to fly apart and somehow to precipitate ineffable harmonies. They qualify as decorative in the way that climbing a Himalayan peak might be deemed recreational.

Price was born in Macon, Georgia, and decided to become an artist while in the second grade. Straight out of high school, he served four years in the U.S. Navy, chiefly to take advantage of the subsequent G.I. Bill financing of his art studies at Middle Georgia College (now part of Middle Georgia State University) and the (recently defunct) Art Institute of Washington, in Arlington, Virginia. He's a Brooklynite today. These and other data points pepper an interview, in the *Financial Times*, that was conducted last year by the Nigerian American critic Enuma Okoro. A "dance with whiteness" is how Price describes his thinking behind work that he made during a residency in London. He regards himself as "political, but not overtly," aiming to "make people comfortable with being uncomfortable," both aesthetically and by way of any worldly association that occurs to them.

Price said that he shuns all social media: "Too much looking and not enough thinking." The abnegation pays off. Inexhaustibly surprising smears, blotches, fugitive lines, and incomplete patterns feel less applied than turned loose, to tell enigmatic stories of their own. The effect is redoubled in his exuberant, earthy drawings in which, often, faces and figures share spaces with visual equivalents of improvisatory jazz. I can think of no precedent for Price's style-defying style except in the spirit, though not the look, of certain decomposed compositions by Cy Twombly. There are occasional longueurs, as seen in dotted lines that seem overly calculated to knit a surface. But even these glitches evince Price's compulsion to risk all manner of painterly tropes. To think is to do, for him. Staggeringly prolific, he recalls Oscar Wilde's doctrine of mastering temptations by succumbing to them.

You must physically encounter Price's paintings to grasp their dynamics. Scale is germane: both internally, in the jostle of mismatched marks and textures, and externally, relating to the proportions of your body. This may be true in general of any effective painting, but it is essential in this case. It enables an exhilarating sense of participation, as if, by viewing a work stroke by stroke, you create it yourself. The artist has left you alone with it as he departs toward something not quite altogether but manifestly else, starting from scratch again and yet again.

Published in the June 13, 2022, issue of *The New Yorker*, with the headline "Scaling Up."

A FREQUENTLY MISUNDERSTOOD AMERICAN MASTER

In town with some summer hours to spare? Visit "Dakota Modern: The Art of Oscar Howe," the overdue retrospective of a remarkable Yanktonai Dakota painter, who died in 1983, at the age of sixty-eight. The show graces the always enthralling New York branch of the Smithsonian's National Museum of the American Indian, housed in the Alexander Hamilton U.S. Custom House—a prodigy of Beaux-Arts architecture by Cass Gilbert, from 1907—hard by Battery Park. It's admission-free. Too few attend. (Some days, you may have the place and its spectacular collection of Native American art and artifacts almost to yourself, except for the occasional school group.) Howe is a frequently misunderstood American master. He bridged ethnic authenticity and internationalist derring-do, though condescension from establishment institutions and proprietary tribute from some sectarian advocates have hindered his recognition as a straight-up canonical modernist. Really, go see.

In Howe's *Sacro-Wi-Dance (Sun Dance)*, from 1965, sacrificially self-wounded male celebrants are seen from an improbable viewing point, below and looking up, as they tumble from a foreshortened, serpentine rendering of the rite's lofty, horizontally striped central pole. The vertiginous composition incorporates tropes of Surrealism and Abstract Expressionism, which, having become second nature to Howe, hardly vitiate the intensity of this particular religious rapture. A palette of russet, yellow, and black has precedents in the Lakota and Dakota crafts of hide painting and beadwork. But racial identity wasn't so much asserted as baked into Howe's pragmatic appropriation, and advancement, of sophisticated aesthetics. In *Bear Dancer* (1962), illustrative details—a bear's head, a wielded spear—lurk unobtrusively amid cubistically distributed abstract forms. Yet more peekaboo are bits of figures in the plangent gallimaufry of *Dance of the Heyoka* (1954). Such paintings embody no rationale except their own.

Howe owed the flowering of his genius to silver-lined childhood bad luck. Born in 1915, with the tribal name Mazuha Hokshina, on an impoverished reservation in South Dakota, he was shipped off, seven years later, to one of the United States' federally run boarding schools. At the time, these schools harshly endeavored to suppress Native youths' ancestral ways. He spoke no English when he arrived. Beset by eye and skin diseases and, in 1924, traumatized by news of the death, from an illness, of his mother, he contemplated suicide. The school let him leave to convalesce. He spent roughly a year back on his home reservation with a sage grandmother, Shell Face, whose exciting stories imbued him with a profound knowledge of tribal history and myth. Such matters were alien to his father, who scorned his artistic aspirations. (Manual labor was then the all but obligatory horizon of ambition for most reservation-raised boys.) Howe subsequently returned to the school, which, in the interim, had undergone humane reforms. After graduating, in 1933, he enrolled in a trailblazing art program at the Santa Fe Indian School, in New Mexico.

Howe quickly became a leading light in what was dubbed the Studio Style, which originated at the school, elegantly arraying linear tribal motifs in negative space with sparing touches of color. One example in the show, *Blue Antelope* (circa 1934–38), delicately represents the eponymous animal beneath a floating, austerely geometric arch. By the early fifties, after the Studio movement had begun to devolve into gift-shop fare, Howe was onto something rangier, informed by an avid appreciation of Western modern art, if at first only by way of reproduction, while being sustained, in South Dakota, by teaching jobs and, eventually, by commissioned work on public murals.

Howe served in Europe as an Army artillery soldier during the Second World War, almost never speaking of the experience except sardonically.

(His unflagging goal, he remarked, was to avoid earning a Purple Heart.) Returning to the U.S. in 1945, he was joined two years later by his fiancée, a German woman named Heidi Hampel, whom he had met and courted during the war. She was to be an astute and redoubtable partner for the rest of his life. The couple reunited in New York and, travelling west by train, married during a stopover in Chicago, to elude a law against miscegenation in South Dakota, where they settled. Howe resumed teaching and achieved B.A. and M.F.A. degrees at universities there and in Oklahoma. Their daughter, Inge Dawn, who was born in 1948, still administers her father's legacy.

"Dakota Modern," crisply curated by Kathleen Ash-Milby, consists almost exclusively of works in tempera, watercolor, gouache, or casein on paper. The execution is phlegmatically deliberate. Photographs of Howe, always neatly dressed and placidly industrious, usually seated at a table, consort oddly with the power-packed compositions and aggressive hues of his pictures. The upshot is a channelling of sheer, visionary imagination, as if the artist were taking dictation from an unseen demiurge. Do some of the effects seem cartoonish, with figuration that anticipated popular styles of graphic fiction which took hold in the nineteen-seventies? Perhaps. Still, generic characters in melodramatic poses strategically depersonalize subjects to the benefit of thematic punch and decorative finesse. The results exalt audacity and breathe beauty. Howe seldom repeated himself. Each work can feel one-off, fulfilling a special mission to a fare-thee-well. If any quality is consistent, it's suddenness.

Howe's topics are rarely historical or patently political, with the main, sensational exception of the gouache *Wounded Knee Massacre* (1959–60), which, at twenty-two inches high and twenty-eight inches wide, is smallish but feels monumental. It depicts a firing line of soldiers along the edge of a ditch, who are riddling defenseless Lakota men below while, in the distance, bluecoats decimate other groups with weaponry that includes a sinister rapid-fire Hotchkiss gun. (One rifleman, neglecting to shoot, gazes askance with an enigmatically goofy grin. He haunts me.) Howe said that his intention here was strictly reportorial, born of an urge to acknowledge the atrocity that, in 1890, effectively ended Native military resistance to white conquest.

One other picture in the show, *Fleeing a Massacre* (1969), may also allude to that event, if not to some other in the United States' annals of exterminatory violence. A panicked young woman is seen on a galloping but bloodied and overstrained horse, the image framed in lyrical arabesques. Collective tragedy is a given, not an issue, for Howe, who strove neither to outrage nor to comfort anyone.

His was a lonely course, incurring resistance even from compatriots who routinely hailed him. As late as 1958, he was denied consideration for a prize in an annual show of Native artists because the new painting that he submitted, *Umini Wacipi (War and Peace Dance),* was declared "not Indian," despite its indubitable subject matter. (It is reproduced in the fine catalogue of "Dakota Modern," but its present whereabouts are uncertain.) He responded with the sole publicized polemic of his career, a letter to an organizer of the show which mocked the tourist-bait "pretty, stylized pictures" favored by the officially sanctioned authorities. "Are we to be held back forever with one phase of Indian painting, that is the most common way?" he wrote. "We are to be herded like a bunch of sheep, with no right for individualism, dictated as the Indian has always been, put on reservations and treated like a child . . ."

Another setback to Howe's autonomy, though it increased his fame, occurred in 1960. He travelled to California with *Wounded Knee Massacre*, at the urging of the actor Vincent Price, who had collected work by him, for a show of Native art in Hollywood. The exhibition took place, but the personal invitation proved to be a ruse, to trick the artist into appearing on the television show *This Is Your Life*, which made a shtick of surprising featured guests with sentimental exposures of their life stories. Having thus been ostracized on the one hand and then exoticized on the other, Howe stood alone.

Howe took as little interest in political contestation as he did in commercial pastiche. But he had to be conscious of the drama that he enacted through his forthright embrace of his Dakota heritage without either parochial constriction or outward rancor, however justifiable that rancor might have been. He proposed, and exemplified, a tough but open-ended imperative for Native American artists of all stylistic stripes—looking back with fealty and sideways with candor while forging ahead—in a statement that he published in 1959: "This is our art . . . and here is where we are making our last stand. . . . The least we can do is to fight this last battle, that Indian Culture may live forever."

Published in the July 11 & 18, 2022, issue of *The New Yorker*, with the headline "Modern Lore."

FAULT LINES IN AMERICA AND UKRAINE

"Art and Race Matters: The Career of Robert Colescott," a clamorous retrospective at the New Museum, bodes to be enjoyed by practically everyone who sees it, though some may be nagged by inklings that they shouldn't. For more than three decades, until he was slowed by health ailments in the two-thousands—he died in 2009, at the age of eighty-three—the impetuous figurative painter danced across minefields of racial and sexual provocation, celebrating libertine romance and cannibalizing canonical art history by way of appreciative parody. He was born in California, the son of musicians from New Orleans. His mother, certainly, and possibly his father, who worked as a railroad waiter, had enslaved ancestors, but both of them—and Colescott—could pass for white. As Matthew Weseley, the co-curator of the show with Lowery Stokes Sims, recounts in the splendid catalogue, Colescott's mother insisted on the ruse, which he adopted. The mild-mannered modernism of his early works, sampled at the New Museum, affords no hints to the contrary.

This changed explosively when Colescott turned forty during a spell, between 1964 and 1967, of sojourns in Egypt, where he imbibed old and new African cultures. From that epiphanic moment on, he went all-in on the complexities of his racial identity. Being an American Black man, whatever else he was, became the dominant conceit—and license—of his subsequent art, which he imbued with perhaps penitent, palpably vengeful irony, for the rest of his life. By not sparing himself from a pageant of caricatural mockeries, he offered no distance, let alone escape, from the fault lines of race in American democracy. As a bonus, he was freed to burlesque, with terrific energy, motifs of past Western art that he had always revered.

In a mood to be rattled? Contemplate *Eat Dem Taters* (1975), an all-Black recasting of van Gogh's early tableau of impoverished Dutch peasants sharing a frugal meal, *The Potato Eaters* (1885), with an aura of minstrelsy. How could Colescott—or anyone, really—have expected to get away with that or, from the same year, with a race-switching pastiche of Emanuel Leutze's nationalist chestnut *Washington Crossing the Delaware* (1851)? A bespectacled George Washington Carver, the pioneering botanist, stands in for the nation-founding hero of the Revolutionary War. A gleeful fisherman at the bow of the boat reels in a catch. A banjo player strums in the stern.

Not yet sufficiently affronted? Throw in *A Winning Combination* (1974), in which a perky white majorette, backed by a rippling Stars and Stripes, is naked from the waist down. Add *Beauty is in the Eye of the Beholder* (1979), a self-portrait of the artist distracted by a disrobing white model while repainting Matisse's hedonist masterpiece *Dance*, from 1910. Still with me? How about *The Judgment of Paris* (1984), in which a clothed Black protagonist is lasciviously vamped by a nude white Venus, to the disgruntlement of white and Black rival goddesses? Rather than angrily or mournfully critiquing racist stereotypes and associated taboos, Colescott shot the moon with them.

A lot goes on in these pictures, starting with how they are executed, in a fast and loose, juicy Expressionist manner and by means of a blazing palette that runs to saturated pink and magenta and thunderous blue. Along the way, Colescott pillages the distinctive hues of Willem de Kooning's iconic *Woman I* (1951) with *I Gets a Thrill, Too, When I Sees De Koo* (1978), in which the face of a grinning Black woman wearing a head scarf replaces that of the Dutchman's generic white female. (The title kidded a redoing of de Kooning the previous year, *I Still Get a Thrill When I See Bill*, by the Pop artist Mel Ramos.) Colescott shrugged off abstract and conceptualist fashions of the late nineteen-sixties and early seventies, guaranteeing himself a marginal status in the mainstream art world as a special taste or, let's say, anti-taste. As if in sweet revenge, his atavistic style and what-the-hell nerve began to influence younger artists of many backgrounds in the late seventies and continue to do so today. Without the spur of his breakthrough audacity, it's hard to imagine the recent and ongoing triumphs of, among others, the fearlessly satirical artists Kerry James Marshall and Kara Walker.

The choice of Colescott to represent the United States at the 1997 Venice Biennale initiated a general surrender to his ineluctable power, though most of America's upper-crust institutions have yet to capitulate. The New Museum's presentation of "Art and Race Matters" is a previously unplanned addendum to a tour that débuted in Cincinnati and, having travelled to Portland and Sarasota, was set to end in Chicago. Roberta Smith, who reviewed the show in the *Times*, properly declared the implicit squeamishness a disgrace to our major New York museums, whose lip service to diversity characteristically stops short of anything that isn't respectably theorized and may be just too roguishly irreverent.

As freewheeling in life as on canvas, Colescott married six times, twice to the same woman, whom he accordingly twice divorced, while studying and then teaching at a series of West Coast and Southwest schools and colleges. After wartime service in the Army, he attended a class in Paris led by Fernand Léger and, in 1951, earned a master's degree from the University of California, Berkeley. In the catalogue, erudition, wit, and wisdom mark a lively selection of his occasional writings, in which he proves to be his own most discerning critic. His last position, before retiring, in 1995, was as a tenured professor at the University of Arizona, Tucson.

Is there something to be said against Colescott's untrammelled temerity? If you wish—I, for one, am hospitable to argument—but resistance isn't easy while you're feeling delightfully knocked about like a sensitized pinball in rooms crowded with the artist's most aggressive creations. The effect is comic in a key beyond outrageous. Inrageous? Metarageous? I'm reminded of the liberating shock of Mel Brooks's flabbergasting movie *The Producers*, which happened to coincide, in

1967, with the onset of Colescott's painterly insurgency. Undeniably, while trashing American iniquities and insulting compensatory inhibitions, he let—or, more accurately, made, at a volume to wake the dead—freedom ring.

"Women at War," at the Fridman Gallery, astounds. I wish everyone could see it. The show assembles drawings, photographs, paintings, a print, and video installations by a dozen excellent Ukrainian artists, none familiar to me. All are women, many of them young. Several hail from the ravaged Donbas region. Two remain in Ukraine. Others have only recently left the country. Apart from one historical piece—a linocut portrait from 1963 of the nationalist poet Ivan Svitlychny by Alla Horska, an artist and activist who was murdered, reputedly by the K.G.B., in 1970—everything postdates the Russian seizure of Crimea, in 2014. Throughout the show, instances of steely discipline ennoble dramas of suffering and defiance.

An outsize oil painting made by Lesia Khomenko in March of this year, *Max in the Army*, tenderly depicts the partner whom, in her flight first to Poland and then to the U.S., she has had to leave behind. Looking both resolute and terribly vulnerable, he is lovable. She loves him. To behold three beautiful watercolors of sylvan landscapes by Anna Scherbyna—one painted per year from 2016 to 2018 and almost inconspicuously featuring ruins in the Donbas, of an airport and two hospitals—you must lift little dun-colored curtains. Olia Fedorova's photograph *Defense* (2017) shows a row of white anti-tank obstacles, or "hedgehogs," ranged along a snowy slope. They are made of paper, which bespeaks both a presentiment of futility—premature, as it has turned out, impressively—and a lionhearted will.

These are tough-minded creators whose moral fibre should humble those of us who are cozily remote from a cataclysm that adapts repertoires of international art to the lived truths of a convulsed, actual place. Some disturb. The most unsettling, by Dana Kavelina, are deliberately crude pencil drawings executed on crumpled white paper punctuated by internal rips colored blood red. A number of them allude to rape. A sketch of a woman using a fetus's own umbilical cord to hang it is titled "woman kills the son of the enemy" (2019). A climactic image suggests the birth of an assault rifle.

But the versatile Kavelina, a rising star in her late twenties, has also created an elegiac, desperately moving video projection. The nearly twenty-one-minute, wide-screen *Letter to a Turtledove* (2020) montages archival film footage of coal miners in the Donbas with expressive women's faces and hypnotically stylized, almost meditative, fiery explosions. The work engulfs the viewer in a sort of minor-key visual cadenza that sounds the heart and very soul of a nation that has come to awareness of itself—past, present, unknowable future—under unspeakable conditions. Its beauty becomes a Ukrainian weapon as bestirring, if not as practicable, as a donated howitzer.

Nothing in the show is either hortatory or sentimental but only hard-won, such as a series of drawings by Alevtina Kakhidze that begin in 2014 and narrate her contact with her mother in the occupied territory of Donetsk. The mother died of a heart attack in 2019 while crossing the frontier to secure a Ukrainian government pension. Reminiscent in spirit of Kavelina's video, a suite of ink-jet prints by Yevgenia Belorusets, *Victories of the Defeated* (2014–17), seeks melancholy solace in nocturnal or befogged views of workers who labor at various tasks amid dismal circumstances. The subjects could be anybody, even ourselves if our existence entailed an interminable state of emergency.

The show is elegantly and, above all, eloquently installed by Monika Fabijanska, an independent art historian and avowedly feminist curator who hereby does Ukraine, and any of us who willingly pay attention, a cathartic service.

Published in the July 25, 2022, issue of *The New Yorker*, with the headline "Confrontations."

WHEN NEW YORK RULED THE WORLD

This is where I came in. A spectacular historical show of art and documentation, "New York: 1962–1964," at the Jewish Museum, addresses the exact years of my tatterdemalion arrival, from the Midwest, as an ambitious poet, a jobber in journalism, and a tyro art nut. I gravitated through the time's impecunious Lower East Side poetry scene into the booming though not yet oligarchic art world. Artists, writers, dealers, patrons, and assorted intellectuals, alert to momentous changes in the world at large, rubbed shoulders at parties that were a lot more stimulating than those attended by my second-generation New York School coterie.

It was an era of season-to-season—at times almost monthly or weekly—advances in painting, sculpture, photography, dance, music, design, fashion, and such hybrid high jinks as "happenings." The exhibition honors poetry, too, by displaying some of the scrappy, mostly mimeographed little magazines that agitated for vernacular language in verse, anchored by a copy of Frank O'Hara's definitive book, *Lunch Poems* (1964), and by piping in recorded readings. My favorites were and remain Ron Padgett and the late, exquisitely laconic artist-poet Joe Brainard, both from Oklahoma.

With Pop art and nascent Minimalism, New York artists were turning no end of tables on solemnly histrionic Abstract Expressionism, which had established our town as the new wheelhouse of creative origination worldwide. Instrumental to the moment was a brilliant critic and curator, Alan Solomon, who died too soon, at the age of forty-nine, in 1970. As the director of the Jewish Museum during the years bracketed in the present show, he consolidated what he called "The New Art," mounting the first museum retrospectives of the trailblazers Robert Rauschenberg and Jasper Johns and elevating such newbie Pop phenoms as Andy Warhol, Roy Lichtenstein, and James Rosenquist in tandem with aggressively large-scale, radically formalist abstract painters like Frank Stella and Kenneth Noland. Solomon organized the U.S. exhibition at the 1964 Venice Biennale, where Rauschenberg was awarded the Grand Prize for painting, a coup that cemented New York's ascendance. If you weren't here, you all of a sudden risked seeming provincial.

Poor Paris, where I spent most of a disillusioning year, spanning 1964 and 1965, was slow to recover from a tantrum of (to apply the appropriate phrase for it) lèse-majesté. As late as 1983, a prominent book by the French-born art historian Serge Guilbaut, *How New York Stole the Idea of Modern Art*, elided the truth that, following the Second World War, "the idea" had been up for grabs. (Finders keepers.) Guilbaut attributed the transatlantic larceny to conspiratorial interventions by the U.S. government, some agencies of which did, to be sure, view American expressive liberty as a soft weapon in the Cold War and supported its exposure overseas, at times covertly. That's accurate enough as far as it goes, but it was only one among many converging circumstances.

In truth, New York rainmakers like Solomon, the quick-witted dealer Sidney Janis, and the European-émigré power couple of Leo Castelli and Ileana Sonnabend—whose split, in 1959, resulted in separate galleries (one in Manhattan, one in Paris) that amplified the sway of their bold and exacting, complementary tastes—needed no cloaks or daggers to broker art that made every decisive case by and for itself. Open-minded young Germans, Italians, Eastern Europeans, Latin Americans, Asians, and even certain French artists were electrified. An influx to New York of foreign talents which had started by happenstance in wartime swelled to an invasion. Some, such as the Bulgarian-born Christo and his French wife, Jeanne-Claude, became stars. Others encountered tough sledding. In 1973, after fifteen eventful but lean years, the sensual, often environmental Japanese sculptor Yayoi Kusama retreated to her homeland and began a rise to international eminence that is still under way.

"New York: 1962–1964" was conceived by the globe-trotting Italian critical macher Germano Celant, before his death, in 2020, as a sampler of exemplary works surrounded by pictorial and written evidence of coincident political and social contingencies. A curatorial team at the Jewish Museum, along with Celant's studio, has seen his eclectic scheme through. Civil-rights campaigns, the sexual revolution, emergent second-wave feminism, the Cuban missile crisis, the J.F.K. assassination, forebodings of disaster in Vietnam, and much else, torn from the period's headlines, make their pressures felt. (I might have thought that I was done with shedding tears at Martin Luther King, Jr.,'s 1963 "I Have a Dream" speech, but a wall-size projection of it in the show proved otherwise.) The global contexts rhyme in energy if not in direct relevance with an insurgent avant-gardism in New York which, while rarely polemical (art for art's sake remained a persistent ideal), rejected modernist detachment in order to engage lived realities. As Solomon observed, "television commercials, comic strips, hot dog stands, billboards, junk yards, hamburger joints, used car lots, jukeboxes, slot machines, and supermarkets," channelling "probably most of the aesthetic experience for 99 percent of Americans," became regnant almost overnight.

Emblematic of this, in the show, are items from *The Store* (December, 1961), by the recently late, and lamented, Claes Oldenburg: a pop-up storefront emporium, on East Second Street, of consumer goods represented in lumpy plaster and slapdash paint. Poeticized by uselessness, the work bridges gee-whiz delight and sardonic irony, seeming at once to brag of and to complain about the virulently commercialized culture that was both crowning and roughing up America's peak power, prosperity, and—face it—hubris. I must admit to a false memory, now that I reflect on it, of having seen *The Store* and a number of Solomon's rousing exhibitions in person. I was way too disorganized even as I was absorbing the period's torrential excitements—soundtracked by Bob Dylan and Motown—at first vicariously and then by way of a nascent career that I had never imagined for myself.

The eruptive early sixties launched many folks on all sorts of trajectories. After intriguing for a trice, some quickly flamed out or stalled, suggesting to me a theory, which I kept to myself, of Temporary Meaning in Art: get it while it's hot or miss it forever, at a cost to your sophistication. Others, at the margins of fame, hung fire for unjustly belated recognition, as demonstrated in this show by the achievements of the Spiral Group, a cadre of Black artists who banded together in 1963 and were led along different but likewise terrific stylistic tracks by the populist collage specialist Romare Bearden and the surpassingly versatile abstractionist Norman Lewis. The group attained some art-world renown, but it was fleeting. Meanwhile, few women at the time were given their due, which should accrue to them in retrospect. New to me is a garish relief painting, from 1963, by the underknown Marjorie Strider, of a glamour girl chomping on a huge red radish, that could serve as an icon of Pop glee and sexual impertinence crossed with proto-feminist vexation.

Strengths of the show include recorded performances of the dance revolutionary Merce Cunningham; photographs of the irrepressible live-action provocateur Carolee Schneemann, who liked cavorting naked to oddly ennobling effect; and the orgiastic, often officially censored film *Flaming Creatures* (1963), by Jack Smith. The last signalled a seething gay underground that Susan Sontag touched on, the following year, in her depth-charge essay "Notes on 'Camp.'" Apart from such highlights, I was annoyed at first blush by the surrounding profusion of non-art-historical matter that I knew very well already. Of course, I had been on hand for the precipitating events, consuming newspapers (there were at least seven dailies in Manhattan back then) and television (in black-and-white, suitable to the avuncular charisma, which I sorely miss, of Walter Cronkite).

I imagine, and quite hope, that numerous teen-age school groups will visit the show and be introduced to a time line that undergirds worldly and creative developments, enthralling or distressing or both at once, across the subsequent six decades. Personally, recalling the chaos of my early-twenties existence checkers my nostalgia for much of that. But I urge you who are young (most everybody these days, relative to me) to explore the exhibition and to imagine what experiencing the rampant stormy weather that it invokes would have been like for you.

Published in the August 8, 2022, issue of *The New Yorker*, with the headline "Time Capsule."

THE MYSTERIES OF MONDRIAN

Pablo Picasso and Piet Mondrian are, to me, the twin groundbreakers of twentieth-century European pictorial art: Picasso the greatest painter who modernized picture-making, and Mondrian the greatest modernizer who painted. (They call to mind an earlier brace of revolutionaries from the southern and northern reaches of the continent: Giotto, in Italy, humanized medieval storytelling, and Jan van Eyck, in the Low Countries, revealed the novel capacities of oil paints with devout precision.) The case for Picasso makes itself, with the preternatural range of his formal and iconographic leaps—forward, backward, and sideways—in what painting could be made, or dared, to do. The brief for Mondrian is harder to extract from a cookie-cutter modernist narrative ("Next slide, please") of marching styles, from the artist's modest-looking Dutch landscapes in the eighteen-nineties to the riveting abstractions he made in the decades before his death, as a wartime expatriate in New York, in 1944. But style for him, from first to last, served a quest to manifest soul-deep spirituality as a demonstrable fact of life. His aim, he said, was not to create masterpieces, though he did that, too. It was "to find things out." He reduced painting's uses and procedures, the whats and the hows, to a rock-bottom why.

Piet Mondrian: A Life (Ridinghouse and Kunstmuseum Den Haag), by the late Hans Janssen—a former chief curator at the Kunstmuseum Den Haag, with its matchless collection of the artist's work—is the first thorough Mondrian biography since the nineteen-fifties to be published in English (translated, from the Dutch, by Sue McDonnell) and unlikely to be supplanted. It is audacious in structure. Janssen, who died last year, at the age of sixty-seven, drew on his profound knowledge to dispense with strict chronology and to write not only about his subject's prodigious mind and eye but also from within them. He openly employs devices of fiction to parse intellectual insights and emotional states and, now and then, to cobble together imagined conversations between Mondrian and some of his significant contemporaries, with lines taken verbatim either from Mondrian's own writings and letters or from the diaries, letters, or recollections of others, such as the American sculptor Alexander Calder. The readerly effect is a bit uncanny, recalling Marianne Moore's definition of poetry as "imaginary gardens with real toads in them."

Mondrian fully justifies heterodox analysis of his famous abstract paintings of sparse black lines or bands and of blocks of primary color, his predominant repertoire after the early nineteen-twenties. There's obdurate mystery in his powerful combinations of hermetic sensibility and formal clarity, which dumbfound even as they command attention. Mondrian's character as a man is enigmatic, too: cognizant of his times, but, with rare exceptions, living and working stubbornly alone. He never married. He and Picasso cohabit no world except the whole one. Picasso's sphere is Dionysian, saturated with his personality. That of Mondrian is Apollonian, evacuated of anyone's. People will have things to say about Picasso forever. I expect that Janssen's book will remain sui generis for Mondrian.

Mondrian was born in the province of Utrecht in 1872. His father was a headmaster with a specialty in drawing instruction. The young Mondrian used to paint and draw in the Dutch countryside in the company of an artist uncle. His early landscapes exercise modes of naturalism, verging on Impressionism, but restlessly, with a palpable yen toward unusual nuances of beauty. After studying at the National Academy of Fine Arts in Amsterdam, where fashions ran to provincial emulations of Symbolism, Mondrian took to adapting such avant-garde demeanors as the blazing palettes of French Fauvism, but with a latent fealty to nature. His *Evening; The Red Tree* (1908–10) is feverishly brushed and plenty fiery but achieves the very quiddity of leafless tree-ness. Always, there's a drive to reach beyond appearance to something unbound by precedent.

For Mondrian in these years, frustration and self-doubt alternated with intimations that he was on the right track, by whatever route seemed viable. Decisively, in 1909, he encountered a show in Amsterdam of pictures by Paul Cézanne. Cézanne's game-changing translation of visual reality into equally emphasized lines and daubs electrified Mondrian. The look didn't matter to him. What did was the self-abnegating intensity.

Mondrian came into his own during his first sojourn in Paris, from 1911 until the onset of the First World War, where he hungrily absorbed Cubism, with reservations. He regarded the illusory bumps and hollows in pictorial space of even the most radical works by Picasso and Georges Braque as surreptitiously conservative, and he took no pleasure in their overlays of collage. True to the formal logic of Cézanne, he would keep things righteously flat. Among my favorite of all art works—I want one!—are his "plus and minus" paintings and drawings from the war years, made back in Holland: oval arrangements of short, often crisscrossing horizontal and vertical black lines. Poetically evoking ocean wavelets and starry skies, they give me, however fleetingly, a sense of coming home to a refuge of all-forgiving grace. No big deal, because the results are vouchsafed by humility. Recoiling from anything in art that smacked to him of "vanity," Mondrian evinced a sincerity like that of no other modern except his compatriot predecessor Vincent van Gogh, whom he appropriately revered.

Mondrian was caught up for much of his life in Theosophy, the anti-materialist mythos that was initiated in 1875, in New York, by the much travelled Russian occultist Helena Petrovna Blavatsky. Its pantheistic mysticism seemed to resonate with everything he craved in both art and life. Theosophy's tenet of an ascent from the natural by way of the spiritual toward a union with the divine was right up Mondrian's temperamental alley. He was most immersed from about 1908 to 1912, when he painted metaphysically supercharged flowers and frankly weird totemic figures. In the years that followed, he shrugged off the aspects of the movement that seemed pedantic and nebulous rather than liberating and practical, not to mention its mediumistic hocus-pocus, but he never regretted the influence. He remarked later, "One cannot call oneself an atheist without really having experienced some form of religion." He kept painting flowers, however, with unfailing virtuosity but waning enthusiasm, as a stock-in-trade to support his experimentation with frontal, vibrant geometric patterning.

Mondrian boiled down his religiosity to a belief in the intrinsic potency of the craft of painting, in and of itself. His voluminous writings on the subject grope, not very cogently, toward possible theories but mainly expatiate on forms that he had intuited with brush, pencil, palette knife, or ruler in hand. Intuition was everything for him—versus "instinct," which he deplored as an ego-inflating snare and came to associate with, among other derangements, the brutally repressive mystique of Nazism. He was ever eager to explain what he did, after he had done it, with an ingenuous presumption that anyone else might pick up the thread and accomplish as much. Mondrian wrote in an appreciative letter to an admiring critic, in 1914, "By not wishing to say anything human, by completely ignoring oneself, the artwork becomes a monument to Beauty: transcending the human; and yet human in its depth and generality!" That's as mordant an aesthetic verity as I know, but Mondrian's guileless confidence in being understood is touching. He seemed genuinely to want other artists to be as good as or better than himself. Only, for that to happen, they would have to be him.

In 1917, after he'd returned to the Netherlands, there began a spell of public collaboration—propagating ideals and commercial applications of abstraction—with Theo van Doesburg, the crackerjack designer and gifted promoter, if lesser artist, eleven years his junior. Their movement was dubbed De Stijl, after a magazine that van Doesburg published. Mondrian preferred the rubric neo-Plasticism, to identify painting with the flexible manipulation of its naked means and ends. This led him to limit himself to strictly horizontal and vertical lines or bands, echoing a canvas's edges, and delimited zones of solid color. Many-layered blocks of white advance to the eye, melding with the surface rather than representing negative space. He felt, Janssen speculates, that "'beauty' was not the same as 'truth.' The 'beauty' of the New Plastic was more 'beauty-as-truth'." You can't go looking for that. Work hard enough, though, and it may find you.

Janssen notes as a transitional step to the artist's mature methods the work *Composition with Grid 9: Checkerboard Composition with Light Colors* (1919). Jarringly simple for its time, it presents uniform small squares, thinly outlined in black and painted watery red, blue, yellow, or gray. In a darker version from the same year, *Composition with Grid 8: Checkerboard Composition with Dark Colors*, Janssen's seasoned eye notices variant hues of "cyan, magenta or chromate yellow" in addition to off-white. (Such discriminations lose force, as do the truly crucial factors of objecthood, scale, and directed brushwork, in photographic reproductions.) A year earlier, when holding a painting by one of its corners, Mondrian hit by accident on the potency of diamond formats—square or squarish canvases rotated forty-five degrees—to hint at the extension, invisibly, of rectilinear layouts beyond their material bounds, perhaps to infinity. He needn't portray the complete universe. He could imply it.

Van Doesburg, clinging to a metaphysics of art that his friend was casting off, seemed not to have grasped Mondrian's increasing rigor. The formerly fervent friendship cooled. Mondrian's uniqueness revealed itself as fate: solitary but not lonely. He mingled in whatever art scene he encountered and, given sparks of commonality, formed the agreements with colleagues that Janssen schematizes in his little one-act dialogues, mosaics of ping-ponging ideas. Among the voices is that of Calder, who was affected by a visit to Mondrian's Paris studio in 1930. He suggested that Mondrian add physical motion to his forms. Mondrian replied, "No, it is not necessary, my painting is already very fast"—a remark, regarding stolidly stable compositions, that had to refer to a kind of subliminal velocity. It's as close as Mondrian comes to illuminating the introspective incentives that he could only show, not enunciate. You need receptive eyes to remind you why his discourse should interest you in the first place.

On the sparsely documented front of Mondrian's personal life, Janssen is at pains to counter a caricatural image that he traces to a 1956 biography by Michel Seuphor, a proprietary Belgian apostle. Seuphor had cast the artist as, in Janssen's paraphrase, "an ascetic, who did not relish the company of friends, behaved strangely towards women and was obsessively focused on a strict and geometric attitude to art and life." Janssen establishes by abundant testimony that, when not holed up working, Mondrian was an ebulliently convivial charmer and, although chary of commitment, had affairs. Albeit formal and reserved, Mondrian was always elegantly dressed, cordial and kind in manner, and, of special note, an avid recreational dancer, adept early on in the one-step, the foxtrot, and the Charleston. Janssen reports that among women in Amsterdam the young Mondrian "developed a reputation for interesting, prolonged kisses, sometimes lasting for more than half an hour." In 1911, he broke off an engagement to an Amsterdam merchant's daughter, and in 1932, at sixty years old, he was rebuffed, to his acute distress, by a loving but ultimately reluctant Dutch woman who was much younger than him.

Mondrian enjoyed and profited from friendships with women. You might expect a strain of puritanism from an individual who was raised Calvinist in what Janssen terms "perhaps the most traditional communities in one of the least forward-looking of countries." The effect on the country boy of his move, in 1899, to Amsterdam's "Quartier Latin," a district of "bars, nightclubs, cabarets and brothels," as Janssen tells it, can only be imagined. But, as much or as little as Mondrian plunged into the nocturnal tumult, he kept his art and his life as remote from each other as possible, to the point of destroying most of the letters that he received after reading them. Janssen, for all his sleuthing, finally confesses that Mondrian's amours remain "more or less a closed book."

Yet there was a doubleness about him in matters of eros that chimes, for me, with the latent ardors and explicit constraints of his painting. In 1941, according to the diary of a valued but inconveniently smitten journalist and painter, Charmion von Wiegand, whom he allowed to assist him in the studio and to watch him paint, he admonished her, saying that sex is "not unpleasant while it lasts—but only a communion of ideas leaves a memory." She failed to see any compelling logic in that, but the two stayed friends.

Mondrian arrived in New York, by way of England, in 1940, on a convoy that had lost five ships to German submarines en route. The New York painter Harry Holtzman, an impoverished aesthete when he introduced himself to the artist in Paris, in 1934, but now flush with money by marriage, was the first in line to greet him. The move occasioned a dramatic shift in Mondrian's art. After briefly continuing the noble astringency that he had pursued on his stopover in London, as seen in the majestic *Trafalgar Square* (1939–43), he loosened up sensationally, displacing his customary black bands with chains of syncopated squares in plangent colors. The dazzling *Broadway Boogie Woogie* (1942–43) and the unfinished *Victory Boogie Woogie*, which he started in 1942, were climactic. The latter retains the tentative bits of tape and strips and patches of colored paper with which Mondrian worked out compositions in a self-critical process of continual revision that could take months or even years to satisfy him.

The spur was jazz, a passion and a wellspring for Mondrian since his return, in 1919, to Paris, where he favored clubs that featured Black American performers. He adored Josephine Baker and ignored her box-office brand as a civilized "savage." Rather, he deemed Baker's improvisatory dance, song, and costume (or lack of it, in one routine, but for a few pink feathers) galvanic fine art. At a concert in 1934, in Paris, Mondrian thought Louis Armstrong already old hat except for the trumpeter's "long lines," he said. But he was transported "into a state of ecstasy," Janssen writes, by Armstrong's pianist Herman Chittison, who "allowed the bass line played with his left hand to fall out of sync, contrasting with the rhythmically varied 'melody' played by his right hand"—boogie-woogie in utero.

Janssen's expert citations of parallels in music for Mondrian's art are a treat and a revelation for a musical doofus like me. Janssen likens the artist's frequent motif, in the mid-nineteen-thirties, of paired horizontal black bands to the bass line running under the saxophone cadenzas of Armstrong's group and others. (Thereby alerted, I see and spectrally hear it.) If, in Janssen's telling, one dynamic recurs throughout Mondrian's aesthetic adventuring, it is rhythm, incipient even in his youthful renderings from nature. Underlying toccatas impart physicality to works that have too often been taken as dryly cerebral. Thought, if any was needed, followed touch.

Mondrian's favorite outings in New York were to Café Society, on Sheridan Square, and to Café Society Uptown, on Fifty-eighth Street, the city's only unsegregated white-owned clubs, which shared the slogan "The Wrong Place for the Right People." (Want to know from racism? At other venues, according to Janssen, Black patrons, should there be any, had whatever glassware they'd used smashed and tossed out.) Janssen persuasively relates Mondrian's new liberties to his almost certain exposure, in New York, to jam sessions featuring the young Thelonious Monk, a keyboard augur of bebop and beyond, who unclenched "abrupt variations in tempo, rapidly switching chord patterns and sudden, unexpected changes in key." So complex are the possible correspondences that I get lost trying to track them. But there can be no mistaking the analogous energy.

Mondrian loved the relative impersonality of the finest jazz, exalting form and technique over seductive performance—not that he minded fun. Jazz left you alone with your perceptions, even as it might bring you to your feet in joyous motion. A master like Monk built cloud castles with many rooms and startling passageways. Hearkening, you might believe that he played for you alone. I remember, poor in the sixties, standing one dank night outside the Five Spot on St. Mark's Place and seeing and hearing him, clearly, through the club's large windows. Then he stood up from the piano, as regular a person as you or anyone. But something had changed that could not change back.

Through it all, there were dance floors, where Mondrian could blissfully lose himself in up-to-the-minute mass culture. Immune to snobbery, he relished the animation, and the pathos, of Walt Disney's *Snow*

White and the Seven Dwarfs, and the novel ubiquity of the jukebox. Noncompetitive, as far as I can tell, he respected the successes of other artists, or, at least, compassionately rued their vagaries. He had acquaintances but few intimates among the hosts of hero-worshipping colleagues that accumulated, starting in Europe and burgeoning in America, most of whom spent years presuming to match or extend the gravitas of his art. Their reward? Style. They run changes on the anatomy but lack the pulse. Not that Mondrian begrudged them. Like his fellow-exiles Marcel Duchamp and Fernand Léger, he was keen to meet and to encourage American artists, unlike the standoffish European Surrealists who had also wound up in New York. It's good that he lived long enough for a foretaste of the New World that would prove worthy of his singular spirit and refractory intelligence.

A delicious tale of modern art and a testament to Mondrian's personal character transpired when, in 1943, he served as one of the jurors for a group show at Art of This Century, a New York gallery directed by the fabulously rich heiress and aspiring doyenne Peggy Guggenheim and devoted chiefly to works by celebrated European émigrés. The episode is drawn by Janssen from published accounts that rely on firsthand testimony refracted through memory and muddled through retellings at, no doubt, dozens of cocktail parties.

Janssen describes Mondrian walking from painting to painting, "slowly and a little stiffly," until he comes to a halt in front of one. "Pretty awful," Guggenheim says. "That's not painting, is it?" Mondrian, who does not stop staring at it, eventually responds, "I'm trying to understand what's happening here. I think this is the most interesting work I've seen so far in America." The piece is Jackson Pollock's *Stenographic Figure* (circa 1942). Guggenheim objects, "You can't compare this and the way you paint." Mondrian replies, "The way I paint and the way I think are two different things." Later, when the other jurors have filed in, Guggenheim drags them over to the Pollock, saying, "Look what an exciting new thing we have here!"

Mondrian had known a little of Pollock, Janssen asserts, through Lee Krasner, a favorite youngish dance partner and the volcanic American's wife-to-be. (They married in 1945.) She later recalled that her fast, ingenious pas de deux with Mondrian, initiated by him and elaborated upon by her, made them the center of attention on several occasions, delighting him. He commented tactfully on her tentative, Picasso-influenced works of the time. But his special fascination with the Pollock painting seems no politic nod but an authentic and, to me, crystal-clear response: he saw a rare fellow-painter striving, in this preliminary instance with tropes cribbed from Picasso and Joan Miró, toward a rule-breaking merger of form and feeling and mind and body, brimming with unforeseeable possibilities.

Janssen surmises an ulterior motive for Mondrian's remarks, positing them, somehow, as a bargaining chip to persuade Guggenheim and others on the jury to consider paintings by Harry Holtzman. (Though shy of patronage, as of anything entailing obligations, Mondrian had succumbed to accepting, from immediate necessity, an offer by Holtzman to pay the rent for an apartment on East Fifty-sixth Street at First Avenue.) The insinuation of nepotism by Mondrian in favor of Holtzman puzzles me. Granted, we enter shadowlands of alluvial art-world gossip. And perhaps Janssen viewed Abstract Expressionism without much enthusiasm. (He doesn't say.) I perceive a firm affinity between Mondrian's fastidiously self-abandoning cultivation of what Janssen calls "organised looseness"—fuelled by jazz—and Pollock's seething, more gestural equivalents: fusions, in the eventual major drip paintings, of sullied surfaces and the depthless music of the spheres. I'm moved by what I can only believe was Mondrian's magnanimity to a tyro who, as he may even have sensed, would usurp his place atop avant-garde royalty.

Intent on Mondrian's internal reckonings, Janssen scants what it's like for a viewer to confront one of the artist's great abstractions. It's kinesthetic for me—gut-felt. Gravity is key, the force that urges everything on Earth toward horizontality. In regard to that, a diagonal is a mere anecdote: something propped up or toppling. Verticality is how, standing, we stalemate gravity, with autonomic, tiny adjustments of balance. Paintings by Mondrian have seemed a mite wonky to my eye when hung on the curved walls along the slanting ramp of the Guggenheim Museum. Certainly, they oppose the weightless modes of abstraction that were advanced by the Russians Vasily Kandinsky and Kazimir Malevich, which would look fine in outer space as a Mondrian couldn't, with its occult memory of Dutch upright entities (windmills, lighthouses, a church) on low-down terrain. He augmented the simple physical reality of his works in the third dimension by thrusting canvases forward of recessed frames.

The complexities of a Mondrian register all at once, with a bang that can hold up to even the most quizzical inspection ever after. It's no cinch to argue with something that has happened to you. Because they are typically asymmetrical, the compositions may trigger slight bodily crises. If we look long and hard enough, we may feel that the slightest displacement of a line or corruption of a color could compromise the stability that prevents us from falling down. Test this the next time you are in person with a Mondrian. Try speculatively altering any detail and see what happens. The effect is a condition of subjectivity without subjects. No one's feelings, starting with those of the artist himself, are either addressed or ruled out.

Though he quailed at ever meeting Picasso—I'd have been nervous of that, too—Mondrian admired him, and Picasso may or may not have returned the favor. (He held "non-figurative" art in contempt, arguing that any mark on a surface constitutes a figure.) Janssen writes that Duchamp, another contrary genius, "had a weakness for the Dutch master of ultimate simplification." The choice of the word "weakness" intrigues. It is precisely at points where we stand aghast at our inability really to know, and fully to understand, anything cosmically pertinent that Mondrian looms like a menhir in a desert, silently replete.

Janssen successfully quashes any tendency to regard Mondrian as an oddball, or to rank him pragmatically with the many other moderns whose legacies have informed developments in fine and applied arts. Did he routinely paint the walls of his studios stark white and on them pin, in scattered array, oblongs of vivid color? Yes, with endless imitative ramifications for minimalist interior design. But it was not a statement. Simply, the scheme aided his concentration, which was imperilled by outside urban noise—cacophonous at times in Paris and New York—and by vicissitudes of ill health. Mondrian had chronic bronchitis, among other maladies, which came to include arthritis and hardened arteries. Bedeviling him incessantly were floaters in his ocular fluids that he saw as drifting and darting threads, like radio static in the broadcast of a sonata. Rarely entirely well, he suffered spells of incapacitation, even as he credited fevers with helping him see things more vividly, between bursts of creative and social vitality. He died, of pneumonia, at the age of seventy-one.

Mondrian passed away four months before the D Day landings and the subsequent liberations of his beloved France and native Netherlands. The title of *Victory Boogie Woogie* was his first and last reference to the war or, as far as I know, to anything political; Picasso, by contrast, gave us *Guernica* (1937). But, no less than Picasso, Mondrian counsels against capitulation to tyranny. He never wavered from a heartfelt adherence to the vision of civilized progress, tensed against the big-time barbarisms, that will always memorialize the twentieth century. He transcends world events, not to mention changes in artistic fashion. Critical attention to him may rise and fall. For anyone undertaking to pay it, though, there can be no ups or downs in Mondrian's importance, relative to other artists past, present, and to come. There is only a steady state of inexhaustible meaning, beggaring comparison and defying definition. Even the critically consummate Janssen, with his magnum opus of a biography, can merely dance around, and not penetrate, the adamantine conundrum of the Dutch magus's dead stops in lived time.

Published in the October 3, 2022, issue of *The New Yorker*, with the headline "Dutch Magus."

THE POLYMORPHOUS GENIUS OF WOLFGANG TILLMANS

"To look without fear," the immense, flabbergastingly installed retrospective of the German photographer Wolfgang Tillmans, at the Museum of Modern Art, persuades me that the man is a genius. There's a downside to the concession—it dampens my quarrels of taste with certain items, among the show's predominantly brilliant several hundred, that I do not like. Geniuses alter the basic terms of the fields of art or science which happen to engage them. Criteria that once applied no longer compel. The ground zero at MOMA is "art photography," its former autonomy diluted in a tsunami of images from Tillmans, in wildly varying sizes, mediums, and formats, which are often mounted from floor to ceiling, and may less risk than exalt banality. Almost violently sociable, the work retroactively mainstreams such precedents as the stark intimacies of love and loss in photographs by Nan Goldin—though the irrepressibly positive-minded Tillmans is never as downbeat as Goldin.

Fifty-four years old, the third child of parents who ran an export business in a city near Cologne, Tillmans soared to fame in the early nineties for work that he had begun a few years earlier: an ostensibly scattershot but, in truth, acutely selective documentation of soulful youths whom he encountered on night-life outings, chiefly in Berlin and London, before and during his art-school studies at Bournemouth, in England. As with Goldin's unhappy couples, his party scenes are like panes of glass dropped through the middle of symbioses. Beholding, you are at once viewer and viewed, at instants that are well served by fast, blurry takes. (Tillmans employed a 50-mm. S.L.R. until he went exclusively digital, in 2012.) His initial body of work put him on the art-world map, but he has somewhat downplayed it in his choices for the present show, perhaps from exasperation at being lazily identified with a fleeting Zeitgeist that determined only the opening gambit for a game that he has conducted in no end of other directions.

Tillmans returns now and then, but glancingly, to themes of social and sexual fluidity. His gayness is a given, not a battlefront. He has lived with H.I.V. since 1997, and has been motivated by gratitude to past pioneers of liberation who made his freewheeling life and art possible, rewarding him with near-incessant exhibitions and speaking gigs around the globe. I was skeptical of *Wolfgang Tillmans: A Reader*, a volume, mainly of interviews, issued by MOMA along with the show's dazzling catalogue, but what do you know? It yields ur-texts of extraordinary intelligence, responsiveness (he listens!), and wit.

Tillmans, strikingly even-tempered, is outspoken in support of liberal causes and communities, but with a spirit more citizenly than activist, as could be seen in the pro-E.U. posters and polemics, a reflex of his cosmopolitan ideals, that he produced during the Brexit referendum. He morphed for a spell in those months, he wrote at the time, "from an inherently political, to an overtly political person," spurred by "an understanding of Western cultures as sleepwalkers into the abyss." Usually, he humbly preserves his detachment as an artist, pushing boundaries only when it makes immediate sense to him. Intermittent provocations—genitalia male and female, the one-off shocker of a guy pissing onto a cushioned chair, a prevalent intimation that whatever clothes are seen may be doffed in the near future—exemplify phenomena that he addresses bravely but sparingly, intent on fact rather than on ideology or sentiment. He stoutly shuns the liberal fallacy of mistaking hope for reality.

In a critical context, Tillmans obliterates Pop dialectics of "high" and "low" art. He observes no distinction, in the show's arrangement, between self-generated and commissioned works, original and appropriated images, framed fine prints and taped- or pinned-up photocopies, deliberate and accidental darkroom misadventures, and, in matters of content, the politically committed and the purely aesthetic. (The show has been organized by Roxana Marcoci, MOMA's senior curator of photography, but Tillmans was closely involved in its production. He spent sixteen days installing the show—an engulfing art work in itself—with a crew of his own.) He is playful on principle, to usually exciting but sometimes redundant effect. Looking without fear entails for him an occasional resignation to tedium, which viewers are free to tolerate or to resent. It does pose problems.

I am left cold by Tillmans's cameraless forays in abstraction, which he has been making since the nineties, either by exposing photosensitive paper to colored light or by feeding it through faulty copying devices. The results, albeit often smashingly decorative, feel painterly but lack the partnership of mind, eye, and hand—conception, envisioning, touch—that distinguishes painting. They evoke but pointlessly sacrifice strengths of his early heroes Gerhard Richter and Sigmar Polke, whose jeux d'esprit are anchored in paint's materiality. Also dismaying to me are tabletop montages, however elegant, of photocopied pages from newspapers and magazines, from 2005 on, collectively titled *Truth Study Center*. A related, wall-mounted assortment, *Soldiers: The Nineties* (1999/2022), beguiles with its outtakes of young soldiers during that relatively pacific decade. Tillmans hates war, he has said, while being mightily attracted to men in uniform. The subjects look more like lads at a summer camp than apprentices in lethality.

I confess to only quickly scanning the complicated table works, which smartly anticipated today's torrent of information via institutional and social media—and its numbing effect. Enough of too much induces apathy. And any one person's sorting of the data seems essentially interchangeable with anyone else's. Nor was I thrilled by Tillmans's videos, mainly of rotating disco balls set to techno music that he has composed, though in this case my resistance may be a blind spot of generational sensibility.

But genius. Everything by this artist—be it the image of a pair of jeans draped on a stair post or a man and a woman perched in a tree and modelling vinyl raincoats while otherwise naked, or fifty-six snapshots taken from urban ground level of the airborne Concorde (some minus the plane but persuasively atremble with its roar)—springs from an idea that, once thought, demands execution. If the upshot is boring, so be it. I'm put in mind of Einstein having to fill in the workaday math relevant to his eurekas. There's an obviousness of a sort that baits the disgruntled: "Nothing new," they may as much as declare. ("Besides, I thought of it first.") Tillmans is drastically—and coolly, calmly, and, indeed, fearlessly—self-aware. I keep trying to catch him not knowing what he's doing. No dice yet.

Tillmans's most powerful images veer away from kinship with photographic genres and conventions. Consider his portraiture, usually of friends but at times of celebrities appearing as nobody special, such as the British supermodel Kate Moss, the composer Philip Glass, and the musician Frank Ocean, for the cover of his 2016 album, *Blonde*. Tillmans's empathetic figures, often shown standing and sometimes larger than life, project improbable conflations of confidence and vulnerability. Captured in each is a moment—always a moment, present tense—of disequilibrium between the inside and the outside of an individual existence. The subjects tend to be attractive. Why gaze at them otherwise? (Tillmans is a self-admitted sucker for beauty, which extends to a color sense that battens on variants of complementary red and green or blue and yellow.) But none comes off as truly glamorous, because all are so downrightly human.

I'm amused by one portrait, *Irm Hermann* (2000), of a red-headed, aging but invincibly charming collaborator of the late filmmaker Rainer Werner Fassbinder. To my perception, she overcomes the gotcha gawkiness of an averted gaze and an off-kilter smile with a self-possession that is all and inaccessibly her own. (I feel that I must know her from somewhere.) But even that picture immortalizes an unrepeatable nugget of a singular biography.

Then there are the still-lifes of remarkably unremarkable windowsill miscellanies: some random fruit and bits of studio gear transfigured by a happenstance of daylight. A specialty that harvests the abandon of Tillmans's partying—in the past and occasionally recurrent, by his account—is a series of unpeopled interiors that are littered with empty beer bottles and other morning-after detritus. These photographs shouldn't amount to much, but to me they are stunningly lovely and, with only trace elements of melancholy, poetically more telling of communal ecstasy than any shots of the originating events could be. Think about mornings. They're when the purest sense of what we are doing, or not doing, with our temporary habitation of the Earth sinks in.

Speaking of planets, Tillmans has been an enthusiast since boyhood for sights of night skies and telescopic spectacles: the ultimate intensification of our infinitesimal and brief—and therefore to be cherished—share in the universe. My favorites in this line are filtered closeups of the sun looking like a pink balloon, each one bearing a tiny black spot: a transit of Venus. It feels trivial to call Tillmans a photographer. Rather, he is an artist who uses photography to the verge of using it up. His wheelhouse, a guarantor of his sincerity, is simple interest and an appetite for surprise. Will he sustain it? That's to be seen, after the undoubtedly exhausting self-scrutiny of the MOMA extravaganza, a rare consent by him to a retrospective rather than, as is usually his policy, an ad-hoc show centered on what preoccupies him at any given time. But what he has done is already so splendid a gift to us, come what may.

Published in the October 10, 2022, issue of *The New Yorker*, with the headline "Stilled Life."

ACKNOWLEDGMENTS

The New Yorker was Peter's home for twenty-four years. David Remnick hired Peter as the magazine's art critic in 1998 and championed his writing throughout his illness. Cressida Leyshon, Peter's trusted editor since 2017, shepherded the pieces that comprise *The Art of Dying* into print. Before Cressida, there was the wonderful Virginia Cannon. Warm thanks to Steve Martin, for his foreword, and Jarrett Earnest, for his introduction. Gary Morris of the David Black Agency and Eric Himmel at Abrams Books made the book happen.

—Brooke Alderson

INDEX